Modernist Travel Writing

Modernist Travel Writing

INTELLECTUALS ABROAD

David G. Farley

University of Missouri Press
Columbia and London

Copyright © 2010 by
The Curators of the University of Missouri
University of Missouri Press, Columbia, Missouri 65201
Printed and bound in the United States of America
All rights reserved
5 4 3 2 1   14 13 12 11 10

Cataloging-in-Publication data available from the Library of Congress
ISBN 978-0-8262-1901-5

∞™ This paper meets the requirements of the
American National Standard for Permanence of Paper
for Printed Library Materials, Z39.48, 1984.

Design and composition: Stephanie Foley
Printing and binding: Integrated Book Technology, Inc.
Typeface: Goudy

To Johanna, for making travel such a delight these many years

And to Lucy

Contents

Acknowledgments

T RAVELING WITHOUT GUIDES IS FOR THE ADVENTUROUS AND the intrepid, among whom I do not count myself. I would like to thank two of the most outstanding guides I could have hoped for as I set out, Holly Laird and Robert Spoo. They shaped this project in particular and my own outlook on modernist literature in general in more ways than I can say. I am forever indebted to them. Johanna Dehler has read the manuscript through many times over the years as it has grown and transformed and has always helped me to sharpen my ideas and my presentation. I would also like to thank my family for the dinner-table conversations from which, in some obscure way, this project grew. A special thanks to my sister Margaret Farley for her expertise and for fielding many a random phonecall.

At the University of Missouri Press, I would like to thank Clair Wilcox for his sage advice and tremendous patience in ushering this project along. Thanks as well to John Brenner and Sara Davis and to Tim Fox for his careful eye. I would also like to thank the anonymous readers for their thorough reading of the manuscript and encouraging feedback. Their comments resulted in me clarifying my argument at several key points. Any lingering errors are of course my own.

I would also like to thank the following people and institutions: The National Portrait Gallery, London, for permission to reproduce Wyndham Lewis's drawing of the head of Rebecca West; Lisa Aguilar at the University of Texas Libraries, The University of Texas at Austin for permission to reproduce the map of Morocco from their collection; Omar Pound for first making available to me a copy of Ezra Pound's 1921 passport and The Lilly Library, Indiana University, Bloomington, Indiana, for the reproduction; Ezra Pound's passport is reproduced with permission of New Directions, agents for the heirs of Ezra Pound; Lori Curtis, formerly of the University of Tulsa McFarlin Library Special Collections, for her help in navigating the Rebecca West Collection; Neelam Mughal, whose feedback and advice was of enormous help at a crucial stage of this project; I would also like to thank my colleagues at the Staten Island campus of St John's University, especially Harry Denny and Connie DeSimone, for their patience, advice, and help in big ways and small.

Finally, to the many guides I have had over the years, looking back, and considering, I feel it fitting to say "with thanks."

Modernist Travel Writing

TRAVERSING THE SPACE BETWEEN

History? How can you get history in the making, on the
spot, as it happens? There were several histories all going on
together, unconnected, often contradictory narratives that
met and crossed, and—they were all "history."

—Lincoln Steffens, *Autobiography*

Somehow the furthest parts of the world have the finest
things in them.

—Herodotus, *The History*

T RAVEL AND TRAVEL WRITING TRANSFORMED LITERARY MODERNISM
as surely as they were transformed by it. The fragmented forms,
montage techniques, and streams of consciousness that are the salient
and distinguishing features of modernist style and experimentation owe much
to the foreign scenes, exotic locales, wrenching perspectives, and uncanny
displacements that were the result of a generation unmoored from convention
and enlivened by foreign travel. Those modernist writers in particular who
were forged in the smithy of the London vortex—that concentrated energy
that drew together writers and artists in the early years of modernism's
flourishing—were influenced as much by dispersal as by concentration, by
real and foreign landscapes as much as by the surreal inner landscape of the
subconscious or by any group dynamic. We need only to recall the itinerary of
cities in T. S. Eliot's *The Waste Land*, the place names and foreign languages
that punctuate Pound's *Cantos*, or the foreign terrains and transgressed

boundaries of Virginia Woolf's *Orlando* to get a sense of the importance that travel had on the creative consciousness of the period.

At the same time, however, it is important to distinguish between modernist works that employed the vocabulary of travel indirectly through the citation of foreign literary works and traditions (the internationalism of modernism remains one of its most distinguishing features) and works that drew directly on the experience of foreign travel. Thus, for example, Eliot did not journey to Jerusalem, Alexandria, or Carthage to gather material for his poem, nor need he have done so in order for these foreign cities to function as the signposts of civilization or the coordinates of culture pointing to contemporary desuetude. Nor do we as readers feel that by visiting these cities, or the sites on which they stood, the notorious difficulties of *The Waste Land* would be dispelled or the fragmentary nature of the poem suddenly coalesce into meaning. On the contrary, Eliot's poem maps a distinctly literary and cultural terrain, and to assist readers in navigating this terrain, he appended footnotes that point to literary sources, suggesting that his poem is firmly grounded in textual signifiers, not in geographical locales.

We likewise need to draw a distinction as Helen Carr has recently done in her survey of the voluminous and varied body of travel writing that appeared between World War I and World War II, between "*travelling* writers" and actual "*travel* writers."[1] While many scholars have noted how traveling itself became a much more common, almost obligatory, activity for a generation of writers freed by the advances in transportation technologies, the modernist features of travel writing during this period are much harder to see. In Carr's view, the increased tendency for the present day travel book to draw as much on a fragmentary interiority as on an objective reality, had its origin during the modern period: "In the twentieth century [the travel book] has become a more subjective form, more memoir than manual, and often an alternative form of writing for novelists" (74). More than an "alternative form of writing," the travel book became an important genre in the hands of certain modernist writers, and Carr helps us see the ways in which modernism and the travel genre intersect in important ways, an intersection that needs to be examined more closely.

In *Modernist Travel Writing*, I likewise examine the particular features of the travel genre through the modern period—the thirties especially, but also in the years around World War I—in the travel writing of four authors who were variously associated with literary modernism, the movement that emerged in the early years of the twentieth century. I first discuss—as a kind of preamble, but also as a way of addressing critical genealogies of modernism—Ezra Pound's views on modern travel, and I examine the one travel book he wrote as he was fashioning his literary identity before the First World War. Pound abandoned the travel genre early on, but his interest in travel and the use of the information thus gathered would continue to inform his work for the rest of his life. Pound's shift away from the travel genre toward the epic, though, helps to introduce the more substantial travel books of the other authors I examine, all of whom saw travel writing as important for recording their impressions of a modern world that was undergoing major upheaval. These writers saw the travel book as a fit vehicle for their modernist style. I examine E. E. Cummings's account of his 1931 trip to Russia in *Eimi*; Wyndham Lewis's book about his 1931 voyage to Morocco, *Filibusters in Barbary*; and Rebecca West's seamless narrative of the three trips that she made to the former Yugoslavia throughout the thirties, *Black Lamb and Grey Falcon*.[2]

In examining the ways that these authors confront the tumultuous political and social landscape during the modernist period, I seek to better understand the intersection between literary modernism and travel writing. These writers, all deeply invested in modernist precepts and versed in modernist style and experimentation—whether this was the difficulty and obscurity of Cummings's prose, Lewis's satire, or the complex nightmare of West's historiography—turned to the travel genre as a natural extension of their imaginative work, even as their views on the modern world were being transformed by the events of the period. In the hands of Pound, Cummings, Lewis, and West, the travel narrative becomes an important genre in the modernist canon. Pound, Cummings, Lewis, and West traveled not to escape but to better understand and assess the complicated political and social landscape of the modern world, and they saw the travel book as an important genre for both this understanding and this assessment, even if this understanding only came in fits and starts and this assessment was transmitted through a style that still bore with it the traces of an earlier optimism about the role of art in the modern world. Even within this admittedly narrow array of authors, however, there are differences in how they saw the purpose and usefulness of the travel genre. The qualitative distinction that Pound often made, for example, between poetry and prose and the respective abilities of either to represent the modern world and "include history"—to paraphrase Pound's definition of the epic—and his ultimate rejection of the travel book as a fit vehicle for modernist style help to shape my argument about the travel books of Cummings, Lewis, and West.[3]

I begin with Pound in part because he is frequently seen as a central figure in modernism's inception as well as its troubled history, but also because Pound's nostalgia for travel as it was possible before the First World War is central to his views on the role and function of literature after the war, and this shift can help us understand, to some degree, the impact that the changing nature of travel had on modernist writers during the period leading up to the Second World War. In beginning this way, I do not mean to suggest that Pound presided over the intentions of these other writers (although he claimed to do so with Cummings to some degree, a point I will develop in my chapters on Pound and Cummings) or that the distinctions he made between poetry and prose are directly applicable to these other writers; rather, I argue that the problem that Pound noted of how literature in the modern period could record and assess a modern world where boundaries were no longer Romantic thresholds, but instead bureaucratic checkpoints that demarcated national borders and regulated economies, as well as the problems of representation that this entailed, is often echoed in *Eimi, Filibusters,* and *Black Lamb and Grey Falcon.*

If, however, the division that I make between Pound on the one hand, and Cummings, Lewis, and West on the other, seems too sharply drawn, this is in part because Pound remained the most vocal in his regret for a lost age of unrestricted travel, a regret that sounds most clearly in his later work. This study sees the main contribution to the modernist travel genre in the works of Cummings, Lewis, and West, and attempts to show how these works contribute both to our understanding of the travel genre and to our understanding of how literary modernism developed throughout the thirties. The works by Cummings, Lewis, and West are important instances where these writers conveyed their impressions of the period between the wars through the modernist styles that they had developed earlier in their creative and imaginative works. They stand as important moments when the brash enthusiasm of the early manifestos had not yet transformed into the elegiac tone of a later modernism. These travel books, I argue, offer alternative ways of both "including history" and of recording current events, as these writers witness the fading afterglow of revolution, the effects of empire, and the consequences of the upheavals of war as they simultaneously ponder the polysemous nature of cultural artifacts, the contradictory messages of political reality, and the opposing arguments of history.

MODERNIST TRAVEL/TRAVELING MODERNISM

This study is positioned at the intersection of two current and evolving critical trends regarding the literature of the early to mid twentieth century: that of modernist studies, which in recent years has seen special focus on the literature written closer to the Second World War—what has come to be known as "late modernism"—and travel studies, which, despite its mostly transhistorical nature, has also seen significant contributions that focus on this period between the wars.

Modernist studies was for many years guided by the same genealogies and narratives that have ultimately served to cut us off from deeper understandings of the literature written in the thirties and beyond. Even though 1939 is often seen in conventional critical approaches as a kind of terminal date to modernism proper, the literature written in the thirties was often read under the auspices of those statements uttered in the early years of the twentieth century, by writers and artists around the First World War, when modernism was still being formed and its interests and precepts still being articulated. It is only recently that the stories of modernism's inception and the pre-war pronouncements of its main practitioners have both come under the scrutiny of critics interested in the changing political and social reality of the interwar years. The focus on "late modernism," generally speaking, is an attempt to situate these modernist writers in a specific political and historical period rather than seeing this political and historical reality as a backdrop onto which incipient pronouncements of coherence and mission can be constructed and testified to.

Tyrus Miller, in *Late Modernism: Politics, Fictions, and the Arts between the World Wars*, provides the most sustained analysis of this new designation, which he appropriates specifically for literary studies.[4] Resisting the temptation, and precedents, to see works of the thirties written by traditional modernist authors as merely souvenirs or "cultural curiosities," or the critical focus on them as merely acts of recovery, or the time period as nothing more than a weigh station between modernism and postmodernism, "rather, [these works] mark the lines of flight artists took where an obstacle, the oft-mentioned 'impasse' of modernism, interrupted progress on established paths. Facing an unexpected stop, late modernists took a detour into the political regions that high modernism had managed to view from the distance of a closed car, as part of a moving panorama of forms and colors" (13). The language of travel employed here by Miller metaphorically in his reference to the paths and landscapes of the modern world, as well as the vehicular analogy that binds this image together, speaks to the importance that travel had as a way for modernist writers to engage the modern world more directly. But the larger claims of Miller's study are more directly applicable to a study of the travel genre in that one of the key features of late modernism that Miller describes is its rejection of rigid form of the kind seen in the traditional modernist masterworks such as Joyce's *Ulysses* or Eliot's *The Waste Land*. Instead, late modernist works are characterized by a "struggle against what they perceived as the apotheosis of form" (19). In the travel books I examine here, we can see the vestiges of this preoccupation with form coupled with what becomes a deep suspicion of form itself.

In *Modernism and World War II*, Marina MacKay similarly describes the new lineaments of a late modernism and suggests that "an adequate definition of modernism needs to take account of this self-referential and historiographic late phase."[5] Building on Miller's argument, MacKay helps us think through the implications of what she calls the "experimental form and political impurity" of the literature of the period. For MacKay, late modernism opens up a new realm of inquiry where the public sphere in Britain, ravaged by political and social upheaval, and the private domain of modernist experimental writers can be examined with more detailed historical and material particularity. Although she does not discuss the travel genre in her book, travel itself and the struggle to transform the experiences of travel into a form that registers the complexity of this experience is perhaps what she has in mind when she suggests that "focusing on late modernism is a way of reading modernism through its longer outcomes rather than its notional origins" (15).

The other field with which this project aligns itself is that of travel studies in general and studies of travel during the interwar years in particular. Over the past decade or so the field of travel studies has grown exponentially. Transnational and transhistorical in approach, but suited as well to period studies or studies of individual figures, travel studies has helped shed light on, if not always reconcile, MacKay's related comments about "experimental form and political impurity." In particular, the period between World War I and World War II has proven fruitful for studies of the travel genre, as the very nature of travel was so rapidly and substantially altered by technological, political, and social developments. Paul Fussell first brought attention to the genre during this period in his seminal *Abroad: British Literary Traveling between the Wars*, a book that set the tone for travel studies during the period for many years, seeing it primarily as a genre of escape and simultaneously seeing the interwar years as a period to be escaped from, as a time of enervation and anxiety.[6]

More recently, Bernard Schweizer has revisited thirties travel writing in *Radicals on the Road: The Politics of English Travel Writing in the 1930s*, where he similarly examines British writers and travelers during these years, but focuses more rigorously on their political engagement.[7] Picking up where Fussell leaves off, Schweizer simultaneously challenges the notion that the writers of the period were guided by any such determined pessimism. As a rejoinder to Fussell's bleak assessment of interwar travel, Schweizer argues that "pessimism was too passive an attitude to suit the dynamic, rebellious impulses of young intellectuals who had been educated in the nation's elite public-school system in the 1920s" (8). He goes on to say, speaking mainly of the writers of Auden's generation, that the positive beliefs these writers sought out were an "antidote to the anxieties and perplexities of the period, just as travel was pursued as a means to clear the fogs of political confusion and to bring about ideological clarifications" (8). If these efforts at clarification often resulted in a "heightened sense of political anxiety," they also resulted in more politically engaged travel books that more accurately reflected the political landscape. Schweizer doesn't address modernism directly, though some of the writers he discusses, especially Rebecca West, have modernist affiliations that he addresses in depth elsewhere, but the implications of his study jibe well with the description of late modernism as put forth by Miller and MacKay.[8] Most importantly, the dovetailing of these two approaches can help us see how "experimental form and political impurity" often came together and often came into conflict, but left us with works that can help us see both modernism and the modern world through fresh eyes.

ENTRE DEUX GUERRES:
THE AGE OF NEW COMPLEXION

The years between World War I and World War II were indeed rich for travel and travel writing. As a result of the industrial and technological advances of the nineteenth century that improved the infrastructure of the European continent and facilitated trade and transportation thereby causing a boom in the tourist industry, casual travel was no longer only for the intrepid or the wealthy.[9] Already by the beginning of the twentieth century, however, the rise of tourism and travel as recreational activities was darkly paralleled by the rise and spread of global conflicts made possible by these same advances in technology and transportation as well as by the competition for foreign markets they created. As Carr points out, these technological developments were not simply "disinterested" advances, but the mechanism for "empire building, trade expansion, and mass migrations" throughout the nineteenth century (70). The spread of modern war and a generation mobilized into military action were the concrete yet nightmarish manifestations of an age of progress and travel, even as the age of empire itself entered a period of slow decline.

During the First World War, governments more and more attempted to control travel, as the unregulated flow of people across borders was seen as a potential threat to national security. Both the United States, whose isolationism was central to its foreign policy, and Great Britain, which throughout the nineteenth century had become increasingly drawn into the European concert, grew ever more concerned about the permeability of their borders and took various steps to shore them up. The degree to which travel was seen as a threat to national stability as much as an opportunity for education or enlightenment can be seen by the introduction during these years of tighter travel restrictions and regulatory measures such as the Defense of the Realm Act in Britain, written into law in 1915, and the World War I Travel Control Act, enacted in the United States on May 22, 1918, a year after America entered the war.[10] Although these wartime measures were not without precedent, their effects lingered long after the cessation of conflict. The discretionary power of the passport division of the United States government, for instance, was such that it was all but impossible to travel in the nineteen twenties and thirties without first securing the necessary documents. Such measures prolonged the atmosphere of wartime alarm and contributed to the mood of post-war malaise.

The First World War defined a generation—both for those on the battlefield and for those who remained at home—and it has to a large degree defined our view of the imaginative writing of the period. The aftermath of the Great War was a breeding ground for even further trauma and anxiety that was manifest in much of the thought and literature of the age as well as in the political and social atmosphere. The treaty signed at Versailles in 1919 ushered in an uneasy and controversial armistice that even at the time was criticized for the disproportionate measure of retribution it meted out to a beaten Germany. In *The Economic Consequences of the Peace*, first published in England in 1919 and in the U.S. in 1920, the British economist John Maynard Keynes described the treaty as damaging to the psychic health as well as to the economic well-being of all Europeans: "If the European Civil War is to end with France and Italy abusing their momentary victorious power to destroy Germany and Austria-Hungary now prostrate, they invite their own destruction also, being so deeply and inextricably intertwined with their victims by hidden psychic and economic bonds."[11] These psychic bonds are so intricately interwoven in Keynes's estimation that should either side have taken advantage of its respective role, he warned, it risked being transformed into its opposite, thus wrecking the already precarious balance of European unity. By the late twenties, Keynes's predictions had proven accurate, as the armistice had become a tenuous fact and Germany had capitalized on its role as victim to legitimize its rearmament and reassert national pride and power. Versailles had become more of an occasion for resentment than a foundation for peace or stability.

Along with the General Strike in Britain in 1926, the crash of the stock market in the United States in 1929, and the widespread unease over Germany's resurgence, the feeling that Europe itself was either in decline or cycling toward another catastrophe pervaded the social and intellectual atmosphere in Britain, in America, and on the European continent. One of the most widely read works at this time, both among intellectuals and among the wider reading public, was Oswald Spengler's *The Decline of the West*, a comprehensive history of the West from ancient Greece to the present day published in Germany at the end of the First World War and translated into English by 1926.[12] Spengler claimed to see in the First World War as well as in the subsequent disintegration of European unity the inexorable fulfillment of the laws of history: "The future of the West is not a limitless tending upwards and onwards for all time towards our present ideals, but a single phenomenon of history, strictly limited and defined as to form and duration, which covers a few centuries and can be viewed and, in essentials, calculated from available precedents" (39). Whereas Keynes cautioned about the dangers of the post-war restructuring of Europe, Spengler's work verged on doomsaying. In *The Decline of the West*, Spengler purported to offer positivist proof of the fate and ultimate demise of the West and belied the naïve hope of a permanent end to war that many dared to hope for with the inception of the League of Nations. Although Spengler's book was the subject of much debate, his propositions gave voice to a growing feeling of uncertainty that pervaded the period.[13]

Such pervasive gloom was present as well in the imaginative literature of the period, and given voice to perhaps most famously in T. S. Eliot's *The Waste Land*. Eliot's 1922 poem portrays the ennui and despair of the post-war years in a fragmented and highly allusive manner. The imagery of *The Waste Land* consists of broken and disjointed glimpses of cities peopled by disembodied subjects, no man's land and the homeland conflated. The names of these cities echo through the poem like the intonation of a ghostly train conductor: "Jerusalem Athens Alexandria/Vienna London."[14] This litany of cities serves as a dreamlike itinerary of urban environments seen through the weary eyes of the modern traveler, for whom all cities are alike in their contours, their shuffling populations, their phantasmagoria, and their ultimate dispersal and decline.[15] *The Waste Land* is, however, not a poem of travel so much as it is a poem of stasis in a modern world in which travel no longer afforded either a rejuvenating connection with the past or intriguing glimpses of the new. Keynes's economic assessment of the post-war world, Spengler's historical account of the West's decline, and Eliot's elegy for the modern world, reiterate and even codify the anxiety and trauma that had been brought about by the events of the First World War. In their works, Spengler, Eliot, and Keynes thus assessed the contemporary world by describing respectively the distant but describable past (Spengler); the chaotic, at times unrecognizable present (Eliot); and the uncertain and ominous future (Keynes).

In this context of post-war malaise and increased government regulations and surveillance, travel was surrounded with an aura of transgression, as borders were more and more marked not by natural boundaries but by human law.[16] World War I had put an end to unrestricted travel while at the same time making it a thoroughly modern enterprise. Writers and artists in Britain and America were not immune to the effects of this malaise or to the travel restrictions bound up with it. Fussell calls the period after World War I in Britain "the final age of travel," a phrase that suggests the apocalyptic anxiety many writers felt that travel had forever lost its Romantic luster and was beginning to lose its capacity for imaginative replenishment.[17] In Fussell's view, authors frustrated with the enforced insularity of British life during the war and burdened with the paperwork involved in obtaining visas and passports saw the temporary easing of travel restrictions after the war—a luxury not shared by Americans—as an opportunity to seek relief and escape abroad: "After the war something new and recognizably 'postwar' surfaces in British intellectual and imaginative life. . . . Departure is attended by the conviction that England is uninhabitable because it is not like abroad" (15). Fussell sees post-war travel here as a kind of profligacy, a reaction to the claustrophobic domestic situation created by travel restrictions, as well as the result of the recognition that a way of life had passed in Britain.[18] In this view, England after the war was all but abandoned by a generation of writers seeking out more exotic locales. Not surprisingly, this sudden evacuation by writers and artists of Great Britain sparked an increase in travel writing, as writers were eager to have their discoveries and impressions read by those back home.

Samuel Hynes, in *The Auden Generation: Literature and Politics in England in the 1930s,* similarly suggests that the travel genre has a special relationship to the literature written during these interwar years.[19] He argues that the travel book was a requisite genre for the generation that lived through the war and that travel writing during the thirties was remarkable for the way authors "turned their travels into interior journeys and parables of their times, making landscape and incident—the factual materials of *reportage*—do the work of symbol and myth—the materials of *fable*" (228). Hynes's description of the intermingling of external, physical travel with internal psychological journeys aptly describes one of the chief features of modernist literature as well and points to one of the perpetual anxieties of the practitioners of both travel writing and modernism: that both the external world and the individual had been irrevocably altered by the Great War. Whereas Fussell sees travel writing as the expression of a combination of long overdue release and escapism, Hynes sees it as a genre that alternately projected and internalized the losses incurred during the war. Both critics, however, limit themselves for the most part to British writers, even as they see the travel genre as uniquely suited to the needs of the post-war generation and take the First World War as the defining event of the period.

The term "post-war," however, with its connotations of aftermath, disillusionment, and even post-trauma, gives a deceptively uniform sense to the entire period between World War I and World War II. So too the designation "between the wars" has become a convenient historical and critical category that, even as it has opened vistas into this era of literary complexity and obscurity, imposes limits on our critical approach to the literature of the period, especially, as we have seen with Fussell and Hynes, on our critical understanding of the travel book. For Wyndham Lewis, the "post-war" was a separate, distinct period that required special attention primarily because those who most assiduously insisted on it, he felt, were deliberately perpetuating its effects as much as they were describing a lived reality. In his 1937 autobiography, *Blasting and Bombardiering*, Lewis attempts to reclaim the phrase "post-war" in order to exorcise it:

> I call "post-war" between the War and the General Strike. Then began a period of a new complexion. It was no longer "post-war." We needn't *call* it anything. It's just the period we're living in today. Some people would call it one thing, some another. Best perhaps to call it nothing, until we see what it turns out to be. (1)

Lewis felt it necessary to designate a terminal point for the post-war years— here 1926, the year of the General Strike in Britain—so that people would not be lulled into taking as inevitable a category that he felt was largely constructed. After analyzing what he defined as the "post-war" in his books of the twenties, such as *The Art of Being Ruled* and *Time and Western Man*, where he specifically criticizes Spengler,[20] Lewis attempted to analyze this age of "new complexion," a process that can be seen to have begun with his 1931 trip to Morocco.

For Lewis, as for Cummings and West, the desire to travel was in part bound up with the desire to recognize and identify the events that could potentially lead to another war, in order to avoid the seemingly inexorable course that had led toward conflict in the first place. This particular motivation was not unique to these writers. The twenties and thirties also saw a proliferation of travel accounts by journalists and intellectuals, in addition to the literary travel writing that Fussell and Schweizer discuss. Accounts by writers such as Walter Duranty, Emma Goldman, Eugene Lyons, John Reed, and Lincoln Steffens testify not to post-war malaise but rather toward an enduring interest in current political events on the part of the public, a fervid need-to-know that was by all accounts saleable. Reporting firsthand from the scene gave these writers greater credibility and authority in the eyes of their audiences back home, an important selling point in an age in which distant events could be reported with ever greater speed.

While the four authors I discuss here are not primarily known as travel writers, their use of the travel narrative to describe and analyze the complicated realities and histories of the countries they visited, as well as their complicated reactions to what they saw, gives us a new perspective on how travel writing and modernist literature are inextricably linked. In each of these books, we can see the various ways in which these authors employ modernist techniques as they confront the landscape of the modern world and feel the urgency to communicate what they saw to an audience that they see similarly schooled in the difficult and allusive style of modernist literature.

Russia, Morocco, and Yugoslavia through Modernist Eyes

Travel writing is important to our understanding both of the literature written between the wars in general and to literary modernism in particular, despite the view expressed by Fussell that travel was in its final throes or that travel was primarily a form of escapism, just as it is important beyond the examples of British writers discussed by Fussell, Hynes, and more recently by Schweizer. While certainly a valuable way to chronicle the exhaustion of a beaten world, writers employed the travel genre as much for inquiry as for elegy. And while certainly a valuable way to examine the fading of British empire in the face a nascent transnationalism, there is as much continuity between the travel genre and modernist literature as there is rupture. For many writers of the period, modernism was always about crossing borders and posturing imaginatively against a backdrop of a modern world grown beyond the boundaries of nation, even as the legal boundaries were being redrawn (in the case of Central Europe) and newly inscribed (in the case of the Middle East) after the First World War. This desire for a new internationalism in the arts in the face of this political reordering of international boundaries was especially expressed by Pound, who had left America early on to explore the various and foreign centers of culture, news of which had reached him overseas through books and contacts. Although Pound never completed a full-length travel book, opting instead for the summative voice of the epic poem over the descriptive and desultory style of the travel narrative, he saw travel as a vital way of connecting with the past and always insisted on the importance of firsthand observation for all kinds of literary work. Pound grew to resent the increasing obstructions and frustrations that went along with modern travel—particularly, passport and visa regulations—and he spoke out against these bureaucratic nuisances repeatedly in newspaper articles and letters; but for Pound, travel remained an important way to obtain reliable information about foreign cultures, people, and artworks.

He was less sanguine, however, about the ultimate ability of prose to transmit the information that was thus gathered. In a 1918 essay on Henry James, he defines the "root difference" between poetry and prose as follows: "Most good poetry asserts something to be worth while, or damns a contrary; at any rate asserts emotional values. The best prose is, has been a presentation (complicated and elaborate as you like) of circumstances, of conditions, for the most part abominable or, at the mildest, amenable" (*Literary Essays* 324). Pound's distinction between mere presentation and outright assertion is one of degree: he sees the value of prose residing primarily in its ability to reflect the ills of society, whereas poetry asserts positive values and provides society with a blueprint for the future. In a 1941 essay, "Augment of the Novel," Pound elaborates on this distinction, appropriating a term from medical discourse and ascribing to prose a primarily "diagnostic" function. The prose works that he discusses—James Joyce's *Ulysses*, Lewis's *The Apes of God*, and Cummings's *Eimi*—"diagnose a state of society, which has led per force to the present conflict," although these books are unable, in Pound's estimation, to offer cures for what they diagnose.[21] For Pound, the ability to record and the manner in which this record was made were central concerns throughout his poetic career.

Pound saw the diagnostic function of prose emerging from the faithfulness and accuracy with which the author recorded their perceptions. Pound always relied heavily on faithful and accurate accounts from prose writers who documented their experiences abroad, writers such as Henry James and Thomas Hardy, as well as Joyce and Lewis, to provide the foundation on which *The Cantos* could assert the positive values and necessary remedies for the modern world, what Michael Bernstein, in his discussion of Pound's epic ambition, calls the "curative" power of poetry.[22] Whether or not Pound's distinctions can be uniformly applied to the modernist writers I discuss here, the empirical aspect of prose is particularly important to bear in mind when discussing the travel genre since the travel narrative relies primarily on what the traveler sees on the spot, and gains its authority from the reliability of the traveler's eyewitness testimony. How Cummings, Lewis, and West assert this authority, how they transmit what they see, and how they similarly relate both history and current events in the course of their travelers' tales are important questions to consider when approaching these texts. Cummings, Lewis, and

West all make explicit, by means of the travel narrative, the contradictory messages of eyewitness testimony and secondhand reports, and they are all aware, to varying degrees, of the way that history prescribes their immediate perceptions and the perceptions of those around them.

Pound's journey to Southern France prior to the outbreak of the First World War was in part pilgrimage, undertaken so that he could see for himself the landscapes crossed by the writers that he admired and was translating. The countries that Cummings, Lewis, and West visited promised no such literary connections. The Soviet Union, Morocco, and Yugoslavia were linked in various ways to Europe and America, largely due to the events of the First World War, and this is their reason for their journeys. Cummings witnesses the consequences of the communist revolution as the euphoria of Lenin's utopia was being supplanted by the claustrophobia of Soviet society and the deeper oppression of Stalin's totalitarianism. He traveled to the Soviet Union in part at the prompting of his friend John Dos Passos, who instilled in him a curiosity about the nature of government subsidies for the arts in Russia, and took copious notes on his tour. Cummings describes the publication of *Eimi*, however, as an afterthought, as a hurried assemblage of these notes. Cummings was one among many American writers who traveled to Russia in the thirties to report on the Soviet experiment. In *Eimi*, Cummings confronts a political system that was being promoted in the West by artists and journalists as a modern-day utopia but which he finds to be stifling and restricting. Rather than being an objective or journalistic account of the workings of the Soviet system, however, Cummings filters his experiences through his dense prose and complex narrative, both of which make it difficult to determine what it is that Cummings sees. On his journey, he assumes various roles and guises—tourist, artist, and journalist, among others—as he travels through Moscow, amidst what he comes to see as the oppressive atmosphere of the communist system. These shifting roles, which he at times assumes and at other times has thrust upon him and which often seem as much defensive stance as artistic posture, along with the dense style, provide Cummings with the different perspectives and voices that he needs in order to make sense of his journey even while he clings anxiously to his identity as an artist and as an individual.

Morocco in 1931 was a French Protectorate, a colonial space occupied by a variety of religious and ethnic groups. The country was also at this time (as it had been in the early years of the twentieth century) a political and diplomatic battleground for the European powers. Lewis traveled to Morocco in part because he felt that a change of scenery would allow him to complete the subsequent installments of his 1928 novel *The Childermass* that he had promised to his publishers, Chatto & Windus.[23] In this regard, his trip was an escape; however, he also sought a wider context for the arguments he was expounding in that imaginative work, and his trip was as much an extension of his ideas as it was a break with his milieu. After having railed against his peers specifically and "Western Man" in general in his polemical works and novels of the twenties, Lewis sought further evidence and fresh insight for his opinions on the margins of an empire. In a letter to his publisher, Lewis wrote that his intention in going to Morocco was "to show the unsatisfactory operation at a distance of a crooked political system" and proposed this journey as above all "a *satiric* enterprise" (*Filibusters*, xvi, Lewis's italics). In the chapter on *Filibusters*, I examine Lewis's use of satire, a complicated word in Lewis's lexicon, and his use of the first-person narrator in this satire. The first-person narrator is a common enough feature in a travel book but one unusual for Lewis outside of his polemical works. Lewis's assessment of the French presence in Morocco and the political lesson that he finds for England and Europe at this critical moment between the wars are revealed through the descriptive prose of his travel book. His portrayal of the colonial space of Morocco and the manner in which he maps the history of the French and European presence onto Morocco's geographical terrain suggest that his interest was less in the exotic or the picturesque than it was in the various ways in which order could be maintained in an otherwise chaotic environment, a persistent interest of Lewis's throughout his career. *Filibusters* is an important, if not always successful, example in Lewis's career where he attempts to utilize his own modernist techniques and style in his cultural critique. In this case, his use of satire, the idea of which he took such pains to articulate and the practice of which he is so well known for, became a way for him to savage not merely an artistic community (as he did in *The Apes of God*) but an entire political milieu and an entire time period.

The country that West knew as Yugoslavia came into existence as a political entity only after the First World War, a makeshift solution to the nationalistic, religious, and ethnic tensions of the fractious Balkan states. It was the site of the beginning of the First World War with the assassination of Archduke Franz Ferdinand of Austria on June 28, 1914, and it looked to many as if it would be the site of the beginning of the second. West's journey is, of the three authors I treat here, the most deliberate and thorough undertaking, and her book is the most comprehensive rendering of its subject. West traveled to Yugoslavia on three separate occasions in the thirties and wove elements of these separate journeys into the single unified narrative that is *Black Lamb and Grey Falcon*. After having been invited to Yugoslavia by the British Council for a lecture series, West was so enamored of the country that she returned twice more. Her stated purpose in traveling to the region, in which transpired the events that directly led to World War I, was to map the convoluted and tortuous route by which events at a distance made themselves felt at home in London, as well as to discover the role of the intellectual in the modern world:

> I had to admit that I quite simply and flatly knew nothing at all about the south-eastern corner of Europe; and since there proceeds steadily from that place a stream of events which are a source of danger to me, which indeed for four years threatened my safety and during that time deprived me of many benefits, that is to say I know nothing of my own destiny. (21)

In my chapter on West, I examine how she interprets events that she witnesses, hears about, or reads about as she considers the various ways in which both history and current events are mediated. I also focus on her attempts to account for her own fascination with what she sees as she ponders "that quality of visibility that makes the Balkans so specially enchanting" (202). But more importantly, I examine the way she enacts this interpretation and performs this inquiry through a text that bears the marks of an earlier modernist style, particularly the modernist concern with the cunning passages and nightmarish manifestations of history, and how this history is transformed into myth.

Modern Literature and The Conditions of Visibility: Travel Writing and Historiography

My discussion of modernist style is not intended to be comprehensive; rather, it provides a specific entry point to the travel writing of Pound, Cummings, Lewis, and West. For each of the latter three writers, I focus on one particular aspect of modernist style or method that predominates in their travel narratives: with Cummings this is the obscurity and difficulty of his prose; with Lewis it is his satire; and with West it is her historiography. These various techniques or methods are clearly present in all of the works to some degree, but what they share is a reliance on the visual. The obscurity of Cummings's prose replicates the obscure nature of Soviet society while serving as well as a shell that encases his artistic persona, providing as much a vantage point as a defense. Lewis's satire is always grounded in the visual, and his focus is, as it was in all of his satire, on "the *outside*" of things, on the carapace of the human being and the exotic picturesque landscapes onto which they are projected.[24] For West, the travel narrative is a screen onto which the beauty of the world is testified to, even as the chaotic present is guided by the unseen forces of the past. This history must likewise be made manifest in order for it to be known.

Eimi, Filibusters in Barbary, and *Black Lamb and Grey Falcon* are richly layered texts that highlight the ways in which truth values are negotiated, history is transmitted, authority is both asserted and questioned, and audiences are configured—all issues important to any discussion of modernist literature. The travel book was for these writers a means not only of portraying or diagnosing the countries they visited but a vehicle for reconsidering the nature and impact of empirical and historical evidence during the strife-filled period between the wars. These authors accomplish this in a variety of ways with varying degrees of success, but what they share, partly by virtue of being travel writers and partly through their affiliation with modernism, is a special, sometimes vexed, relationship to the visual—both in the sense of what can be seen and in the sense of what can be portrayed—and to the ways that subjective experience, tethered always to the objective world, could be transmitted to a particular audience back home.

This reliance on the visual is a part of the history of modernism as well, as this revolutionary movement evolved through the period between the wars. For modernist writers who were developing styles that they hoped would reflect the complex and chaotic modern world in the early years of the century, visual perception and empirical data were of primary importance. This is as true of an author such as James Joyce, who took acute observation and realism to their utmost logical conclusions, as it was for the writers I examine here. Ezra Pound also stressed the importance of the visual when articulating the tenets of imagism in 1913 and then again when describing the poetic method (closely related to imagism) that he called "phanopoeia" and defined as "a casting of images upon the visual imagination."[25] These phanopoetic images, Pound said, could "be translated almost, or wholly, intact," from one language to another, suggesting by this that the visual imagination transcends cultural and linguistic boundaries.[26]

The reliance on external objects or events that have their source in sensory perception was also central to T. S. Eliot's famous "objective correlative," which he defined as "a set of objects, a situation, a chain of events which shall be the formula of that *particular* emotion; such that when the external facts, which must terminate in sensory experience, are given, the emotion is immediately evoked."[27] The objective correlative serves as a common ground for the author and reader, and it provides testimony both of the external world and of the internal authority of the poet. Virginia Woolf wrote similarly in her 1923 essay, "Mr. Bennett and Mrs. Brown," of the need for some external verifiable object to correspond with internal emotion: "The writer must get into touch with his reader by putting before him something which he recognizes, which therefore stimulates his imagination, and makes him willing to cooperate in the far more difficult business of intimacy."[28] For Woolf here, as for Eliot, the object or formula under consideration, while prompted by sensory data, is more than simply a visual image, and sight itself is in part a metaphor. Woolf goes on to say, "It is of the highest importance that this common meeting-place should be reached easily, almost instinctively, in the dark, with one's eyes shut" (Scott, 638). Nevertheless, both writers rely on some recognizable visual object or event when formulating their artistic principles.

In *A Genealogy of Modernism*, Michael Levenson sees this modern dependence on the visual developing alongside a growing skepticism over the ability to describe the external world objectively.[29] Citing Joseph Conrad's famous statement at the beginning of *The Nigger of the Narcissus* that the role of the artist is to "make you hear, to make you feel . . . before all, to make you *see*" (qtd. in Levenson, 1), for example, Levenson suggests that Conrad here is not endorsing objective, empirical observation so much as he is questioning the authority of vision itself. Levenson sees Conrad's interest in the visual as symptomatic of a shift from the omniscient narrator of nineteenth-century fiction to the separate, "more modest" zones of narration characteristic of modernist fiction. Conrad, Levenson argues, calls into question *what* it is that we are seeing, even as he takes this as his primary criterion for artistic success. For Levenson, the "impressionist" school of writing, of which he takes Conrad to be an exemplar, was thus engaged in a dual-pronged critique both of the omniscience of the narrator and of the verity of inner subjectivity. Modern fiction, Levenson suggests, is located between these poles: "Part of every fiction is *physis*, the elaboration of an external physical space, and part is *psyche*, the construction of an internal psychological space" (7). The dialectic tension between these two, so characteristic of modern writers, was, according to Levenson, the result of the "abrupt contact between subject and world" (20).

This "abrupt contact" between subjectivity and objectivity manifested itself in various ways among modernist writers as we have seen. In recent years a number of critics have explored the consequences of this abrupt contact not for its aesthetic manifestations but for how it shaped the political and ideological ideas of modernist writers. Both Vincent Sherry and Reed Way Dasenbrock, for instance, take the visual and visual media as central to the writing of Pound and Lewis, seeing these as important elements in their political entanglements and increasing authoritarian stances during the thirties.[30] Focusing on the role of the visual arts in the literature of the period, Dasenbrock examines Vorticism, the artistic and literary movement Pound and Lewis launched in London in 1914. According to Dasenbrock, Vorticism provided literary modernism with a vocabulary that drew heavily on the visual arts. This influence, however, functioned primarily as a negative example as Pound and Lewis, swayed by the power and immediacy of visual art, came to see the necessity of keeping the arts separate and distinct. As Dasenbrock suggests, "Each art, in Pound's account, has an essential element not found in other arts, such as the image in poetry, and form in painting. The best work in each art is that which relies exclusively upon that element, the primary pigment of that art, because it creates the most concentrated, most intense kind of art" (17).[31] Although intensity was Vorticism's chief goal, the relationship between Vorticist paintings and perceived reality is a tenuous one, according to Dasenbrock: "Vorticist painting is marked by its geometric bias. Lines demarcate angular shapes, which are manipulated for compositional reasons, not out of any fidelity to optical perceptions" (41). The persuasive power of visual immediacy and discrimination attracted both Pound and Lewis, who were attempting to find the "primary pigment" of modernist literature. Dasenbrock suggests that the literary experiments of the Vorticists were more significant than their painterly equivalents and encourages us to see modernist prose as something other than a striving toward realism, psychological or otherwise.

Sherry also examines the importance of the visual to modernist writers but goes further than Dasenbrock in drawing direct connections between the aesthetic of visual immediacy and the political ideas that Pound and Lewis espoused in the twenties and thirties. He traces the origins of Pound's and Lewis's thought around the time of the First World War to the influence of the French "ideologues," who in the aftermath of the French Revolution articulated a physiological approach to aesthetics in order to ground their political and social theories. This linking of aesthetics with politics, in what Sherry calls the "pseudo-scientific language of the ideologues," had its logical outcome, he argues, in the high modernism of Pound and Lewis where, as with the French ideologues, "the physiology of the eye accounts both for a new literary language—a vocabulary of ultravisual immediacy—and the faculty . . . of dictatorial command" (7). The attempt to apply "optical standards into a linguistic medium," Sherry argues, had its counterpart in the political sphere (58). The "severing" effect of visual discrimination, which clearly demarcates objects within a space and foreground from background, establishing as well the necessary detachment between subject and object, sharply contrasts, for example, to the affective power of music. Thus, the lessons of the visual arts, as they were translated into a literary medium, became charged with a new political valence and led to, or were the preconditions for, Pound's and Lewis's political affiliations during the thirties and forties. According to Sherry, "The modernists' new standard of visual immediacy in words led them to esteem (what they saw as) a superior directness in the political cultures of Nazism and fascism" (7). This severing effect as well as the focus on the visual, and, especially, the function of art as a conduit for such radical political ideology might also be applied to the opposite end of the political spectrum that Sherry describes, as we see evidenced in the social realist art of the Soviet Union. The physiology of the eye, as Sherry describes it, and its relationship to modernist literature, would seem to be of use mostly as a way of describing how modernist writers made this transition from an often obscurely scripted interiority to a starkly presented external representation, whatever the nature of the resulting ideology might be. Pound himself, for instance, as we will see in the next chapter, seemed for a period to be drawn as much to the possibilities of the Soviet Revolution as he was to the order of Italian fascism.

While neither Sherry nor Dasenbrock discusses travel literature specifically, their arguments regarding visual perception and political thought are important to keep in mind when discussing the travel genre during this period, especially since the works I examine all describe the political as well as the geographical landscapes of foreign countries, and these writers frequently incorporate polemical arguments into their narratives. Travel writing depends on the visual in this way, both in the sense of what the traveler sees and in how they make what they see apparent to others. Cummings, Lewis, and West all accomplish this in various ways as they navigate the perilous political landscape of the thirties. These writers construct representations of the foreign that were often intended to be read as political metaphors or allegories for those back home. If the early modernists were attempting to occupy some "still point," in order to examine the modern world more accurately—as Dasenbrock says of the Vorticists (26)—the onset and aftermath of the First World War and the subsequent social and political upheavals required, paradoxically, that at least some movement was necessary in order for this examination and inquiry to proceed.

The word *history* derives from the Greek *istor,* meaning "eye-witness," and it is above all this paradoxical idea of a confrontation with what has passed or is passing that preoccupied the modernist writers of the period, from Pound's imploring us to see history as an "it" in his call to "make it new," to the cunning passages of Eliot's formulation in *Gerontion,* to Joyce's Daedalian nightmare. In *The Mirror of Herodotus: The Representation of the Other in the Writing of History,* François Hartog describes the complex ways in which "history" (what has passed) and "eye witness" (what passes before the eye), so seemingly at odds in their linking of the past and the present, the conjectural and the manifest, interact in the work of the Greek historian Herodotus in a way that can help us read these modernist texts.[32] Echoing a common view of Herodotus throughout the ages, Hartog refers to him as "the father of history and also a liar—if not, indeed, the father of all liars" (xviii). This double appellation arose partly as a result of Herodotus's giving equal space in his work to eyewitness testimony and secondhand reports as he traveled around the known world. Hartog, however, attempts to reconcile this fractured view of the Greek historian by reading Herodotus's *Histories* not as unmediated historical truth but rather as a multilayered text that makes explicit the ways that historical knowledge and current events are transmitted to particular discursive communities. Hartog de-emphasizes the eyewitness testimony on which Herodotus's work is ostensibly based and focuses instead on how he "translates" both what he sees (autopsy) *and* what he hears (hearsay) into information for his audience back in Greece.[33] Hartog's main goal is to examine through Herodotus's writing how the Greeks perceived the "Other" in what he hopes will be a contribution to "an archaeology of historical perception," by which he means, partly, a study of the uses to which people put eyewitness testimony (268). By drawing attention to the nature of historical evidence, Hartog's reading of Herodotus is a useful model for my study because he sees Herodotus's *Histories* as grounded in firsthand accounts but proliferating in a variety of discursive practices that complement and even challenge the very authority of vision upon which his *logoi* are ostensibly grounded. Hartog focuses instead on the more complex, layered narrative structure of Herodotus's text.

Thus, from Hartog I would like to borrow the notion that rather than rendering truth, the travel genre asks the question, What is truth?: "It is more a matter of pondering what is visible and the conditions of visibility. What is it that is visible? Not *what* have I seen, but *what is it* that I have seen?" (267). What qualifies as an event? How are events reported? And how do we read them? According to Hartog, for positivist historians "writing history meant consulting archives and unfolding long chains of events, all in the past" (266), and they frowned on the presence of the historian in the text. The authenticity and persuasiveness of the travel books I examine, while ostensibly grounded in the belief that firsthand knowledge is of primary importance, are caught up in this same tension between subjectivity and objectivity that Hartog sees as important in Herodotus and that was so important to the early modernists. Understanding this tension entails as well understanding the variety of discursive strategies that these writers employ, including but not limited to journalism, satire, and history, as they transmit what they see and hear on their journeys. Like the writers I discuss, Herodotus was writing between two wars: the Persian Wars, which ended when he was still young, and the Peloponnesian War, the beginning of which he lived long enough to witness. This focus on firsthand testimony and the layered representation of what these writers see jibes well with the intersection between the critical fields of late modernism and travel writing.

SETTING OUT

The subtitle of my study, "Intellectuals Abroad," is meant to suggest the sense of mission with which these writers traveled, however vaguely conceived, but it is meant at the same time to recall the naïve travelers of Mark Twain's *Innocents Abroad,* who are on a fundamental level unable to shed their own sense of home long enough to appreciate what they are seeing. I derive this title more directly, however, by way of Cecil Frank Melville, a British critic of Oswald Mosley and English Fascism, who, in reference to Lewis in his 1931 book *Hitler,* accuses Lewis of being an "Intellectual Innocent Abroad," of distorting what he sees. He suggests that Lewis has been duped by the popular fascist appeal of Adolf Hitler.[34] Melville argues that Lewis's idealism permits him to see only a Great Man while remaining blind to Hitler's political opportunism:

> Such a mixture of idealism and opportunism in politics is, of course, inevitable. Hitler would appreciate this, naturally enough. . . . But Mr. Wyndham Lewis, looking in the Hitlerist mirror and seeing therein the reflection of the familiar features of Mr. Wyndham Lewis, has not yet, it would seem, been able to recognise such a necessity. (6)

In their works, Cummings, Lewis, and West are all guilty to various degrees of creating images of foreign countries that are in some respect in the service of their own beliefs and desires. However, to various degrees they all remain aware of this danger, and the travel genre is ideal for representing if not resolving the paradox this situation necessarily involves. It is a danger that Hartog describes as well regarding Herodotus: "The *Histories* are a mirror into which the historian never ceased to peer as he pondered his own identity: he was the looker looked at, the questioner questioned" (xxiii). This danger is a distinguishing feature of both historiography and travel writing, especially borne as the latter is of this admixture of idealism and innocence.

In *Ezra Pound and the Monument of Culture,* Lawrence Rainey offers his own diagnosis of the state of literary criticism, borrowing a phrase from Jürgen Habermas as he does: "To confront 'what is foreign'—the heterogeneous testimonies of history, the world that informs cultural works, both past and future—is a task that has been largely evaded by literary studies in our time."[35] Confronting what is foreign is the chief exercise of this study—both the foreignness of other countries, in the works of Cummings, Lewis, and West, and the foreignness of literary modernism itself. In both cases, these experiences are mediated: latterly by critics who have constructed canons, traced genealogies, and established historical periods; and formerly by Cummings, Lewis, and West themselves, whose accounts of foreign lands are always permeated by their concerns for home and by attempts to make sense of events which grow ever more ominous, events which to a large degree are still with us today.

According to Habermas elsewhere, the concept of modernity needs to be rethought, not abandoned. In his view, "modernity" is an attempt to arrive at a deeper sense of community, and in this light he proposes the notion of "communicative rationality" as a means for making truth claims, both normative and legal. In doing so he does not appeal to a transcendent and always valid truth, but a local and negotiable one, suggesting that any attempt at communication is an attempt to make oneself known to another:

> The concept of communicative rationality does contain utopian per-spective; in the structures of undamaged intersubjectivity can be found a necessary condition for individuals reaching an understanding among themselves, without coercion, as well as for the identity of an individual coming to understanding with himself or herself without force.[36]

Cummings, Lewis, and West all struggle to understand events that often seem to exceed understanding. In their travel books, their styles are infused with the characteristic idiosyncrasies of modernist texts, as they attempt to portray not only the countries they visit but also the process of their own understanding. These works enact the double goal of coming to terms with a larger, chaotic post-war community facing the prospect of another war and with their own at times equally chaotic perceptions. Cummings, Lewis, and West all grope for order and meaning in foreign countries where what they see is conditioned by the histories of the countries they visit, by a host of conflicting voices, cultures, political systems, and sights, as well as by the anxiety that what they say will have an impact on those back home. Representation itself becomes an issue as they attempt to rethink the role of the artist in the modern world. Cummings, Lewis, and West not only record what *had* happened in the pasts of these countries and what *was* happening in their present, but also try to determine what might *yet* happen in their futures and the future of the West in general. These writers, who were variously associated with a movement that had tried to create a language with which to record and reflect modern life, now employed that language to create a new way of seeing.

"DAMN THE PARTITION!"

Ezra Pound and Modern Travel

And at places where no frontiers could possibly be, in the middle of a square, or on a bridge linking the parts of a quay, men in uniform step forward and demand passports, minatory as figures projected into sleep by an uneasy conscience.

—Rebecca West, *Black Lamb and Grey Falcon*

A little passport is my life.

—E. E. Cummings, *Eimi*

IN THE SPRING OF 1912, EZRA POUND EMBARKED ON A WALKING TOUR OF southern France during which he visited more than a dozen towns and cities in the span of a few weeks. While traveling, he kept with him a journal in which he recorded what he called in another context the "luminous details" of his trip.[1] This journal, scrawled in a series of notebooks and on more informal scraps of paper, was to form the basis of a prose work that would be a compendium of his firsthand experiences in the Midi, observations on the lives and works of the troubadours, and Pound's thoughts about the modern world. He intended to call this work *Gironde*, after a river that flows through Toulouse. Pound had traveled in part because he hoped that seeing the Provençal landscape firsthand would enable him to decode the *trobar clus*, or "closed poetry," of the troubadours, a verse form notable for its complex structure, involved sonorities, and obscure meanings.[2] As Richard Sieburth, who transcribed and published the notebooks, points out, Pound's scholarly methods were, at the very least, unconventional, as they involved "shuttling back and forth between the realm of real topographical referents and the domain of written signifiers."[3] Although the impetus for Pound's journey came from his reading of the troubadours, he didn't merely take their works as a Baedeker for the territory so much as allow the words on the page and the landscape laid out before him to feed off one another. What he saw and experienced on the road helped him solve some of the difficulties of the texts, just as what he read in the works of the French *jongleurs* helped him recognize what he was seeing on the road, so that neither book nor place held priority. This "shuttling back and forth," as Sieburth calls it, along with the projected *Gironde*, in which this shuttling would somehow be recorded, also revealed the uncertainty that Pound felt as to the path that his own literary career would take, whether it would be in poetry or prose that he could best contain the results of this method and portray the modern world.

Although Pound had come to Europe from America with great literary ambitions, it was not yet clear to him whether his true métier would be prose or poetry. In addition to several books of verse, he had published significant prose works, such as *The Spirit of Romance*, his 1910 study of the middle ages. In 1911, Pound showed his recently published book of poetry, *Canzoni*, to Ford Madox Ford (then Hueffer). Instead of the encouragement that he had hoped for, however, Pound described, whether fancifully or not, the sight of the editor of *The English Review* rolling on the floor in disgust over the antiquated and stilted language.[4] Years later, Pound would recall this scene as an important moment for him: "that roll," he wrote affectionately on the occasion of Ford's death in 1939, "saved me at least two years, perhaps more."[5]

Undaunted by Ford's critical exhibition, Pound sought out his advice a year later in 1912, after his walking tour in Southern France, this time regarding the proposed travel book. Ford's comments on this occasion, although harsh, were not as dismissive as his roll, nor were they without encouragement. In a letter to Dorothy Shakespear on September 14, 1912, Pound wrote: "I went over the first 80 pp. of 'Gironde' with Ford yesterday, he says its [sic] as bad as Stevenson and that is very violent for him, he is however pleased with the Ripostes—and his criticism of the prose is very helpful and the stuff is not precisely hopeless or past revising."[6] After struggling further with the manuscript, however, Pound eventually gave up on the project, unable, it seems to yoke the "real topographical referents" to the "written signifiers." Disheartened, he wrote to Dorothy a week later, "I've hung about the 1st 1/3rd of 'Gironde' on my west wall as a sign that I'm dam'd if I bother much more with revising it." (161). He wrote of the manuscript one last time the following spring, in what seems to have been a final effort to revive his own flagging interest in the travel narrative: "I've got a damn rotten prose thing, neither fish nor feather, a walk in the troubadour country with notes on the troubadour lives etc. Awful hash. . . . sort of muddle" (qtd. in Sieburth, xiii). The hybrid *Gironde* eventually sank without a trace into the recesses of Pound's mind, although the memory of unfettered travel that it conjured and the luminous details that it recorded would periodically offer up ideas and oddments for his later poetry. Pound seems to have decided that travel writing was an insufficient genre with which to express the modern world. While he continued to write both poetry and prose, from this time on Pound's main work would be his "poem including history," *The Cantos*.[7] Travel would continue to have an impact on his poetry, although his subsequent travel experiences would not always be as picturesque as were the roads of southern France in 1912.

Only a few years after Pound's decision to abandon *Gironde*, the freedom to travel that he enjoyed in 1912 was curtailed as the result of the travel restrictions prompted by the exigencies of the First World War, such as the Passport Control Act of the United States, which required all citizens traveling abroad to have with them the necessary documents.[8] After having traveled extensively without visas, passports, or other paperwork, Pound was understandably perplexed by these laws. After the war, when the government failed to repeal these measures, Pound's perplexity grew to outright frustration. His American passport proclaimed a nationality that he was eager to keep, but it also became for him the symptom of all that was wrong with the modern world, a world that was becoming overrun with bureaucracy and pointless regulations (see figure 1).

Pound's frustration over passport regulations during this time grew along with his frustrations over other bureaucratic and governmental matters that he similarly saw as obstructionist and wrongheaded, including obscenity statutes, copyright law, and postal censorship. Reference to these issues becomes more frequent in Pound's writings throughout the teens and the twenties, and his tone in regard to them became increasingly vituperative. Many critics have noted the prominence that these matters assumed for Pound as well as the peculiar way that they were linked in his mind. Robert Spoo calls the obscenity statutes, copyright law, and postal censorship a "trinity of legal forces that [Pound] believed was crippling the progress of literature and enlightenment in the United States" (634).[9] To this trinity could well be added the legal force of passport regulations, whose effects more literally crippled the casual traveler. What these issues shared for Pound was their inhibition of the freedom of the artist and of the spread of the arts just at a moment, he felt, when the modern world was ripe for a renaissance. In his repeated denunciations of these matters, however, we can also see the outlines of Pound's more strident

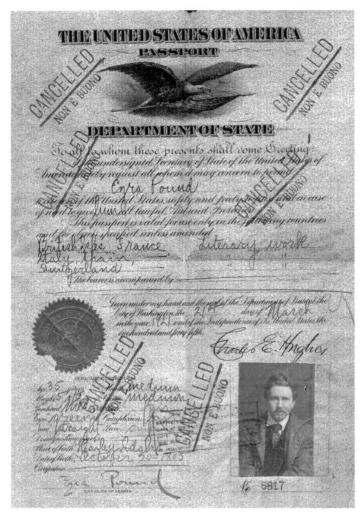

Fig. 1. Ezra Pound's 1921 passport. Courtesy, The Lilly Library, Indiana University, Bloomington, Indiana.

and fixed concentration on the larger political and economic issues that were to preoccupy him throughout his life.

As E. P. Walkiewicz and Hugh Witemeyer point out, Pound's interest in Social Credit and Italian Fascism was not entirely discontinuous with his earlier interests in, for example, the statutory matter of passports: "Underlying Pound's prescriptions on both cultural and economic issues is a vision of healthy, unobstructed circulation within and among national communities— circulation of ideas, publications, works of art, consumer goods, money, and people."[10] Pound's early travels remained an important touchstone for this vision of "unobstructed circulation," even as his interests broadened beyond the boundaries of France and the middle ages. As a sign of this gradual elision from the strictly cultural to the broadly political, Walkiewicz and Witemeyer note one interest in particular that came to preoccupy Pound in the twenties, that of the diplomatic recognition of the Soviet Union.

Residing as he did in Rapallo in the late twenties, Pound could observe firsthand the development of Mussolini's Italy, and he had direct access to Italian journals and periodicals. Through his contacts with numerous writers, artists, and politicians in America, Pound also felt that he had a fairly clear idea of the economic and political scene there.[11] The Soviet Union, however, remained a closed book, and Pound was forced to rely on the testimony of others for his assessment of the political events that had been transpiring there since at least the 1917 Revolution, events which were being discussed at great length in the West. The accounts of those who had traveled there, especially those by John Reed, Lincoln Steffens, Senator Bronson Cutting, and E. E. Cummings, as I will show, were a crucial ingredient in his portrayal of the modern world in *The Cantos*. While the empirical method that Pound had privileged on the roads of southern France was important to *The Cantos*, equally important were the descriptions of foreign scenes by other travelers.

Pound felt that the modern renaissance he had been proclaiming since before the war could only occur if people had access to the monumental works of the past and were fully informed of the political events that were transpiring throughout Europe and America. For Pound, travel provided a more direct and vital contact to these literary works and to these present events than simple scholarship or mere reportage could. *The Cantos* were intended, in part, to foreground this double contact simultaneously, fusing firsthand observation with secondhand reporting—one reason perhaps for their notorious difficulty. Commenting on this difficulty, Guy Davenport, using Pound's own words, has described *The Cantos* as a periplum, "not as land looks on a map / but as sea bord seen by men sailing."[12] This approach to *The Cantos*, which takes travel as a metaphorical voyage both through a unique literary tradition and through a modern world all but unrecognizable in the postwar years, helps make sense of this difficult poem, the terrain of which is still so foreign. However, although the metaphorical use of travel was important to Pound and can be of use to readers of *The Cantos*, few critics have examined the ways in which Pound's own travel experiences and the travel experiences of others both influenced his views on modern literature in general and helped shape his own work in particular.

Both kinds of travel—Pound's own and the travel of others—had an impact on his development as a writer, and both kinds of travel were to play important roles in Pound's forty-year epic. In what follows, I first describe in more detail Pound's early travels during which he began to formulate the distinctions between poetry and prose that were important to him as he was beginning his literary career, insisting on what he called the "diagnostic" properties of prose. I then show how Pound responded with increasing frustration to the travel restrictions of the First World War by obscurely encoding his own encounter with the "passport nuisance" in Canto 7. I also examine Pound's use of the travel accounts of other writers, especially Lincoln Steffens and his reports on the Russian Revolution at the end of Canto 16. While important to Pound, the travel genre was useful primarily as a source for economic and political realities but not as a way of containing and expressing the modern world. It would take the epic poem to order and contain this material. I then discuss Pound's subsequent interest in the diplomatic recognition of Russia, especially as he expressed it in his correspondence with Senator Bronson Cutting of New Mexico, who had traveled to Russia in 1930. This issue of the diplomatic recognition of the Soviet Union and Pound's subsequent promotion of Cummings's *Eimi* paved the way in the thirties and forties for a reemphasis on Pound's part of the distinctions between poetry and prose. I examine this distinction both for what it says of *Eimi* and also by way of introducing my discussion of the modern travel books of Lewis and West. Throughout his career, from his early travels to his residence in Italy and eventual incarceration in St. Elizabeths hospital in Washington, D.C., the theme of travel and the conditions and possibilities of recognition between people and states pervaded Pound's conversation and writing. Perhaps one reason Pound remained so nostalgic for those early years before the war, on the roads of southern France, was that he was then so sure of what he was seeing.

"Damn Rotten Prose Thing": Pound's Early Travels and *Gironde*

Pound saw his identity through the dual prisms of the life of the artist, which he defined by a delight in travel and wanderlust, and the life of a European, which defined itself by its nationality and deep historical roots. Born in Hailey, Idaho, in 1885, he first traveled to Europe at the age of twelve in the company of his Aunt Frank in 1898. The two journeyed throughout the continent, seeing Cologne, Nuremberg, Paris, Lucerne, Genoa, Florence, Rome, Naples, and Venice, ending up in Tangiers in Northern Africa after crossing the Strait of Gibraltar. Such a whirlwind tour must have been as arduous and exhausting as it was edifying, especially since Aunt Frank carried with her "an enormous quantity of assorted baggage" that the two lugged from point to point.[13] Any ardor or exhaustion they felt on their journey, however, was surely due to the rigorous itinerary and to the amount of luggage they carried with them, not to any difficulties they had with obtaining the correct paperwork, since there was none to obtain. The travelers took for granted the ease with which they could cross borders and go where they wanted, not having to worry about visas or passports.

Pound acknowledged the importance of this early voyage many times. After his walking tour of Southern France in 1912, as he was learning more about the lives and work of the troubadours and discovering for himself the pleasures as well as the difficulties that must have attended their own travels, he wrote to Aunt Frank, "I have come to realize how much work those preliminary tours saved me" (Carpenter, 33). He remembered this 1898 trip again toward the end of his life, along with some touching, hitherto latent details when, in a postscript to the 1968 reissue of *The Spirit of Romance*, that prewar paean to the Middle Ages, he wrote:

> A fellow named Smith put me on the road which led to the publication of this book—my first published prose work. He was a Philadelphia travel agent whom I had first seen as a boy, in 1898, when my great-aunt Frank had taken us on a grand tour of Europe. . . . Looking back, and considering, I feel it fitting that this new American reprint be dedicated: "to 'Smith' with thanks."[14]

It is tempting to see Smith as a Tiresias who provides Pound with early guidance as he embarks on his journey; but what Pound remembers here is not the arcane instructions given to a would-be Odysseus but the simplicity of planning a trip, the ease of travel, and the connection between travel and literary work ("the road which led me to the publication of this book"). This memory further attests to the fact that from the beginning, Pound's literary career was closely linked to travel.

In 1909, Pound moved to London to establish himself on the literary scene, having found nothing in the American geographical or cultural landscape that could serve as the launching pad for an artistic career. He returned to the states briefly in 1910–1911, however, and from this trip gathered material for a series of essays that were published in 1912 and 1913 in *The New Age*. He had at one point planned on combining these essays, collectively known as "Patria Mia," along with *Gironde*, into what Sieburth calls a "diptych" that would juxtapose the Middle Ages and the modern world, Europe and America (Sieburth, xii). In "Patria Mia," Pound expresses his early enthusiasm for both travel and literature, addressing his native country like some poor relation to European greatness: "America, my country, is almost a continent and hardly yet a nation, for no nation can be considered historically as such until it has achieved within itself a city to which all roads lead, and from which there goes out an authority" (101).[15] Pound's *rappel à l'ordre*, however, was prompted not by despair over what he saw but by optimism for America's future. Pound believed that the modern world was on the brink of a new renaissance, one in which artists and writers would lead the way to a transformed society by forging connections between the old world and the new. It was crucial to Pound in "Patria Mia" that the roads he envisions radiating from the metropolis should be accessed freely in order for this modern renaissance to be realized and for the arts to circulate and flourish.

Later in "Patria Mia," Pound describes in more detail the artist's role, again making a connection between travel and literature, but also seeing this role in relation to national interests: "Letters are a nation's foreign office. By the arts, and by them almost alone do nations gain for each other any understanding and intimate respect" (109). Such a project of mutual understanding, respect, and recognition was possible at this time because travel itself, although rigorous, was nonetheless free of bureaucratic interference. Pound, for instance, had traveled to America, then back to London, and was to begin his trip through southern France all within several months, never bothering to obtain travel documents. In Carpenter's words, Pound at this time "would travel about Europe with a minimum of premeditation and an absolute disregard for bother about tickets or currency, rarely troubling to supply his intimates with more than the barest details of his next address, if known" (154).

Pound delighted in the ease of travel again when, residing in London, he set out alone on the more ambitious walking tour of southern France previously mentioned that was to result in the abandoned *Gironde*. During this trip, Pound traveled with a Baedeker of southern France and a book on the troubadours, Justin Smith's *The Troubadours at Home* (1899), but otherwise was led only by his interests in their lives, poems, and the landscape. Decrying the passport system in a 1927 article in *The Nation* (where he misremembers the year of this journey as 1911), Pound recalls that the only paperwork he traveled with on this occasion was "an unstamped membership card to the Touring Club de France," which helped him "get into a small inn at Chalus when covered with twenty miles of mud."[16]

During his walks through Poitiers, Chalais, and Toulouse, and along the Languedoc coast, and as the roads took their toll on him, Pound came to realize the difficulties that travelers in the thirteenth century must have faced without modern amenities: "My left shin denying me further assistance, not wishing to remain longer at Chalus, I went by train to Rochechouart & Limoges, filled with the moral reflections on the inconvenience of travel in a time when such assistance would have been denied one & when like mishap might have befallen oneself or ones [*sic*] beast" (Sieburth, 30). These inconveniences were due to the rigors of the journey, to the material conditions of the road, and to the physical limitations of his body. Pound felt that from these inconveniences he was learning not only about the lives of the poets but about the content and form of their poetry. While traveling through Chalus, for example, Pound speculated that the troubadours' notions of heaven and hell most likely emerged from the numerous irritants and irritators of daily life:

> Certain engaging people in their eagerness to deny that the race has progressed tell us that what we have gained in material comfort we have lost in spiritual riches. The number of interruptions to life, mental, moral or physical,—interruptions wholly beyond one's own control, must have been in the middle ages such that no belief save that of divine mercy for oneself & an eternal hell for ones irritators would have been tenable or satisfactory. This for the discomfort of the rd. and boredom in the castles must easily have been such as to warrant a special form of verse "Envez" [or] "envoi" to express it. (Sieburth, 30–31)

In a 1913 essay entitled "Troubadours, Their Sorts and Conditions," which also emerged from his 1912 walking tour, Pound discusses specifically the obscure and difficult form of the *trobar clus*, in a way that again links poetic form to living conditions: "No student of the period can doubt that the involved forms, and the veiled meanings in the 'trobar clus,' grew out of living conditions, and that these songs played a very real part in love intrigue and in the intrigue preceding warfare."[17] The *trobar clus*, or "closed poetry," was characterized by its complexity and obscurity, and had an aura of the hermetic about it for Pound, as if this meaning were intended to be accessible only to a select few. But Pound here gives an additional reason for the obscurity of these poems. The veiled meanings of the *trobar clus* were not merely obscurity for obscurity's sake but were direct reflections of material conditions and thus could not be solved by textual scholarship alone without reference to these conditions. According to Sieburth, Pound had a particular theory in mind regarding the forms of the troubadour's poetry:

> He was testing a rather daring (if unfounded) theory about the text, namely, that the erotic riddle of the *dompna soiseubuda* in fact veiled Bertran's military designs on the network of castles occupied by each of the ladies whose charms he celebrated—the troubadour language of love

merely making a power play against male rivals for the strategic control of territory. (xiv–xv)

This view of poetry as an encoded map of a terrain on which love and war compete for the attention of the reader was appealing to Pound's romantic sensibility and his penchant for hermetic, obscure verse. Clearly, real living conditions had for Pound a direct impact both on the subject matter of poetry and on its form, a fact that was to contribute directly to the way in which *The Cantos* "include" history. These difficult poems provided important models as Pound was attempting to find a poetic form that would best reflect the modern world.

It is also in the notes to this tour that we first see Pound establishing a hierarchy between poetry and prose. We see as well an early mention of the "diagnostic" function of the novel that was later to become so important to Pound:

> Let me accept the designation realist . . . but with this secession. Not everything is interesting or rather not everything is interesting enough to be written into novels, which are at all but the best a dilution of life. It is excellent doubtless for future sociologists that certain diagnoses of certain strata be recorded, but it is work for encyclopedists or else it isn't. (Sieburth, 7)

This application of the term *diagnosis*, as well as the grouping of novelists together with sociologists and encyclopedists, indicate the anxiety that Pound felt over the role of the poet in the modern world, who had the dual responsibility both to cleave to realism and yet to retain the intensity of life that the novel dispersed. Pound's subsequent poetry is notable for the way he struggles to avoid the "dilution of life" that he saw as characteristic of the novel, although, as we will see, certain novelists remained important to him as he was beginning *The Cantos*.

EP and the Question of Obscurity

Pound always acknowledged his debt to novelists, even as he anxiously relegated them to secondary status, but nowhere does he express a more thoroughgoing admiration for a novelist than in his 1918 essay on Henry James.[18] In this essay, Pound praises James's attempts to bridge the gap between America and Europe in his fiction, what he calls James's "labour of translation, of making America intelligible, of making it possible for individuals to meet across national borders" (296). This labor involved on James's part the close study of characters and milieux and necessitated the often complex forms and dense narrative, at once sociological and encyclopedic, that are characteristic of the James novel. However, according to Pound, the price of this labor was James's subsequent alienation from his homeland, which all but ignored James's efforts. Of *The American Scene*, James's 1904 travel book, Pound says that it is nothing less than a "creation of America" (327). This creation was not completely out of nothing, but it was, in Pound's mind, a project that had hitherto never before been attempted:

> The desire to see the national face in a mirror may be in itself an exotic. I know of no such grave record, of no such attempt at faithful portrayal as *The American Scene*. Thus America is to the careful observer; this volume and the American scenes in the fiction and memoirs, in *The Europeans, The Patagonia, Washington Square*, etc., bulk large in the very small amount of writing which can be counted as history of *moeurs contemporaines*, of national habit of our time and of the two or three generations preceding us. (327)

It is no coincidence that Pound saw one of James's most successful works in his travel book, or that he saw James's most significant achievement in his attempt to make two cultures mutually intelligible and mutually recognizable despite the cultural and historical chasms that separated them. Such an effort struck a chord with Pound, whose early attempts in *Gironde* (the milieu of which was southern France in the Middle Ages) and "Patria Mia" (the milieu of which was contemporary America) at translating between Europe and America, between the Old World and the New, were at the heart of his vision of the modern world and his vocation as a poet.

Pound's essay on James was also an elegy, both to "the Master" who had passed away not long before, and to the passing of an age when such a feat of translation between nations, Pound felt, was still possible. Pound would complete this elegy in "Hugh Selwyn Mauberley," the 1920 poem that he claimed was "an attempt to condense the James novel."[19] In this sequence of poems, Pound presents us with a portrait of a modern poet "out of key with his time," who may or may not be some version of Pound himself. Pound denied such identification, claiming, "I'm no more Mauberley than Eliot is Prufrock" (qtd. in Espey, 49), a statement rife with equivocation, since Eliot's poetic persona is itself ambiguous. The modern world is presented in "Mauberley" through a series of luminous glimpses without any narrative connections, although there are distinct points of view, and these points of view invite comparison not only with "J. Alfred Prufrock" but also with the narrative style of the two of

James's works that Pound singles out for praise in his essay on James, *The Sacred Fount* and *The American Scene*. In these works, both told in the first person, an unnamed narrator records events not from an omniscient point of view but as they are experienced by the recording subject. In Pound's condensation of the James novel, however, we also see Pound's modernist technique emerging in his penchant for allusions, pastiche, irony, and obscurity, qualities which had hitherto been simply fallout (as Ford had perhaps been suggesting by his roll on the floor) from Pound's masquerading as a troubadour, but which in poems such as "Mauberley" were successfully applied to a modern theme.[20]

In 1919, a year after his essay on James and as he continued to think about the role of obscurity in verse and its relation to narrative sense, Pound wrote an essay on Robert Browning's translation of *The Agamemnon* of Aeschylus, in which he criticized the difficult and obscure nature of Browning's verse translation.[21] The obscurity of Browning's verse, says Pound, is a deliberate attempt to introduce difficulties into the surface of the text. This, Pound says, is a fault: "Obscurities *not inherent* in the matter, obscurities due not to the thing but to the wording, are a botch, and are *not* worth preserving in a translation. . . . Obscurities inherent in the thing occur when the author is piercing or trying to pierce into, uncharted regions; when he is trying to express things not yet current, not yet worn into phrase" (268–69). The convoluted sentences in Browning's *Agamemnon*, according to Pound, are not effective as poetry; rather, the obscurities appropriate to poetry, as he had learned on his walking tour (conjured here again in the reference to travel with the phrase "uncharted regions"), were those that emerged from particular situations and material conditions. He also criticizes Browning for ignoring the true meaning of the text and translating only ideas: "[Browning's] weakness in this work is where it essentially lay in all of his expression, it rests in the term 'ideas'—'Thought' as Browning understood it—'ideas' as the term is current, are poor two-dimensional stuff, a scant, scratch covering. 'Damn ideas, anyhow.' An idea is only an imperfect induction from fact" (267). The "scant scratch covering" of Browning's ideas impedes, in Pound's estimation, empirical observation. Although Browning was correct, Pound felt, in seeking out analogies in the past to the contemporary world, he failed in his translation to find an appropriate modern diction and mode of expression. As influential as Browning was for Pound, especially in his *Sordello*, this essay, in its critical brusqueness, is the equivalent of Ford's critique of Pound's *Canzoni* in 1911. Pound's articulation of the function of obscurity in Browning's verse is important in that it helps us understand its role in his own subsequent poetry.

Soon after Pound wrote the essays on James and Browning and as he was beginning to revise the early drafts of *The Cantos*, he traveled again to southern France, this time with his wife, Dorothy. The two stayed briefly in Paris and then traveled down to Toulouse, Nîmes, Arles, and Avignon, and were joined briefly by T. S. Eliot in Dordogne. As Pound was to discover, however, traveling after the war with the new travel regulations in place was not as easy as it had been in 1912. One particular encounter that Pound had in the American consulate in Paris regarding his travel documents, as he was attempting to return to his London home, was to have an important impact on his subsequent writings and on his view of the modern world.

"Damn The Partition!": The Passport Nuisance

In March of 1920, Pound sent Cantos 4–7, along with *Hugh Selwyn Mauberley* and several other pieces, to Boni & Liveright to be published in a collection that was to become *Poems 1918–1921*. Pound indicated to the American bookseller and patron John Quinn in October of 1920 that this book was his most significant work to date: "It is all I have done since 1916, and my most important book, I at any rate think canto VII the best thing I have done."[22] These new Cantos, which were written mainly during the latter half of 1919, signified the first serious attempt at getting the "long poem including history" under way since the publication of "Three Cantos" in 1917. While he felt that Canto 7 was the best thing he had written, Pound fretted over the difficulty of these poems. In a 1919 letter to Quinn, Pound expresses concern over the intelligibility of his poem: "I suspect my 'Cantos' are getting too too too abstruse and obscure for human consumption" (*Pound/Quinn*, 181). This obscurity, however, as we have seen with Pound's response to the troubadours and in the essays on James and Browning, was an essential part of Pound's poetics, as we can see with one line from Canto 7 in particular.

Traditional readings of Canto 7 take the opening sequence, from "poor old Homer" to the ghostly portrayal of Henry James "weaving an endless sentence," to be an anthology of styles, which, in their grim and inevitable progression, lead to a portrait of an enervated modern world in which "buried beauty" is no longer accessible.[23] The lines "Damn the partition! Paper, dark brown and stretched, / Flimsy and damned partition" are a particularly curious interjection in a canto that seems to be a lament for past times.[24] These lines are often read as conveying Pound's feeling of alienation from some heroic past—Homer's Greece or Ovid's Rome—as if he were forever removed from these ages by the partition of time. However, that this partition is "flimsy" and made of paper suggests that it has no power in itself to act as a barrier. And while there is certainly no reason why this partition could not also function as a metaphor—it recalls, for instance, the "scant scratch covering" of Browning's ideas that Pound had damned in his essay of the previous year—what is most striking about these lines is the vehemence with which they are uttered, as if what had confronted Pound was something immediate and palpable. The outburst "Damn the partition!" has the tone of Cantos 14 and 15, the so-called "Hell Cantos," to which Pound relegates financiers, profiteers, and monopolists. It is more likely that these lines refer to a nuisance of this kind than that they lament a lost golden age. In the article that Pound wrote for *The Nation* in November of 1927 entitled "The Passport Nuisance," where he recalls being covered in mud while in Chalus, he also remembers an incident, still fresh in his mind, that occurred as he was returning to his home in London in 1919, and this recollection helps to explain his cryptic reference.

Pound expressed his disapproval of the passport system in "The Passport Nuisance" in the most severe terms. Of the wartime legislation he says:

> That was 1919, and Europe was, confessedly, in a mess, and errors might be exceptions. But what in heaven's name has that temporary confusion to do with 1924, 1925, 1926, 1927? What has it to do with the unending boredom of waiting an hour, a half hour, three hours, in countless bureaus, for countless useless visas, identities, folderols? (389)

The incident to which Pound refers here occurred in 1919, after his second walking tour of southern France, while he was attempting to return through Paris to his home in London. When he reached the American consulate in Paris, the official there told him that he would be unable to go any farther without the proper paperwork. Irate, Pound suggested that the man consult his superior regarding the regulations. "He disappeared behind a *partition*," writes Pound (my emphasis) in this article, "and returned with a request that I 'get a letter' from my employer, evidently knowing no strata of life save one where *everyone* has an employer" (390). This partition becomes for Pound a division between France and England and between himself and his adopted home. It is this partition, apart from any symbolic meaning it may bear, which he damns in no uncertain terms in Canto 7.

To Pound, the passport system was a relic of wartime Europe that he felt should be done away with. The year 1914, itself a kind of partition from an idealized past with the beginning of the war in Europe, saw the creation of the Defense of the Realm Act (DORA) in Britain, which proclaimed "His majesty in Council has power during the continuance of the present war to issue regulations for securing the public safety and the defense of the realm."[25] This

act increased the government's discretion to intervene in the private domain
and drew the nation's borders more sharply than previously, resulting in travel
restrictions for British citizens abroad and for those traveling within the British Empire. In the United States, which entered the war later, a passport system was already in effect, although it was not compulsory for citizens to have
a passport in order to travel. In December 1914, as a result of a resolution by
William Jennings Bryan and perhaps as a result of growing concern over the
events in Europe, photographs were first required as a part of the passport. On
May 22, 1918, a year after the United States entered the war, the World War
I Travel Control Act was instituted. Section 2 of Public Law No. 154 stated
that it shall be "unlawful for any citizen of the United States to depart from
or enter or attempt to depart from or enter the United States unless he bears
a valid passport" (4).[26] As a wartime measure, such an act was not unjust or
unnecessarily bureaucratic, but the effects lingered long after the war and contributed to Pound's sense of frustration over unnecessary bureaucracy.

In the *Nation* article, Pound refers to government bureaucrats as "hired
janitors who think they own the whole building"; however, he saw the
passport system not as an isolated form of petty bureaucracy but as a symptom
of the growing indifference to the arts that had become evident since the end
of World War I. During this time, Pound wrote numerous articles and letters
to newspapers decrying the passport nuisance, as well as letters to legislators
in the United States, such as Senator Bronson Cutting of New Mexico, in
whom he saw an ally in these matters.[27] In a 1929 letter to the editor of the
Paris edition of the *Chicago Tribune*, also entitled "The Passport Nuisance,"
where he refers to "the passport pest and the visa inanity," Pound writes that
anyone over the age of thirty-five will remember a time when "'foreigners'
i.e. we, were decently treated and walked about the face of civilized europe
[*sic*] without idiotic interference and doing no harm to the scenery."[28] This
unpleasant moment at the consulate was a watershed for Pound, who, as we
have seen, had been used to traveling throughout Europe unhampered by
regulations.

In a letter to John Quinn in December 1919, Pound relates a similar
encounter to the one in Paris, this time in London, and explains how the
issue was resolved: "I had hell's own time about passports last spring, was saved
here because Paul Perry of the propaganda dept. stuck up for me, and said I
represented American magazines here etc. etc. etc. no need to bother you with
long tale of woe [*sic*]" (*Pound/Quinn*, 180). Pound, in fact, did not "officially"
represent any American magazine at this point, and he was writing to Quinn to
request just such an appointment. He felt that getting a letter from Quinn, who
had been acting as a kind of patron for Pound, would prevent future difficulties

when traveling within Europe, thus bypassing the bureaucratic nuisances of passport regulations. This request represents a significant equivocation on Pound's part. Although furious over his treatment at the consulate, he heeded the passport official's advice, trying to get Quinn to sponsor him. He asks Quinn: "Can you appoint me your 'representative,' official buyer, or whatever you like; ANYTHING to have a piece of autographed letter head stationery from some reputable person" (*Pound/Quinn*, 181). Pound here did not seem to make a distinction between "employer" and "patron," perhaps hoping he could salvage a lesson from the indignity visited upon him by the passport official by seeing a connection between the Middle Ages, a time when patronage flourished, and the modern world. This hope faded the more he thought about the encounter and the more that the differences between the two ages made themselves felt.

The obscure way in which Pound chooses to include the issue of passport regulations in general and his own encounter in particular are important for understanding the development of *The Cantos*. Embedded as it is within a list of images of faded beauty, the outburst against his experience at the consulate is attributable to no particular voice and directed at no particular individual or government measure. Pound removes any context from these lines and just presents them. The details of the encounter at the American consulate are not worth recording as poetry, unlike the outburst "Damn the partition!" which is, for Pound, the proper emotional response to an absurd situation. For Pound, as we have seen, this was one of the chief functions of poetry, to record real lived conditions, not in any documentary way but through the curative power of poetry. In the 1918 essay on Henry James, as previously mentioned, Pound had described the "root difference" between poetry and prose as follows: "Most good poetry asserts something to be worth while, or damns a contrary; at any rate asserts emotional values. The best prose is, has been a presentation (complicated and elaborate as you like) of circumstances, of conditions, for the most part abominable or, at the mildest, amenable" (*Literary Essays*, 324). In Canto 7, the contrary that Pound damns is, specifically, the partition behind which the passport official retreated, but generally it is the "passport nuisance," on the occasion of what was perhaps one of his most significant encounters with the modern world.

On February 13, 1946, a specially impaneled federal jury in Washington, D.C., heard testimony regarding Pound's mental fitness to stand trial for treason as the result of wartime radio broadcasts he made from Italy. While testifying for the defense, Dr. Wendell Muncie, associate professor of psychiatry at Johns Hopkins, recited a list of symptoms that had led him to conclude that Pound was not of sound mind. Among these were "fixed ideas . . . verging on the delusional," "grandiosity," "paranoia," vagueness and distractibility, and "confabulation."[29] Along with these symptoms, Dr. Muncie said of Pound, "He has a hatred of bureaucrats which goes back a long way" (158). On cross-examination, Muncie acknowledged that a hatred of bureaucrats was not necessarily evidence of insanity, but clearly Pound was vehement enough during the examination that he felt this warranted mention in court. This diagnosis reveals in its baffled characterization of Pound much that was not only *not* aberrant but that was central to his personality and poetic. As an assessment of Pound's character, this diagnosis was accurate: Pound *did* have a hatred of bureaucrats that went back a long way. For Pound, however, this was not evidence of his own insanity but a natural reaction to the insanity of the modern world.

Perhaps, as I have suggested, one of the reasons that Dr. Muncie felt it necessary to mention Pound's hatred of bureaucrats as evidence of his mental instability during his testimony was that this played an inordinately prominent role in Pound's conversation. In fact, it is difficult to believe that such a trivial, though obviously inconvenient, encounter as the one with the passport official could have had such a lasting impact. From the *Nation* article, we do not learn precisely what the passport official required of Pound in the way of paperwork or procedures, but there is evidence that it was more than a matter merely of filling out a few forms or getting the proper stamps. In his 1919 letter to Quinn, Pound elaborates on his "long tale of woe" while in London: "Pie faced Y.M.C.A. clerk threatening to stop passport unless I went home and 'took up duties of citizenship.' etc. etc."—"home" here meaning not London, but the United States (180).[30]

In 1958, just after his release from St. Elizabeths, before returning to Italy, and almost forty years after his encounter with the passport official, Pound still recalled the incident. During an interview with the *Washington Star* on April 30, Pound, according to the reporter, "flashed back to a moment in Venice in 1898 when he was with his great-aunt and had no bother 'with passports and frontiers and all that malarkey'"—a memory which was also to make it into the 1968 postscript to *The Spirit of Romance*.[31] Then, according to the *Star* reporter, "[a] sentence later, he was in Toulouse [*sic*], date unspecified, trying to get back to London and a 'dirty little squirt' in the consulate was telling him he had to go back to the United States" (145). Surely, this is not in Toulouse, through which winds the river Gironde, but either in Paris, where the American consulate is located, or in London with the "pie faced clerk."[32] In this unguarded moment, Pound, on the verge of leaving the country that had incarcerated him for twelve years, recalls the absurdity of what he faced when attempting to travel in the face of the "passport nuisance." Why he remembered this indignity at this particular moment can perhaps best be explained by the fact that the "passport nuisance" was partly responsible for keeping him at St. Elizabeths. According to his attorney, Julien Cornell, even if Pound had been released from St. Elizabeths earlier, there was no guarantee that the State Department would return Pound's passport to him. As Cornell points out, "The power of the Department of State to withhold a passport was at this time absolute. Not until many years later was this power broken by the United States Supreme Court" (*A Serious Character*, 60–61). Without the prospect of returning to Italy, Pound may not have been eager to be released. The "dirty little squirt" finally had had his way.

This hatred of bureaucrats did indeed go back a long way, as Dr. Muncie pointed out. It was perhaps no accident that Pound eventually chose to begin his forty-year epic with Odysseus' voyage to the underworld where the wily traveler, attempting to get on with his journey, encounters the peculiar bureaucracy of Hell. Canto 1 is filled with procedures and regulations ("Here did they rites, Perimedes and Eurylochous"; "I dug the ell-square pitkin"), moments of waiting and frustration ("I sat to keep off the impetuous impotent dead"), and special injunctions ("Shalt return through spiteful Neptune, over dark seas, / Lose all companions"). Pound's Odysseus does not want to return home to Ithaca any more than Pound himself wanted to return to America in 1919, or remain there in 1958, but to sail outward and away, beyond all boundaries.

Pound's belief that poetry could contain and order the complicated materials of history—"include history," as he was to say, whether this history was personal or public—has been recognized before, primarily by Lawrence Rainey in his exhaustive study of the Malatesta Cantos (XIII–XI) in *Ezra Pound and The Monument of Culture* where he connects the genesis of these Cantos to the ambiguous historical records that Pound consulted when composing them. Rainey traces Pound's condensation of this ambiguous documentary material into their placement in *The Cantos* as unambiguous historical detail. With the example of the passport nuisance and the ejaculation "Damn the partition!" we see Pound similarly reducing the potentially ambiguous, even polysemous nature of his own personal experiences into a stable unambiguous reading of a personal affront writ large. By entering the phrase "Damn the partition!" into the historical record of *The Cantos* while simultaneously removing the context of the utterance, Pound also seeks to preserve his memory of travel as it existed in pristine form before the war, not unlike the rose in amber in the "Envoiz" that ends "Hugh Selwyn Mauberley."

Despite the nostalgia Pound felt, however, he also remained attuned to the opportunities that would rescue the modern world from the perils of bureaucracy. This hope manifested itself with increasing fervor in larger and more important issues than passport regulations, but always with the indignity that he suffered at the Paris consulate fresh in his mind. When Pound saw others successfully negotiating the difficulties of modern travel, he was alert to the information that they had to offer. This was especially true in the twenties and thirties as his interest turned to the Soviet Union, a country that he had never visited, whose language and literature he had never mastered, but which he nevertheless felt was a crucial example for the modern world—not, perhaps, as crucial and as immediately applicable to the situation in England and America as was that of fascist Italy, but important nonetheless.

Pound was to hold to his definitions of the diagnostic function of prose and the curative power of poetry throughout his career, and his distinctions in this regard can help us understand aspects of *The Cantos* that might otherwise seem perplexing, as we have seen with the example of the "passport nuisance." Pound's thoughts on the nature and role of obscurity in verse, as we have also seen, are related to this distinction between poetry and prose, as the transmutation of information into poetry brings with it—through loss of context and lack of narrative logic—a sense of immediate disorientation. But the adherence to these definitions of poetry and prose, this focus on diagnosis and the assumption that the mental struggle with obscurity leads somehow to a cure for societal ills, while useful to Pound's early career when he was seeking to identify the unique features of the modern world, often led Pound away from travel as a means of achieving the immediacy that he so valued. It was also Pound's tendency during the thirties and after to read any and all kinds of prose as a kind of variously charged journalism or reportage that often accounts not only for the obscurity of sections of *The Cantos* as he struggled to include this material in it, but which also led to his idiosyncratic view of the modern world. We can see this with his reaction to Cummings's *Eimi*, where his initial perplexity over Cummings's obscure text is resolved not by understanding Cummings's book as the poetic statement that it so clearly is (as we will see in the chapter on Cummings) but rather by seeing it as an unambiguous registering of fact. For Pound, difficulty, as he described it in the essays on James and Browning, does not result from the ambiguity of signification or the unresolved tensions of a poetic mind, where contraries are allowed to exist together to be resolved in an ultimate beauty that transcends historical particularity, but rather results from the mind confronting unfamiliar terrain where meaning remains locked away to all but the initiate.

Frustrated by his inability to travel with the ease that he had been accustomed to, Pound grew increasingly dependent on the travels of others. But when Pound uses the travel experiences of others as a source for his poetry, as the remaining sections of this chapter will show, his results, while often spectacular as verse, are notable mainly for the ways in which they adumbrate Pound's statements about the value of poetry. In what follows, I show how while travel continued to be important to Pound, the travel genre itself was discarded, hung on the wall like the abandoned *Gironde*.

"I'VE SEEN THE FUTURE AND IT WORKS!": POUND AND THE SOVIET UNION

By the late twenties, Pound had tempered his early optimism for a modern renaissance with the bleak reality of the problems facing the modern world, problems which included political and social upheaval, economic uncertainty, and the relegation of the arts to a secondary status in society as a result of government interference in matters such as postal censorship, lack of copyright protectionism, and, as we have seen, passport law. Although he still saw the poet as the person best equipped to reveal the ills of modern life and to offer remedies to these ills by forging connections between the decaying modern world and the pristine past, it was only the leaders and economists, he was discovering, who could bring about the necessary changes that would reverse this decline. One of the key roles of the poet, Pound gradually came to see, was to advise leaders, to inform them of instances of effective governance from the past, and to translate real, lived experiences into useful examples that would inform policy decisions.

However, in order to inform leaders effectively, Pound had to be informed. For Pound, as well as for many others at the time, the events in Russia, from the revolution to the implementation of Lenin's New Economic Policy, offered an intriguing example of the kinds of transformations that could occur to society in the modern world, although it was frustrating trying to determine with any accuracy just what was transpiring since information was so hard to come by. Pound's views on the Russian Revolution demonstrate his awareness of the difficulties he faced when attempting to translate the secondhand information and hearsay of reporters into material for his epic poem and into useful information for leaders.

The Bolsheviks' seizure of power and the subsequent implementation of Lenin's New Economic Policy resulted from an even more significant political and economic transformation of a society than had occurred in Italy. In the years after the revolution, however, information regarding the new regime and the transformations of Soviet society was strictly limited and eventually reduced to a trickle after Lenin's death and as Stalin consolidated power. According to Whitman Bassow in *The Moscow Correspondents*, "Since 1921, when the Russians opened their borders to U.S. news organizations, only some three hundred Americans were permitted to enter as resident correspondents."[33] So, while the Soviet government did indeed create a center from which radiated an authority, as Pound had recommended governments do in "Patria Mia," it was not yet a center that could be freely accessed. Understanding Pound's method of obtaining information about the Soviet government and its economic and social plans, the manner in which he communicated with government officials, and the way he included this information in his poem is important for understanding both the progress and development of *The Cantos* and Pound's thoughts about the role of literature in the modern world.

Pound first expressed an interest in the Soviet Union not immediately after the revolution, nor during his more politically engaged years in Rapallo in the early thirties, but rather during his years on the cultural scene of nineteen twenties Paris. Back in Paris in 1921 from yet another extended stay in the South of France, Pound was inspired by the energy and bustle of the metropolis, an energy that could barely be contained by the regulatory nature of passport bureaucracy. In 1923, along with Mary and Padraic Colum, he attended a lecture by the famous American journalist Lincoln Steffens, who was famous primarily for his sensationalist, muckraking journalism in the early years of the century. But he was also known for having been in Petrograd during the Russian Revolution in 1917. Along with John Reed, author of *Ten Days That Shook the World*, Steffens was one of only a few western reporters who had actually been on the scene as the Bolsheviks seized power. Steffens had returned to Russia in 1919 as a part of a government committee headed by William C. Bullitt, formed to assess the state of U.S.-Soviet relations. He subsequently reported before the Committee on Foreign Relations in the United States Senate where he described in detail the state of Soviet society: "A new center of gravity seems to have been found. . . . We saw this everywhere. And we saw order, and though we inquired for them, we heard of no disorders."[34] Steffens was in Paris in 1923 having only recently returned again from the Soviet Union.

Whatever the contents of Steffens's 1923 lecture, the effect on Pound was immediate and palpable. In her memoir, Mary Colum remembered Pound's reaction to the lecture distinctly: "Ezra listened to it with rapt attention, his eyes glued to the speaker's face, the very type of a young man in search of an ideology, except that he was not so very young. He seemed to have an intense interest in new political and economic ideas."[35] Pound was spellbound as much by the speaker who had witnessed the revolution and advised the U.S. president as he was by the account of the country itself. Whether at this time Pound was confirming latent beliefs or in search of new ideologies, as Colum suggests, is unclear, but it is enough to say for now that what primarily interested him in this instance was the belief that he was getting authentic information from someone who had witnessed these events firsthand and who had consulted lawmakers in Washington. While we cannot know for sure the subject of Steffens's talk, on this occasion it seems likely that he discussed the events of the Russian Revolution that he had witnessed directly.

In 1925, Pound published *A Draft of XVI Cantos* in a special deluxe edition, and the final canto in the sequence, which is essentially the same as in later versions, ends with a lengthy description of the Russian Revolution based closely on Steffens's account published later.[36] Although Steffens's *Autobiography* is frequently given as a background for this scene (and there we do in fact see all of the elements that Pound here condenses), as Walter Benn Michaels points out, Steffens's book was published in 1931, six years after the publication of *A Draft of XVI Cantos*, so it is possible that Pound built these details on the 1923 lecture.[37] Since one of Pound's purposes in *The Cantos* was to register the transmission of history, it is worthwhile examining this passage in some detail. This section of the canto is introduced by a German voice discussing the "zhamefull beace" of the Brest Litovsk treaty. This treaty, signed in March of 1918, ceded Russian territory to the central powers in a separate peace prior to the armistice and represented a weakening of Lenin's still young government (74). The scene then turns to the events in Petrograd in November 1917 as the revolution was beginning:

> There was a man there talking,
> To a thousand, just a short speech, and
> Then move 'em on. And he said:
> Yes, these people, they are all right, they
> Can do everything, everything except act;
> And go an' hear 'em, but when they are through,
> Come to the bolsheviki. . . .
> And when it broke, there was the crowd there,
> And the cossacks, just as always before,
> But one thing, the cossacks said:
> "Pojalouista."
> And that got round in the crowd,
> And then a lieutenant of infantry
> Ordered 'em to fire into the crowd,
>   in the square at the end of the Nevsky,
> In front of the Moscow station,

> And they wouldn't,
> And he pulled his sword on a student for laughing,
> And killed him,
> And a cossack rode out of his squad
> On the other side of the square
> And cut down the lieutenant of infantry
> And that was the revolution. . . .
>   as soon as they named it. (74–75)

What is important to recognize in this passage is the preponderance of voices: from the man talking to the crowd, to the Cossacks uttering a single word that is taken by the crowd as evidence of their allegiance, to the order of the lieutenant to fire that goes ignored. This scene is constructed out of speech, secondhand reports, and rumor as much as it is of firsthand observation. It gives the impression of on-the-spot reporting and firsthand accounts, but its main preoccupations are in the ways that rhetoric and speech incites action and the manner in which this information is transmitted ("And that got round in the crowd"). This is in sharp distinction, for instance, to the "Malatesta Cantos," where Pound re-creates the past through the fragmentary remains of Sigismundo's postbag, the written documents that record the construction of the Tempio. Here, we have scraps and fragments as well, only in this case fragments of talk and conversations filtered through Steffens's reports. Pound includes this passage as if it were firsthand empirical description, when in fact it is layers of reported speech. This scene is important in Pound's overall intent of "including history," because he makes use of Steffens's objective account to offer a potentially curative solution to the chaos of the modern world. Thus this canto demonstrates the distinctions that Pound had described between poetry and prose, between reported speech and empirical description. The scene is chaotic, but we also see in this chaos Pound's view of how political ideas are absorbed into the population at large. The description of events precedes historical categories: "And that was the revolution. . . . /as soon as they named it."

Canto 16 is often seen as Pound's portrait of the chaos into which the modern world has devolved, and his frustrations and laments for those lost in the war do indeed dominate and give form to the canto in particular and to the sequence thus far as a whole. Pound recalls in this canto the First World War and those who died in it, including his friends the sculptor Henri Gaudier Brezka and T. E. Hulme, among others. He also considers, not for the last time, the causes of war, stopping just short of ascribing blame. He sputters accusations such as: "And because that son of a bitch,/ Franz Josef of Austria. . . . . . / And because that son of a bitch Napoléon Barbiche. . . ." (16). However, it is difficult to read the scene of the Russian Revolution as an example of the decline of the modern world; rather, it seems to represent to him the possibility that social revolution could spread by word of mouth. Canto 16 as a whole is rife with images of pandemonium and chaos, not surprising perhaps if we recall that it directly follows the so-called "Hell Cantos." However, it also contains brief paradisiacal moments: "Then light air, under saplings,/ the blue banded lake under aether,/ an oasis, the stones, the calm field,/ the grass quiet."

Canto 16 ends on a note of frustration over being at a remove from the scene, a frustration that arises from the difficulties of judging from second- or thirdhand accounts. After the rumors of the revolution and the reports of "some killed at the barracks" (75) have spread abroad, we are back in the world of art and society, where these scraps of speech have congealed into rumor: "So we used to hear it at the opera,/ That they wouldn't be under Haig;/ and that the advance was beginning;/ That it was going to begin in a week" (75). The impact of political events on those back in the west was diluted, in Pound's view, by the time it reached the public.

If Steffens was aware of the inclusion of his description of the Russian Revolution in *The Cantos*, he makes no mention of it in his *Autobiography*, where he recalls Pound only briefly from the Paris years, referring to him as a "private, professional propagandist" (833). Steffens's phrase suggests that Pound's forays into politics, during his Paris years, were not the result of someone interested in the value of public information, but the result of a private individual unsuccessfully attempting to assimilate the importance of political events. In a letter late in 1919, Steffens writes in defense of his role as a reporter in a way that sharply contrasts with Pound's view of the objective value and strictly empirical nature of eyewitness testimony and journalistic accounts:[38]

> I assert that "news" now is not merely happenings, but what caused the happenings and what it means; and that this interpretative form of reporting can be given a serial progressive interest, but only by having moving correspondents; the system of keeping a man in one place dulls the man and his news sense. But a correspondent in a group of them who watch the whole world roll and follow its motions can give and keep a sense of evolution of life.[39]

While Steffens's notion of having "moving correspondents" would certainly answer to Pound's desire for the unobstructed circulation of information, and whereas the admonition that "keeping a man in one place dulls the man and his news sense" no doubt spoke to Pound's love of travel, it is difficult to see in Steffen's "interpretative form of reporting" or the "serial progressive interest" of his journalism anything like what Pound had in mind when he was describing the diagnostic nature of prose or the objective value of empirical description and accurate perception. For Pound, news was "merely happenings" and most valuable when it was simply that. It served in this form as the raw material for the epic poet, as we see in Canto 16. Pound was intrigued by the transformations that were taking place in the Soviet Union, though not in the same way as he was intrigued and would be more fully absorbed by the similar transformations taking place in Italy, on the opposite end of the political spectrum. But it was the possibilities offered by Steffens's reporting that allowed Pound to make connections between his developing political thought and his telegraphic modernist prose.

POUND AND SENATOR CUTTING: THE PROBLEM OF DIPLOMATIC RECOGNITION

Although Steffens's account of the events in Petrograd was formative to Pound's developing interest in larger political matters in general and in the Soviet Union in particular, it was insufficient in itself for learning about Russia, especially since events there developed so rapidly. As the West was struggling to maintain economic stability in the midst of the economic depression and labor unrest of the twenties, the Soviet Union, in the wake of the Bolshevik Revolution, had captured the imagination of many Western writers and artists and provided hope for the disenchanted masses. In 1928, Josef Stalin inaugurated another version of the New Economic Policy (NEP). Lenin's 1921 NEP had signaled a retreat from wartime communism, as he granted the peasants the right to own their own land and adjust the prices of their goods according to the principles of supply and demand. This economy resulted in what economists called the "scissors crisis," a situation whereby the peasants were controlling the economy and as a result setting policy. Stalin's version of the NEP introduced collectivization by which the peasants, the kulaks, were deprived of their property and the focus of the economy became industrialization. He called this the five-year plan by which Russia would, in one bound, catch up to the industrial West.

Pound drew his interest in the Soviet Union from sources other than Steffens, as well. In 1930, he began a correspondence with Bronson Cutting, the progressive Republican senator from New Mexico who had argued passionately for the abolition of customs censorship. In addition to sharing views on prohibition and international copyright law, both Cutting and Pound were convinced that recognition of the Soviet Union was vital for the interests of the United States in the postwar period. In the years after the Russian revolution, the U.S. government had initially bungled foreign relations with the Kremlin, granting recognition to the provisional government headed by Alexander Kerensky while ignoring Lenin and the Bolsheviks. To redress this error, Woodrow Wilson formed a commission to assess U.S./Soviet relations, a commission on which Steffens served as adviser. The initial lapse in judgment on the part of the United States government, Wilson seemed to feel, was the result of inaccurate reports on the political situation in Russia, not to mention the inability of lawmakers to recognize the significance of the events that they did know.

Both Pound and Cutting felt that the Soviet Union warranted attention, although Pound's sympathies at this point lay with the similarly transformative programs of Mussolini's Italy. In both cases, Pound saw the role that the arts would play in these respective transformations as crucial to his own ideas about the role of art in the modern world. And before Pound could offer any of the curative verse that would display his own vision of the modern world, he needed to find out more for himself, or, again, have access to someone who could tell him about the events in the Soviet Union. In 1930, Senator Cutting traveled to the Soviet Union on a diplomatic junket, an important point for Pound, who, as we have seen with Steffens, highly valued such firsthand experience. On his return, Cutting delivered a speech before the National Republican Club in New York City on January 31, 1931, entitled "Recognition of Russia," a speech to which Pound contributed. Cutting argued in this speech that "the Russian experiment, like it or not, is one of the fundamental events in world history. We can not ignore it and we can not cope with it through lack of recognition or through suppression or through misrepresentation" (*Pound/Cutting*, 33). Pound responded positively to Cuttings's remarks in a letter of February 6, 1931, where he writes, "I (so far as I see it) agree. I mean we both think there is no Russian peril once they and 'we' have a clear idea of the other's position" (*Pound/Cutting*, 49).

For Pound, however, how to arrive at this "clear idea" was the problem, and the parenthetical caveat "so far as I see" indicated precisely the boundaries of his knowledge due to the fact that living in Rapallo, his ability to "see" what was going on in Russia was limited to what he heard from others. Pound was frequently confused and frustrated, as his letters to Cutting show, by the conflicting reports emerging from the so-called workers' paradise. In a letter to the senator, Pound writes of Henry Wales, one of the first Western reporters to reveal the famine crisis in the Ukraine: "Are the horrors reported by Hank Wales etc. due to some Russian hogging all the best and locking it up, or simply to there not being any more for anyone?" (*Pound/Cutting*, 63). The limits of what Pound could see and the absence of any thorough accounts of the political scene in Russia contributed to his frustration. And though he had some sense of the momentousness of events from Steffens and access to someone in power in America in Cutting, what he still lacked was a full account of the Russian scene. This lack would be filled within a few years as Pound's interest in Mussolini's Italy in the meantime came to occupy his interests.

POUND AND THE NOVEL IN THE THIRTIES

Throughout the nineteen thirties and forties, Pound was frustrated over the inability of Europe and America to learn from recent history and heed the warnings and advice of its artists and intellectuals. Most important for Pound at this time was to get people to recognize the extent of the political and economic morass in which the modern world had found itself. In order to actuate this recognition, Pound, as he had done on so many prior occasions, recommended certain books that, in his opinion, best assessed these perilous years and made manifest the various crises that the world faced. The majority of these books were nonliterary, for example, Brooks Adams's *The Law of Civilization and Decay*, Leo Frobenius's *Erlebte Erdteile*, and Silvio Gesell's *The Natural Economic Order*, as Pound's interests had become almost single-mindedly civic. However, there were three notable exceptions to his nonliterary curriculum: Joyce's *Ulysses*, Lewis's *The Apes of God,* and Cummings's *Eimi*; and while these three books were not the only literary works that he promoted during these years, they are important in that Pound recommended them not solely for their individual literary merits but for their collective diagnoses of the interwar years. In the 1941 essay "Augment of the Novel," Pound wrote that these books functioned as a "triad":[40] "'The Apes of God,' along with 'Eimi' and 'Ulysses,' is one of at least three books that any serious reader in 1960 will most certainly have to read if he wants to get any sort of idea of what happened in Europe between one of our large wars and another" (95). His grouping of these works ran parallel to his interest in political and economic matters throughout the period. In his writings about these three books, we can discern the same distinctions between poetry and prose that he had made during his early travels through southern France, where he ascribed to prose a diagnostic function.

Pound had, of course, championed *Ulysses* since the time he had been reading it in manuscript before it appeared in 1922. He felt that Joyce's work was a singular achievement that all but exhausted the prose genre. However, as the twenties wore on and Pound's interests became more wide-ranging, Joyce's continued experiments in literature in *Work in Progress* left him cold.

In his 1938 *Guide to Kulchur*, Pound dismissed *Work in Progress* and recalled the initial impact of *Ulysses*: "The katharsis of 'Ulysses,' the joyous satisfaction . . . was to feel that here was the JOB DONE and finished, the diagnosis and cure was here."[41] This was an unusual moment for Pound, where he ascribes to a prose work both diagnostic and curative powers. However, frustrated with Joyce's experimentations, Pound sought out other prose works that would continue the job of diagnosis that *Ulysses* had inaugurated.

His attention turned naturally to his collaborator from the *Blast* years, Wyndham Lewis. Pound's critique of Joyce's later work stems primarily from his belief that Joyce had abandoned all fidelity to visual perception in favor of the musical elements of language, which rendered his book useless for purposes of diagnosis. Lewis, on the other hand, had, in Pound's view, brought a new intensity of perception to his work: "From 'The Ideal Giant' to 'The Apes of God' Lewis had used a kind of writing akin to hyper-daylight. Hence the glare, hence the imperception, on the part of weak-eyed and tender-minded, of his activities" ("Augment," 95). *The Apes of God* was important, in Pound's view, for its demolition of Bloomsbury and for its ruthless exposure of the literary and artistic scene of London in the twenties as an art racket. Pound sees the people and events portrayed in *The Apes of God* as realistic but also as symptomatic. These apes are "acts of a time and place, and they form a symbol not only of themselves or a picture of a small bevy of idiots, but do definitely diagnose a state of society, which has led perforce to the present conflict" (96). Whereas Joyce's book marked the end of an era, *The Apes of God* was the ongoing account of the follies of the modern world that Pound felt needed to be revealed.

Pound was hesitant at first when praising *Eimi* because Cummings's testimony was hard to decipher. He had read the selections that appeared in *The Hound and Horn* in 1932 and had heard the reactions of others, but at first he was not sure what to make of the book. In a letter to Cummings on April 6, 1933, we can see Pound sifting through his reactions to *Eimi*, dwelling as he does so on the issue of obscurity:

> I dunno whether I rank as them wot finds it painful to read. . . . and if I said anything about obscurity it wd. far ridere polli, in view of my recent pubctns.

> Also I don't think EIMI *is* obscure, or not very

> BUT, the longer a work is the more and longer shd. be the passages that are perfectly clear and simple to read.

matter of scale, matter of how long you can cause the reader to stay immobile or nearly so on a given number of pages. [. . .]
a page two, or three, or two and one half centimetres *narrower*, at least a column of type that much narrower might solve all the difficulties.[42]

For Pound, here the way the words look on the page is a crucial element of the book: the neologisms and typographical idiosyncrasies give the page a clotted look that would be remedied by the inclusion of more white space. He appeals to Cummings to attend to the visual appearance of the page, to assist the reader by making a document that would appeal to a visual sensibility as well as a readerly one. Pound attributes his initial frustration over the style and odd typography of *Eimi* partly to his own impatience, but he was perhaps partly frustrated as well over his lack of ability to recognize, and by extension, verify what was being described, never having traveled to Russia himself.

As with his reaction to James Joyce's ongoing experiments in *Work in Progress*, Pound was less than enthused at the prospect of wading through another obscure and difficult work, despite the fact that his own poem, as we have seen, was becoming more and more allusive and obscure. At first, in a 1934 essay titled "E.E. Cummings Alive," Pound links *Eimi* not with *Ulysses* but with Joyce's *Finnegans Wake*: "For useful comparison with 'EIMI,' Europe offers only the later Joyce and Miss Stein."[43] This was intended to be a compliment, but Pound was reacting here solely to the stylistic innovation and not to the book's ability to describe what Cummings saw. Pound, however, eventually came to see *Eimi* as less like the Joyce of *Finnegans Wake* and more like *Ulysses* or *The Apes of God*, works which foreground visual perception and diagnosed a particular milieu. This gradual recognition of *Eimi's* importance and its elevation in the ranks of Pound's own curriculum occurred as Pound's own political sympathies grew closer to fascist Italy. The more that Pound saw *Eimi* as the indictment that it was of the Soviet system, the more importance it held for him. Whereas Pound's inclusion of Steffens's reporting seems deliberately ambiguous regarding its stature as political statement, serving in *The Cantos* instead as evidence of the power of individual will, rumor, and the spontaneity of political movements, his recommendation of Cummings's book has the tone of diagnosis about it, even the language of indictment of an entire political system.

In "Augment of the Novel," Pound praised *Eimi*, along with *Ulysses* and *The Apes of God*, for the painstaking detail and technical achievement with which they recorded the social and economic realities of the interwar years, thus allowing readers to judge for themselves the benefits and detriments of modern society. Pound refers to these works as "potwollopers," as if embarrassed by their accidental resemblances to the work of Thomas Hardy or Henry James (95). Their respective virtues lay in their ability to describe clearly and thoroughly a particular milieu. Although prompted in part by the anxieties that attended the composition of his ongoing "poem including history," Pound's comments nevertheless indicate the high regard he had for all three of these works.

Pound's promotion of these three works took on an urgent, imperative tone in "If This Be Treason," a short selection of scripts of Pound's radio broadcasts that aired in 1941. He reiterates, for instance, his belief that *Ulysses* is the end of an era: "It cooked up and served the unmitigated god damn stink of the decaying usury era." He saw these three books as sweeping indictments of various aspects of modernity that exposed the decay hidden beneath its façade. Of Lewis and Cummings, Pound says, "both of 'em used to USING their eyes/ use of the eye assists human beings in making direct observations."[44] Pound's curriculum for the modern world had gradually become transformed into a litany of complaints against this world. The kind of heightened empirical perception that had allowed Pound to recognize in the landscape of southern France parallels between the Middle Ages and the pre-war years was now used to make manifest the follies of the modern world. For Pound, Cummings's *Eimi* was important because it described the Russian scene so accurately that it allowed Pound to feel that he had traveled there himself. And, in a way, in its indictment of a system that Pound had no allegiances to anyway, *Eimi* allowed Pound to cleave closer to his own belief in the saving ideology of Italian fascism.

CONCLUSION:
THE OUTPOST MAN

Pound continued to appreciate the pleasures and salubrious effects of travel even as he continued to experience many of the frustrations associated in a world overrun with bureaucracy and laws designed to impede movement, as when his passport was withheld during his incarceration at St Elizabeths. But more and more, Pound's interest was not in proclaiming the value and importance of unimpeded roads that would provide access to the central authority of the metropolis—to recall his image from "Patria Mia"—but rather in being the still point at the center of that authority and processing the information that was brought to him from abroad, from the margins, from the outposts, by novelists such as Joyce, Lewis, and Cummings.

For Pound, this center of authority was oddly and perpetually split between

America and Europe both in his early essays and travels and later in works such as *Jefferson and/or Mussolini,* where he yokes together two entirely different traditions and political systems in the service of one large idea. But while there is no reason to suppose that these two different traditions could not somehow be brought into focus in service to the rapidly changing modern world in which travel between Europe and America was growing ever more frequent thanks to developments in technology and transportation, Pound's attempt both to promote Italy's fascist government and to defend America's republican past was accompanied by a serious misconception over how these views were being received in America. Such defense and this attendant misconception led to Pound's eventual arrest on charges of treason as the result of radio broadcasts made from Rome. In *Black Sea,* Neal Ascherson, in a different context, describes the mentality of what he calls "outpost people," people who are "faithful defenders of some tradition whose centre is far away and which, often, is already decaying into oblivion." One of the characteristics of the "outpost" mentality, according to Ascherson, is a "skewed and paranoid awareness of the exterior world."[45] This description fits Pound well during these years. Pound's early poetic calling, enlivened by the ease of travel by which he celebrated the foreign works and landscapes that he traversed with equal gusto, had become tinged with messianic fervor as his enthusiasm soured into vituperation. Immobile for the most part in Rapallo for much of the thirties and very early forties and broadcasting his defense of both American traditions and Italian fascism from his outpost there, Pound relinquished the tonic effects of travel in favor of the authority of stasis.

E. E. CUMMINGS

Intourist in the Unworld

A difficult author—Mallarmé, Henry James or Hopkins—would
be no hero in Russia today. Indeed it should be self-evident
that "difficulty" (that is, highly individualised expression) must
be regarded not only as anti-popular, but, since useless for the
purposes of propaganda, a sort of affront like an idle man.

—Wyndham Lewis, *Letters*

Russia was by then so remote behind its Chinese wall of
exclusiveness and secretiveness, it was like thinking of Paradise,
or, as it may seem to others, of Hell.

—Rebecca West, *Black Lamb and Grey Falcon*

I N HIS 1941 ESSAY "AUGMENT OF THE NOVEL," EZRA POUND PLACES E. E.
Cummings's *Eimi* alongside John Reed's *Ten Days That Shook the World*,
a book he refers to as that "first grand rapportage" of the Russian
Revolution.[1] In his firsthand account of the events of 1917 in Petrograd, Reed
sought to demystify for western readers an already complicated political scene
in the throes of revolution in order to begin to establish a rapport between
America and Russia. His narrative framed these revolutionary events as Reed
reported both what he witnessed directly and what he heard from others,
usually through translators. These two concepts of "rapport" (seeking mutual
recognition) and "reporting" (getting the facts straight), both evoked in
Pound's use of the French "rapportage," Pound saw operating in *Eimi* as well,

a book that also relies on both firsthand accounts (autopsy) and secondhand reports (hearsay), to recall François Hartog's distinctions regarding a more ancient historiography.[2] Cummings's testimony, however, is harder to decipher than Reed's due to the idiosyncratic style and odd typography of *Eimi*, features which distinguish Cummings's poetry as well. It was this difficult style as well as the subject of the book (Russia more than a decade after the revolution) that recommended *Eimi* to Pound, who, as we have seen in the previous chapter, had demonstrated an interest both in the special forms needed to express the modern world and in the diplomatic recognition of the Soviet Union.

The information that was available regarding these events was scarce in the West due to censorship of news reporting by the Soviet government, though Pound himself had tried to make informational inroads by establishing contacts with writers and politicians.[3] The revolutionary fervor that had swept the region in 1917 and inspired western writers such as Reed and Lincoln Steffens had abated by the late twenties as the euphoria of Lenin's revolution gave way to the oppressiveness of Stalin's totalitarianism, though many western artists and intellectuals on the left still praised the Soviet system.[4] In 1931, Russia was under the leadership of Josef Stalin, who had succeeded Lenin as head of the communist party in 1924. In 1928, Stalin had put the country on the road to industrialization and modernization with the five-year plan, which hinged on the forced collectivization of the kulaks, or peasant farms, and the centralization of power with the communist party to a degree that surpassed even Lenin's original vision. It was in this context that Cummings traveled and recorded his impressions.

Cummings journeys to Russia partly out of curiosity about the Soviet experiment, the relative merits of which were still being debated in the West. The USSR was either praised as a successful utopia or condemned as a fruitless and failed experiment in socialism. He had heard of it most enthusiastically from his friend John Dos Passos, who had visited Russia in 1928 and wrote to Cummings about his experiences in glowing terms. He had also heard about it from the French writer and poet Louis Aragon, another friend and believer in Stalin's vision, who urged Cummings to journey to Russia to witness for himself the communist transformation of society.[5] Cummings heard a less laudatory account of the state of the Soviet Union from Morris Werner, who claimed after seeing the country in 1930 that the living conditions of the average Russian were poor and that society was in shambles.[6] Cummings wanted to determine for himself what the Soviet system had to offer, although as Richard Kennedy points out, "devotee of individualism that he was, he did not expect to be overwhelmed by the joys of collectivism."[7] Thus, Cummings saw Russia not as an objective, unbiased observer but under the influence of a variety of contradictory opinions and with a certain pre-formed view about the realities of Soviet life and the role of the individual.

Eimi is the resulting account of a six-week journey that Cummings took to Russia in the spring of 1931. He traveled by train from Paris, through Berlin and Poland, to Moscow, where he stayed for three weeks. Cummings obtained a special "without party" visa for his trip, which permitted him to travel on his own and not as part of a tour group (Kennedy, 308).[8] Despite this freedom, he spent much of his time doing all of the things that a tourist would do: securing hotel accommodations, visiting the state tourist agency (known as Intourist), changing money, seeing the sites (including Lenin's tomb in Red Square and St. Basil's Cathedral), attending plays and performances, and meeting with both Russian citizens and writers and artists. Cummings also visited Kiev and Odessa in the Ukraine (then a part of the Soviet Union), having agreed to deliver some gifts for a friend who had relatives in Odessa. He eventually left Russia for Istanbul, from where he then returned by train through the Balkans to Paris. Compared to the experiences of John Reed, Cummings's visit was particularly uneventful.

Far from being a straightforward account of this journey, however, *Eimi* is a dense, often cryptic work in which Cummings records his day-to-day life among the Russian people. It is a greatly expanded version of a diary that he kept with him and, on first glance, seems to contain many of the idiosyncrasies of a diary, including abbreviated words, initials for place-names, and unconventional word-combinations, all of which make the book seem to be written in a kind of unfinished shorthand. However, as with his poetry, Cummings saw these features as an integral aspect of his work. *Eimi* contains both moments of lyrical intensity and passages of obscure prose where it is often difficult to determine what Cummings is describing. This stylistic experimentation and innovation rank *Eimi* among the more familiar and similarly experimental works of modernism such as James Joyce's *Ulysses*, Virginia Woolf's *To the Lighthouse*, or Pound's own *Cantos*, although *Eimi* has had a much smaller readership than any of these.

Cummings hesitated to present *Eimi* as a politically engaged work, instead encouraging people to take it either as a casual, even perfunctory, record of his travels in a country and through a system with which he had become increasingly disillusioned, or at most as a self-contained work that displayed the restless play of language that his poetry was known for. In Cummings's own account of the publishing history of *Eimi*, we can see this hesitancy at work, a hesitancy that belies the depth of his feelings about Russia. In an unpublished letter, Cummings records how Pascal Covici, of Covici Friede, solicited the book from him. In response to a general query by Covici,

Cummings reluctantly mentions the notes that he had taken on his recent Russia trip:

> "I have a Russian diary."
> "Great. I know that everybody in the U. S. has been sold lock, stock & barrel on Karl Marx's Paradise."
> "But this book is against Russia. I spent [five weeks] there and I loathed it."
> "So what. Did you write this book?"
> "I sure did."
> "Then I want it." (qtd. in Kennedy, 327–28)

Cummings hesitates offering the book to Covici not solely out of indifference or lack of confidence, as his casual mention of his Russia diary might suggest, but also because he seems to realize that his negative account might alienate him from his readership or his peers. Cummings here deliberately elides the difference between "diary" and "book," unsure, in the logic of this re-created dialogue, of the relationship between personal impression and political statement, as he appears to let himself be prodded into publication. There is a clear political position here as Cummings forthrightly tells Covici that his book is "against Russia." But the "it" from the next sentence indicates that what he loathed was not the Soviet system per se, but rather his time spent there. Cummings does not convert his travel experience into fiction, but there is an element of fiction in his account of the book's publication.

By insisting that *Eimi* was merely a transcribed diary, Cummings maintains that his book was a transparent account of *what* he saw, *as* he saw it. As Norman Friedman points out: "Since the focus is not on *what* happens," since, in fact, so little happens, "but rather on how it appears to the traveler, the book gives the appearance of a lack of selectivity, of an impressionistic completeness and fullness."[9] Friedman cites Cummings's own description of the finished *Eimi*:

> 1—that *Eimi*'s source equals on-the-spot-scribbled hieroglyphics
> 2—that through my subsequent deciphering of said hieroglyphics, not one incident has been revalued; not one situation has been contracted or expanded; not one significance has been warped; not one item has been omitted or inserted "Pour l'artiste, voir c'est concevoir, et concevoir, c'est composer" (Paul Cezanne)." (122–23)

According to Richard Kennedy, however, who has examined the original notebooks that Cummings kept, *Eimi* is "a development and expansion, about ten times the length, of the travel diary he kept during the trip to Russia" (Kennedy, 327).[10] This expanded version retains the freshness, idiosyncrasies, and even confusion of a journal, a fact which would for years mislead scholars into taking Cummings at his word and *Eimi* as a mere transcription of a travel diary. However, despite assuming the role of unwilling author with Covici, in *Eimi* we see one of Cummings's fullest and most elaborate declarations of his identity as an artist, his very own defense of poetry. In this book particularly, he sees language as something that can hold at bay the modern world as he enters into the inferno of the USSR. In the expansion of his Russia notes (if not in their "revaluation") we begin to see an oblique commentary emerging on how his individuality conflicts with Soviet ideology. The travel genre, with its subtle play between interiority and exteriority, as well as the related linguistic play of modernist style, allows Cummings this privileged perspective.

One way Cummings fashions this unique narrative is by complicating the very notion of identity. We see, for example, how he applies various nicknames to the people whom he meets, at first, ostensibly, for the purposes of note-taking, but later, as he translated these notes into *Eimi*, as a way of suggesting the slippery roles that individuals can assume within a system that he sees as denying individuality altogether. In the 1958 preface to the reissued *Eimi*, Cummings further suggests that these nicknames emerged from a desire to avoid the censors and protect people whom he had met from the Secret Police: "thanks to a maker's congenital fondness for metaphor—heightened by Russia's immemorially merciless (once tzarist, now socialist) Gay-Pay-Oo or Secret Police—the persons described in eimi are masked with nicknames."[11] We see this fashioning again in the way he presents his own identity in the text as well as his own narrative persona. The first day he arrives, as he tries to get his bearings, Cummings states his intention of making his presence known, but only indirectly, through stealth: "verily,verily have I entered a new realm, whose inhabitants are made of each other;proudly I swear that they shall not fail to note my shadow and the moving of the leaves" (21). He frequently portrays Moscow itself as disguised, masked by an ideology that he finds to be oppressive and dehumanizing. He describes the city as "dirty," as an "unworld," and repeatedly alludes to Dante's *Inferno* as he makes his way around. We see this, for example, in his description of the crowded streets of Moscow: "with dirt's dirt dirty dirtier with others' dirt" (240). However, despite seeing Moscow as an "unworld" peopled by indistinguishable crowds, there are moments of beauty that manage to pierce the oppressive atmosphere, moments that represent an "actual" world of aesthetic beauty behind the "real" world of ideology. Whereas he frequently sees people fixed in their roles, roles that subsume their individuality, Cummings himself is more than willing to assume various roles and guises himself in order to move within Russian society, thus setting himself uniquely apart from it.

In his statement to Covici, Cummings makes no secret of his dislike of Russia, and *Eimi* can be read both as a denunciation of the Soviet system and as a critique of the way this system was being reported in the West by journalists and intellectuals alike. Cummings couches this denunciation in a style that is both elliptical and obscure, but more importantly it is couched in an aloofness that takes observation as an ultimate kind of authority that transcends the historical and political situation which it claims to register. By coding his experience in this way, by adhering to the role of tourist, and by insisting that his account is no more than a traveler's diary, Cummings deliberately and carefully avoids the complicated and politicized engagement of a writer such as Reed, who became swept up in the events that he reported. Reed's account was intended to persuade readers of the benefits of the Russian revolution by re-creating the immediacy of the scene, whereas Cummings creates a traveling narrator who circulates within society, yet remains distinct, at times anxiously so, from what he is observing. But, just as we will see with Lewis, what begins as a carefully orchestrated narrative tension between subject and object becomes a much more vexed relationship, as Cummings's texts ultimately reveal a particular political reaction to what he confronts in Moscow. In fact it was this reaction, this "diagnosis," as we have seen in the previous chapter, that drew Pound to Cummings's book.

I begin by returning briefly to Ezra Pound's assessment of *Eimi* as one of the works that best diagnosed the interwar years, the Russian scene in particular, and I return as well to his related comments on diagnosis, this time relating it to the detachment that is characteristic of Cummings's style in *Eimi*. I next provide an overview of *Eimi*'s critical reception, limited though it has been, which has tended to see the book as either a self-contained stylistically innovative work of modernist literature on the one hand, or as a work that partakes ambiguously of its political moment on the other. Both the initial reviews and the subsequent critical reception of *Eimi* instantiates a break that was consistently made between the detached artist and the politically engaged writer, a break that we often see as well in the modernist travel writers that I examine here especially, but it is also a rupture that appears similarly throughout Cummings's career. In *The Enormous Room* (1922), for example, a book about his experiences in a French prison camp during the First World War, Cummings straddles this line between engagement and detachment in a way that forecasts his methods in *Eimi*, as I will show.[12] Although *The Enormous Room* is not about the freedom to travel but about the enforced stasis of imprisonment, it is nevertheless an important pre-text when reading

Eimi in that we first see Cummings here translating his foreign experiences into prose that replicates the unfamiliarity of foreign experience.

I examine *Eimi* itself as both a stylistically innovative work of modernist literature, in which Cummings delights in linguistic play, and as a book that needs to be read as a politically engaged work of art that is very much concerned with the world out there, the audience back home, and the authority of firsthand vision. I don't attempt to reconcile these disparate critical views so much as read *Eimi* as a work in which an aloof aestheticism and an engaged political writing exist in uneasy tension often coming into conflict. In this regard, Cummings's use of the conventions of the travel genre is itself where we see his modernist style employed most forcefully and most innovatively. I examine this conflict primarily by exploring the various roles that Cummings assumes—the tourist, the journalist, the artist—and his visits to two prominent tourist attractions, St. Basil's cathedral and Lenin's Tomb. Both of these sites become for Cummings places where conflicting historical and ideological accounts vie for his attention. I also examine Cummings's exit from Russia. Here we see his style at its most obscure and vibrant as he caps his egress from this earthly inferno by reasserting his identity in a world where he can speak as and be himself.

Cummings's testimony, his *cri de coeur* "Eimi" (Greek "I am") is meant to register the fundamental incompatibility between the Soviet regime and his role as an artist and an individual, between what he saw all around him in Russia and what he believed. We should again recall François Hartog's study of the *logoi* of Herodotus, where he argues: "It is more a matter of pondering what is visible and the conditions of visibility. What is it that is visible? Not *what* I have seen, but *what is it* that I have seen?" (Hartog, 267). As Cummings ponders the conditions of visibility in Russia, he finds it necessary at times to assume various guises so that his vision, always mediated, is never entirely obstructed by the boundaries of a rigid role, whether this be tourist, artist, or journalist. In translating *what* he sees and *how* he sees, Cummings employs a style that renders every event obscure in order to foreground the difficulties involved when pondering the "conditions of visibility."

POUND'S MAN IN RUSSIA:
THE ORIGINS OF *EIMI*

Pound's turn in the twenties from civic to political matters (to recall Tim Redman's distinctions),[13] as demonstrated in his increasing interest in the diplomatic recognition of the Soviet Union, and his subsequent interest in the novel as a medium and a genre that would accurately reflect the modern world in all of its political and economic complexity, coalesced in his praise of *Eimi*. However, this interest and his subsequent praise of the book, which he expressed both in print and during the Rome radio broadcasts, developed gradually.[14] By his 1941 essay "Augment of the Novel," Pound had come to see *Eimi* as a necessary component of his modern curriculum. Whereas Cummings, as we have seen, played down his involvement in seeing *Eimi* into print, in this essay Pound accentuates his role in Cummings's decision to travel to Russia:

> I swore that mr. cummings was a fit person to go into Russia. I said he certainly had no prejudice against the regime. Upon which, or at any rate after which, he got his visa and wrote his enormous 'Eimi.' So that for several years I thought perhaps I had erred, though it now appears that I was a hundred percent right, and that he was not only *a* but *the only* fit person to let into Russia. (93)

Pound here figures Cummings as an envoy dispatched to foreign parts to gather information. He sees Cummings as a journalist, albeit one with a highly complex style, whose reports took years to be properly digested. *Eimi* was a perfect example of Pound's description of literature as "news that stays news."[15] It presented information in a form that was necessarily complex and obscure although stable and free from both contingency and the vicissitudes of public opinion. In his recollection of actively encouraging Cummings to travel to Russia, however, Pound revises history somewhat. Cummings did not in fact leave for the Soviet Union "upon" Pound's request, although he did indeed leave "after" Pound had voiced to Cummings an interest in Russia. Although Pound's interest in Russia was significant enough by 1930 that he was corresponding with Senator Bronson Cutting of New Mexico, it seems unlikely that he coaxed Cummings into going traveling, at least according to Cummings in *Eimi*.

Cummings's references to Pound in *Eimi* do not suggest that Pound's role in Cummings's decision to travel was anything but perfunctory. While in Moscow at a dinner party in the apartment of a friend, Cummings is having a discussion with a Russian couple who take turns reciting "propaganda carefully intended to convert the Heathen" (82). The conversation eventually turns to literature. Seeing a copy of Joyce's *Ulysses* on their shelf and grateful for the distraction, Cummings asks the man if he is familiar with Pound's work. When the man says that he has heard the name, Cummings recalls a meeting he had with Pound before he left for Russia. Cummings here describes the extent of Pound's involvement:

("tell them to read cantos" soandso at the Régence who , to my "have you any greeting for the Kremlin?" had replied thoughtfully (more than) glancing (very) keenly past himself into a luminous Everywhere of nowhere)" (83)

In this brief parenthetical recollection, Pound is only casually interested in Cummings's journey. He seems more intent on promoting his own work than in obtaining any information about Russia. He does not demonstrate any of the interest or enthusiasm that he had felt on hearing Lincoln Steffens's 1923 lecture; nor does he urge Cummings to travel nor instill in him any of the missionary zeal that he alludes to in the "Augment" article. Cummings's description of Pound's glance past himself into a "luminous Everywhere of nowhere" borders on the satirical, casting Pound in the role of *distrait* intellectual. Furthermore, Cummings's question to Pound if he has a message for the Kremlin is playfully provocative, if not mocking, knowing as he does Pound's penchant for the big issues of politics and the important political figures of the day. While it certainly could be the case that Cummings's account of Pound's involvement is as revisionist as Pound's own account, it is more likely that as the thirties wore on and for various reasons having more to do with respective self-fashioning than documentary impulse, both men were engaged in creative historiography.

Nevertheless, Pound's figuring Cummings as a foreign correspondent and his subsequent, though gradual, assimilation of *Eimi* into his modern curriculum in the thirties, can be helpful when reading *Eimi*. Cummings wrote his book during a time when the few journalistic accounts that were being published helped shape the view of Russia for many in the west. During his stay in Moscow, Cummings moved in and out of these journalistic circles, and at one point, as I will discuss in detail later, Cummings even passed himself off as a reporter in order to gain access to Lenin's Tomb. For Pound, it was not the translation of sensory input into prose for which he valued *Eimi*, or the immediate transmission of information that was characteristic of the news and wire services, but rather the slow and, in Pound's view, more accurate way in which sensory experience and living conditions were revealed in a work of literature. While for Pound, the speedy and accurate relay of information was important in order to make informed decisions—we even get some impression of this in the way *The Cantos* seem at times to unravel information like a newswire or ticker tape—his gradual appreciation of *Eimi* suggests that he also felt that caution was needed when making sense of historical information and current events. As we have seen in the previous chapter, it was Pound's ideas regarding the role and value of prose that led him to see *Eimi* as simply a gargantuan version of *Ten Days That Shook the World*. While Pound may have been only partially correct in seeing *Eimi* as a "diagnostic" work, he was correct in seeing it as a book that demands both careful and close readings and an understanding of the political and historical context of the period, as well as a book that was most politically engaged just at those moments where Cummings claims the greatest aloofness.

CRITICAL RECEPTION OF EIMI

As slow as Pound's recognition of the importance of *Eimi* was, however, it was rapid compared to the general reception of Cummings's book. Selections from *Eimi* first appeared in 1932 in *Hound and Horn*, the little magazine that had previously published several of Cummings's poems. The brief passages that were included worked well as isolated poems given their form and their removal from the larger narrative. However, when the book appeared in its entirety the following year, reactions to it were for the most part negative. The unusual typography and elliptical style that make Cummings's poetry evocatively lyrical and strangely beautiful did not translate well for many readers into a long travel book about a country about which there was still much misunderstanding. According to Richard Kennedy, *Eimi* "caused a widespread outcry over its stylistic acrobatics." One paper called it "more obscure than Browning's *Sordello*," referring to a work that was Pound's own high watermark of difficulty and obscurity, and one reviewer even "admitted he did not finish the book" (Kennedy, 359). Reactions to *Eimi* by other poets as well as by journalists who had been to Russia, while not as dismissive, were nevertheless equally skeptical about Cummings's style.

In a 1933 review in *Poetry* magazine, Marianne Moore critiqued *Eimi*'s difficult style: "Style is for Mr. Cummings 'translating;' it is a self-demonstrating aptitude for technique, as a seal that has been swimming right-side-up turns over and swims on its back for a time." The peculiar typography, she goes on to say, "is not something superimposed on the meaning but the author's mental handwriting."[16] Moore's praise for Cummings's technique is qualified, however, by her concerns over the self-delusion that such style potentially involves: "A Saint Sebastian—as our Dante probably knows—may be hid by too many arrows of awareness" (279). This image of the martyr obscured by the instruments of his martyrdom Moore offers as a cautionary message to Cummings. For Moore, Cummings's "mental shorthand" is often more confusing than it need be, a particularly egregious mistake in a travel book, which should render a foreign country clearly. As an example of such confusion, Moore cites the word "condesfusionpair," which, she says, is "not hard on the brain but awkward for it" (279–80). Although familiar herself with the inherent difficulties and obscurity of modernist poetry, Moore nevertheless found Eimi to be unnecessarily complex and even self-indulgent in its willful obscurity.

Cummings's style was no easier to decipher for those westerners who were more familiar with the Russian scene and who had suffered the slings and arrows of Soviet life for themselves. In his 1937 book *Assignment in Utopia*, for example, the former United Press correspondent Eugene Lyons recalls reading *Eimi* with a mixture of admiration and perplexity similar Moore's: "What I understood of that book, *Eimi*, was so good, so penetrating, that I still wish he had not written it in puzzlewords."[17] As it was with Moore, so for Lyons, Cummings's style impedes apprehension even as it provides luminous glimpses of meaning. For both Moore and Lyons, Cummings's style gets in the way; it demands either interpretation or deciphering.

This reaction was not limited to the initial reviews of Cummings's book. *Eimi* has left a trail of perplexed readers ever since. In a review of the 1955 reissue of *Eimi*, Francis Fergusson finds beneath *Eimi's* complex, obscure surface a *passeist* quality, like "dead Caruso in a gramophone."[18] The book's precious style conjures for Fergusson a vision of the past, not just a particular Soviet past, but a moment in the history of a generation of Western writers. According to Fergusson, for Cummings Russia is "the end of all that Paris in the 'twenties, 'Paris in the spring,' meant to his generation of Americans in their perennially youthful quest for life and freedom. The contrast between his 'world' and that of the Soviets reveals both a richness and intensity . . . which makes most of the statistical and doctrinaire accounts of the Soviets look frivolous and second-hand" (701–2). For Fergusson, *Eimi* is essentially a document of the "lost generation"; it is a lament for a lost time and the style of the book, in its richness and intensity, is an attempt to recapture this lost youth; but at the same time its density and obscurity harbor an unexpressed belief that such recovery is impossible.

Like Pound before him, Fergusson sees *Eimi* here as a particularly American work. Rather than rendering Russia clear to Western readers, Cummings uses his style, as Henry James used his in *The American Scene*, for example, to record the uncanny contrast between the two worlds. Like James's book, Fergusson argues, *Eimi* is "the intimate record of the impingement of an alien way of life upon a very acute, candid, and individual sensibility" (702). Most importantly, however, for Fergusson, the peculiarities of this "intimate record" preclude any sense of form:

> The book as a whole has ... no form beyond the mere haphazard temporal
> sequence of the author's journey into Russia and out again. The essence
> of Cummings' method is to obey his immediate vision and feeling at the
> expense of all thinking *about* his material, even as much as would be
> required to arrange it in a larger form. . . . In *Eimi* he attempts no such
> ordering or composition. (703)

In his eagerness to account for Cummings's style, Fergusson fails to detect in
Eimi any larger form beyond the mere "haphazard" one of a journal.

As several critics have noted, however, *Eimi* does have a form, despite the
seemingly random surface. Cummings bases his voyage to what he calls the
"unworld" of Moscow on Dante's *Inferno*.[19] He refers to his first guide as Virgil
and to the wife of a friend as Beatrice. As T. S. Eliot has said when describing
the "mythical method" of *Ulysses*, however, these parallels are not a way to
decode the meaning, but rather convenient and ultimately dispensable ways
to organize a book.[20] When expanding his journal, Cummings made use of
these parallels to suggest that these different roles exist in uneasy tension.

Subsequent critics, however, for the most part have concurred with
Fergusson's opinion regarding *Eimi*'s lack of form. In a 1966 article, "Cummings'
Impressions of Communist Russia," Austin Patty sees the book primarily as a
direct translation of Cummings's experiences and thus devoid of form: "When
Cummings simply reported what he saw or heard in Russia, *Eimi* became more
objective and hence more valuable as a criticism of that country. There is every
reason to believe that *Eimi* was written on the spot and that it received little
revision prior to publication."[21] Repeating a common error among critics, Patty
claims that *Eimi* is merely a transcription of the notebooks in which Cummings
recorded these impressions, which would support his argument that Cummings
valued personal experience and eyewitness testimony above all. William Troy
has also perpetuated this belief, pointing to Cummings's linguistic tricks as
evidence that he is simply attempting to reproduce sensory experience:
"Because conventional syntax is historical, that is, based on an arrangement
of thoughts, feelings, and sensations already completed, Mr. Cummings
annihilates conventional syntax and with it conventional punctuation as well.
. . . Typography is also made to perform a dynamic function by approximating
visually the actual thought, object, sensation, being rendered."[22] Both in the
view of *Eimi* as a complex puzzle-book and in the view of it as merely a direct
translation of sensory experience, critics have been slow to grant it a place in
the modernist canon.

This critical reception shows how Cummings's book was uneasily received
by both New Critics, who wanted to see it apart from its historical context, and

critics on the left, who wanted to see in Cummings's narrative an engagement with the economic and political issues of the Soviet Union. Cummings's methods are a way for him to have it both ways: to show how an individual weighs the evidence of history and political reality and how this evidence is then translated into a work of literature. What happens in the course of this translation is what this chapter seeks to explore. Cummings was already familiar with the difficulties of travel and the strangeness of trying to assess a foreign scene. His trip to Russia was not the first time that he had traveled abroad and recorded his experiences in a book whose genre provoked some debate. His most important prior trip, for our purposes here, occurred in 1917 when Cummings enlisted in the army. His experiences during the First World War, when he served in an ambulance corps, formed the basis of his 1922 book *The Enormous Room*. In this earlier work, we can first see some of the themes and methods that Cummings would later employ in *Eimi*.

THE ENORMOUS ROOM:
HISTORY AND FICTION

The Enormous Room documents Cummings's experience in a French detention center in La Ferté-Macé during World War I, where he served time on suspicion of subversive activity. Cummings, however, did not necessarily want his account to be seen as a war book. In his essay "'Brilliant Obscurity': The Reception of *The Enormous Room* (1922)," Paul Headrick notes that initially critics were unsure as to whether to take the work as nonfiction or fiction,[23] an uncertainty that fluctuated over the years, according to shifting critical trends. So, for example, the initial reviews by readers such as John Dos Passos, who insisted that the book was not "an account of a war atrocity" but a "distinct conscious creation separate from anything else under heaven" (qtd. in Headrick, 47), echoed the emerging New Critical standards that saw the work of art as removed from its historical and political context. The value of Cummings's book, in this account, resided in its artistic wholeness and integrity, as Dos Passos asserted, not in its reflection of a political or social scene. Other reviewers, however, railed against the unconventional style and linguistic tricks that Cummings played, the "strainings and obscurities of his style," in one reviewer's words, which avoided any substantive statement on war (qtd. in Headrick 52). On the occasion of the book's reissue in 1933, however, the same year that *Eimi* was published, one reviewer claimed that in *The Enormous Room*, "art and protest were projected together by the same impulse" (qtd. in Headrick, 55). Seeing how art and protest come together in *The Enormous Room* and how Cummings navigates the perilous course between fiction and nonfiction can prepare us as well for reading *Eimi*.

Cummings's decision to join the army was partly prompted by a desire to avoid conscription and partly by a need for authentic experience. In a letter to his father, Cummings explains his reasons for enlisting in a way that suggests this mixed motivation: "It will mean everything to me as an experience to do something I want to, in a wholly new environment, versus being forced to do something I don't want to & unchanging scene. I only hope I shall see some real service at the front" (qtd. in Kennedy, 137). As an enlisted man, Cummings had some say in where he would be stationed and chose a Red Cross ambulance service attached to the French army. The mixed desire expressed in the letter to his father to feel part of something authentic ("real service") but also to obey his own will ("something I want to") characterized his stay in the army and foreshadows his time spent in Russia as a tourist.

On the ship that took him abroad for duty, Cummings met William Slater Brown, a journalism student at Columbia University, and the two became good friends. Brown remembered the first time he saw Cummings in an image that highlights the contradictions we see in Cummings's letter to his father. Headed for service overseas, Cummings was dressed in his college gear—a long fur coat and a crushed "Harvard" hat. The two wound up serving together in the ambulance division where they consistently flouted regulations by refusing to wear standard-issue uniforms and being generally insubordinate. They also remained aloof from their countrymen, preferring to fraternize with the French soldiers (Kennedy, 138). As a result of their repeated insubordination and as the result of a particular letter that Brown sent to his family in which he deliberately provoked the camp censors with statements that were taken as sympathetic to the enemy and potentially subversive, both men were arrested by the French authorities. Although there was no direct evidence as to Cummings's guilt other than his friendship and association with Brown, he spent the next three months in an internment camp as the charges against him were examined. According to Kennedy, this camp was "a Dépôt de Triàge in the nearby town of La Ferté-Macé, a kind of waiting station for aliens who were suspected of espionage or whose presence was generally undesirable during time of war" (Kennedy, 148).

Unlike *Eimi*, *The Enormous Room* is not structured as a journal, although Cummings did, in fact, keep a journal during his incarceration. We see this, for instance, when he describes a fellow Dutch prisoner: "In one of my numerous note-books I have this perfectly direct paragraph : Card table: 4 stares play banque with 2 cigarettes (1 dead) & A pipe the clashing faces yanked by a leanness of one candle bottlestuck (Birth of X) where sits the Clever Man who pyramids, sings (mornings) 'Meet Me . . . '" (96). This passage shows how crucial Cummings's on-the-spot jottings were to *The Enormous Room* and how at certain times Cummings was content to leave these impressions untransformed in his narrative. However, although *The Enormous Room* is presented for the most part in chronological sequence and is loosely modeled on that most teleological of narratives, John Bunyan's *Pilgrim's Progress*, Cummings at the same time distances himself from such teleology. In *The Enormous Room*, he favors instead a pastiche method, common to modernist literature, where he juxtaposes different vignettes and various portraits of individuals. He explains his reasons for this in a conventional aside to the reader:

> To those who have been in jail my meaning is at once apparent; particularly if they have had the highly enlightening experience of being in jail with a perfectly indefinite sentence. How, in such a case, could events occur and be remembered otherwise than as individualities distinct from Time itself? Or, since one day and the next are the same to such a prisoner, where does Time come in at all? Obviously, once the prisoner is habituated to his environment, once he accepts the fact that speculation as to when he will regain his liberty cannot possibly shorten the hours of his incarceration and may very well drive him into a state of unhappiness(not to say morbidity),events can no longer succeed each other: whatever happens, while it may happen in connection with some other perfectly distinct happening, does not happen in a scale of temporal priorities—each happening is self sufficient, irrespective of minutes months and the other treasures of freedom.
>
> It is for this reason that I do not purpose to inflict upon the reader a diary of my alternative aliveness and non-existence at La Ferté—not because such a diary would unutterably bore him, but because the diary or time method is a technique which cannot possibly do justice to timelessness. (82–83)

In eschewing the "time method," Cummings undermines any sense of progression, physical or otherwise, and at the same time, oddly enough, avoids either criticizing the events that led to war or valorizing his own war experience. It is perhaps this that led early reviewers such as Dos Passos to maintain vehemently that *The Enormous Room* was not a typical war book, despite its resemblance to both war novels and to traditional narratives such as *The Pilgrim's Progress*. For Cummings, his most authentic experience happened away from the site of war, in the enormous room.

Cummings's growing awareness of the absurdity of his imprisonment runs parallel to the unfolding and heightening of his perceptions, and thus these external events and his perceptions of them cannot be talked about separately. When he is first arrested, he is unsure exactly of what is happening to him and confused about what he sees and hears. In response to his question of where he is being taken, the guard says "Mah Say" (35), which he hears as "Marseilles" and assumes he will be deported from the French port city. It turns out, however, to be the town of La Ferté-Macé, where the detention center is located. He arrives at the detention center at night in a state of disorientation. Tired, hungry, and cold, Cummings is left in a room that he takes to be a small cell, but whose dimensions remain indeterminate as he struggles to get his bearings:

> all about me there rose a sea of most extraordinary sound. . . . the hitherto empty and minute room became suddenly enormous;weird cries,oaths,laughter,pulling it sideways and backward,extending it to inconceivable depth and width, telescoping it to frightful nearness. From all directions, by at least thirty voices in eleven languages(I counted as I lay Dutch,Belgian,Spanish,Turkish,Arabian,Polish,Russi an,Swedish,German,French—and English) at distances varying from seventy feet to a few inches, for twenty minutes I was ferociously bombarded. (42–43)

This contraction and expansion of space and the ebb and flow of sound that lapses in and out of language further disorient Cummings as he tries to make sense of his surroundings. The "enormity" of the "Enormous" room is not simply hugeness, but an expansiveness that eliminates scale and unfixes dimensions.

The elastic space of the enormous room stabilizes as Cummings wakes up the next morning and his senses gradually recover, but what lingers is the feeling that the space he is in will at any moment collapse. The routine of the detention center acts as a brake against such collapse as Cummings sees, interacts with, and forms relationships with the diverse and changing prison population. The narrative chronicles his struggle against the chaos of overwhelming sensory input from the beginning, throughout his time there, and even upon his release.

When the camp director notifies Cummings of his release and instructs him to "report immediately to the American Embassy, Paris," Cummings is relieved, although it is a relief alloyed with the same confusion that he also felt upon his arrival: "'I? Am? Going? To? Paris?' somebody who certainly wasn't myself remarked in a kind of whisper. [. . .] But how changed. Who the devil is myself? Where in Hell am I? What is Paris—a place, a somewhere, a city, life, to live : infinitive. Present first singular I live. Thou livest" (237).

This statement of living, which foreshadows the title of Cummings's Russia book, "*Eimi*" was a theme throughout Cummings's life and was at the heart of his role as a poet. He complains against those who would put limits on or attempt to negate this living, for example, the camp commander. And while *The Enormous Room* is certainly meant to be a denunciation of war, this denunciation is not directed against war itself but against those who see war as a natural part of the human condition. Cummings's political thought at this stage was still developing, but he did see his wartime experiences as the result of politics both personal and global that were linked in their disregard for the individual. Cummings counters this view through his resistance to taking his own wartime experience as somehow formative on his growth as a writer or as an individual. This resistance manifests itself in the form of Cummings's novel, which undermines conventional teleological approaches to narrative structures.

At the end of *The Enormous Room*, Cummings is released and put on a boat to New York after finally reaching Marseilles. He characterizes this relief, however, as a mere plot device and in the process attempts to dismantle the notion that the narrative he has constructed from notes and memory is true, that it is a history. The final chapter, entitled "I Say Good-Bye to La Misère," begins: "To convince the reader that this history is mere fiction (and rather vulgarly violent fiction at that) nothing perhaps is needed save that ancient standby of sob-story writers and thrill-artists alike—the Happy Ending" (229). He blends aspects of the fictional and the historical, variously taking elements from each in order to structure his book and to make sense of his experiences.

Despite this book's account of Cummings's war experiences, there is an underlying anti-subjectivism to the narrative, as Cummings locates his book delicately between fiction and nonfiction and repeatedly attempts to distance himself from the happiness that he feels upon his release by labeling it as fiction:

> I dare say it all comes down to a definition of happiness. And a definition of happiness I most certainly do not intend to attempt; but I can and will say this : to leave La Misère with the knowledge, and worse than that the feeling, that some of the finest people in the world are doomed to remain prisoners thereof for no one knows how long—are doomed to continue, possibly for years and tens of years and all the years which terribly are between them and their deaths, the grey and indivisible Non-existence which without apology you are quitting for Reality—cannot by any stretch of the imagination be conceived as constituting a Happy Ending to a great and personal adventure. (229)

Although on the one hand, Cummings's book ends with him "quitting for Reality," thus providing a fit narrative shape to his experience and to his book, on the other hand he cannot simply and conveniently shed what he has left behind, whether his own experiences or the reality of those he has left behind. The "Non-existence" in the detention center is "indivisible"; it is not subject to conventional narration that breaks events up into chronological, causal structures. The "reality" to which he is headed upon his release, on the other hand, is highly divisible: fractured, fragmentary, even at times joyous, but permanently infused with the "Non-existence" that he leaves behind at La Ferté-Macé.

Cummings's view of New York as he arrives on board ship after his release is similar to Bunyan's view of the celestial city at the end of *Pilgrim's Progress*. Cummings describes the verticality and ascension of the buildings that greet his eyes, after being for so long confined in a room that hardly offered a glimpse of the sky. He again feels a sense of "aliveness," a feeling which was a credo throughout his career. His appreciation of the vertical structures of New York architecture and the throngs of people are rendered with impressionistic detail:

> The tall,impossibly tall, incomparably tall,city shoulderingly upward into hard sunlight leaned a little through the octaves of its parallel edges,leaningly strode upward into firm hard snowy sunlight; the noises of America nearingly throbbed with smokes and hurrying dots which are men and which are women and which are things new and curious and hard and strange and vibrant and immense,lifting with a great undulous stride firmly into immortal sunlight . . . (242)

Cummings's language is lyrical in this passage. The buildings are personified in that they are "shoulderingly" and "leaningly" striving upwards, an action mirrored in the men and women who hurry about their business and are "lifting with a great undulous stride" into the air and sunlight. The buildings and the crowds are in harmony, and the noises of the people that greet his ears, though indistinguishable, are nevertheless "strange and vibrant." At the end, Cummings hardly seems able to determine which was more real, that which he has left behind or that which he is heading toward, and this offers yet another reason why critics had trouble determining whether this book was fiction or history.

In a 1931 letter to the publisher of his volume of poetry, *ViVa*, a title that again asserts vibrancy and life, Cummings returns to the ideas of space, form, and enormity, as the memory of his imprisonment in La Ferté-Macé still clearly lingers:

There are two types of human beings children & prisoners. Prisoners are inhabited by formulae. Children inhabit forms. A formula is something to get out of oneself, to rid oneself of—an arbitrary emphasis deliberately neglecting the invisible and significant entirety. A form is something to wander in, to loose oneself in—a new largeness, dimensionally differing from the socalled real world. (Kennedy, 319)

Written soon after his trip to Russia where he saw and heard the "formulae" for Marxism all around him, from its promulgation in a play that he went to see called *Roar China* (58) to the propaganda posters he saw throughout Moscow that proclaimed the success of the five-year plan (150), Cummings's statement in this letter regarding the differences between children and prisoners counterpoises rigid formulas (a trap) against form (something in which to "loose oneself"). Like the space of the enormous room, form is elastic and allows the self to be fluid; form promotes and accommodates wandering. The form of the text and the world expressed within is different from the "real world" and yet just as potent, if not more so, than "reality." Cummings will elaborate on this distinction between the formula of, for example, Soviet life and the form (or lack of form, as critics saw it) of his travels and his travel book. Cummings's style attempts to be as faithful to recording "the invisible and significant entirety" of Russia as it does to recording what he sees all around him.

EIMI:
A Tourist's Eye View of Russia

Cummings's protestations aside, *Eimi* needs to be read as a politically engaged work that seeks authority for its perspective precisely at the point of disengagement. Thus the posturing to Covici in Cummings's account of the book's publication is perfectly in line with his narrative persona throughout his travel narrative. The generic uncertainty—that the book is not quite exposé and not quite journal—that this posturing underscores is symptomatic of the larger questions that this current study seeks to explore, including the relationship between vision and authority, clarity and obscurity, as well as the related discussion of the ways in which modernist style can best convey the modern world. And yet, even as Cummings repeatedly evokes Dante's own narrative persona in the *Divine Comedy* in the way that the Italian pilgrim passes through the un-world of Hell while maintaining the substantiality of his own body and the integrity of his own unfolding life, there is a way in which the Cummings of *Eimi*, while striving for a like detachment, often finds himself most lost precisely at those moments where he is most detached. The kind of detachment that Cummings often strives for is a result of the dual repulsion he feels both for the system itself and the mundane reality through which he moves. These divergent though related repulsions don't always get brought into focus let alone reconciled or even explicitly related, the way they do, for example, in *The Enormous Room*. Instead, a kind of desultory record emerges, of a kind much more closely related to the conventions of the travel genre than to the features of modernist prose during the period.

Despite the appearance of the book, in which dates serve as section headings and allusions to Dante's *Divine Comedy* abound—a work that, like *Pilgrim's Progress*, equates narration with both personal experience and historical progression—*Eimi* is even more resistant to teleological narrative norms than *The Enormous Room*. As Norman Friedman points out, "Whereas in the first book he was discovering and defining his values, in the second he is applying them and confirming them. The structure of *Eimi*, then, involves not so much an upward movement of apocalyptic revelation concerning the Delectable Mountains, as an outward movement of grateful escape as Cummings leaves Russia" (Friedman, 111). However, as with *The Enormous Room*, where Cummings resisted the narrative norms that equated his emergence from prison with either happiness or meaning, so in *Eimi* Cummings's "escape" from Russia is not intended to correspond directly with Dante's emergence from Hell. Although his vision of Lenin's body is clearly intended to be infernal and although, as he leaves Russia, his narrative is saturated with the vocabulary of relief and transcendence that most directly recalls Dante's vision of paradise, it would be inaccurate to suggest that Cummings's book relies solely on such structures. Rather, it is with the contrasts that he sees on his journey—both the contrasts between the west and Russia and the contrasts within Russia— that Cummings frames his simultaneous denunciation of Soviet ideology and his assertion of individuality. As Robert Wegner says regarding *The Enormous Room* and *Eimi*, "The noticeable difference . . . lies in the scope of their implications: whereas *The Enormous Room* revealed cruelty and suffering inflicted upon innocent human beings by war, *EIMI* reveals the inhumanity of an ideology imposed upon a people under the banner of materialistic progress."[24] This realization, however, is fragmentary and halting, as Cummings weighs what he sees and what he hears in a style that is obscure and convoluted.

The portrait that we get of the Soviet Union, at least those aspects that Cummings sees (primarily Moscow), is of a country in which a social experiment has failed on a massive scale. Cummings does not visit any of the surrounding regions, or collective farms, or industrial centers that were the centerpiece of Stalin's drive for industrialization, but he does see the distant effects of enforced collectivization while in Moscow. These effects manifest themselves in the people that he meets, the propaganda that he hears, and the bureaucracies that he encounters that make every task, from changing money, to switching hotels, to obtaining travel documents, a lengthy and frustrating process. In this respect, Pound's view of *Eimi* as a work of diagnosis is accurate in that Cummings does not attempt to portray the core or machinery of the economic or ideological structures of the Soviet state—as Reed did, for instance, in *Ten Days That Shook the World*, or as John Scott would do in his account of his time in the thirties in the industrial city of Magnitogorsk in *Behind the Urals* (1942)—rather Cummings is content to show how the symptoms of such radical, revolutionary change manifest themselves in people's day-to-day lives. Cummings also witnesses how Soviet ideology affects art and language, how it affects the stories that people tell about their history as well as about their immediate present.

As when he is first brought to La Ferté-Macé and left in a room in which his senses are overwhelmed by the unfamiliar environment, so in *Eimi* we, as readers, are confronted with a feeling of disorientation as the book opens. Whereas Cummings's initial sensations when imprisoned in France vacillated between a cacophonous expansiveness and a disquieting closeness, in *Eimi*, the initial effect is strictly one of intense claustrophobia. In both cases the disorientation and the obscure style in which Cummings registers this disorientation signal for the reader a break between the narrator's consciousness and the foreignness and unfamiliarity of the external circumstances. To emphasize the closeness of space, *Eimi* begins abruptly with the word "SHUT." This claustrophobia has an immediate source since Cummings is situated in one of the tiny sleeper compartments of the train, a compartment that he likens to a "deuxième coffin" (3); however, it also signals on a larger scale the panic that Cummings will feel throughout his trip regarding the numerous restrictions that are placed on him as he travels about: from the ubiquity of bureaucratic regulations to the pervasiveness of Soviet ideology.

The people whom he meets on the train he describes in a similarly morbid fashion: his cabin mate he labels "funeral director" because of the way that he dresses and his insistence on keeping the window of their "coffin" closed (3). This will be a common strategy of Cummings's, to assign people nicknames based on some distinguishing feature they possess or some role they fill. When he goes to eat, he finds four people already in the dining car, which is even more claustrophobic and reminiscent of death than his sleeping compartment:

> and lunch was more Shut than a cemetery:4 separate corpses collectively illatease:no ghost of conversation. Ponderous grub;because(last night, Shut in a breathless box with a grunting doll)I rushed sidewise into

> Germany(but that swirling tomb of horizontality was less Shut than the
> emptiest rightangledness which calls itself "essen"). (3)

The experience of claustrophobia permeates this passage and the opening
pages, as do the repeated allusions to death, for example the "swirling tomb of
horizontality." The word "SHUT" that begins *Eimi* stands apart from the rest
of the sentence and in fact announces what is essentially a theme for the book,
that of the closeness of space and of the contraction of all dimension. As it
turns out however, this word is also a command given him by one of his cabin
mates but one he at first does not understand since it is in a foreign language:
"SHUT seems to be The Verb." As if to aggravate his claustrophobia further,
he is asked by one of his cabin mates, who insists on smoking, to shut the
window of the train, to which Cummings replies, "don't you think we'll have
too much smoke?" (3).

The position of Cummings's body, as he sleeps, is perpendicular to the
direction of the train, so he rushes "sidewise" toward Russia, a position that
itself belies purposive direction despite the fact that he is being rushed toward
Moscow inexorably on iron tracks. Yet his position as he sleeps also offers a
kind of silent but willful resistance to such inevitable progress and directed
travel. When he arrives in Moscow, Cummings remains confused and weary
from traveling in the tiny train compartment and his senses reach out for some
signs of life: "Alive?arrive? Whenwhere?" (12). The latter word conflates time
and space; he does not know where he is or what time it is. But the confusion
rendered in the rhyme of the first two words "alive" and "arrive" suggests his
struggle to feel that he has managed to escape the death that he felt so strongly
while on board the train.

His confusion continues nonetheless. Thanks to the efforts of the Russian
novelist Ilya Ehrenburg, whom Cummings had met in Paris, he was supposed
to have been met at the train station in Moscow by Vladimir Lidin, a Russian
playwright; but when Cummings disembarks, Lidin is nowhere to be found and
so he is forced to use his limited phrasebook Russian to find his way to the tourist
agency to find lodgings. He goes to the state tourist agency, Intourist, which
regulates all foreign travel within the borders of the Soviet Union and whose
name coincidentally represents a kind of Cummingsesque distortion of language.
The "without party" visa that Cummings had managed to obtain with the help of
Dos Passos had freed him from having to associate himself with any tour groups,
but without any other option and with the help of well-meaning locals whom
he meets at the train station, Cummings finds his way to the Intourist office and
to the nearby Metropole Hotel. As Cummings approaches the two buildings, his
guides point to a sign and Cummings sees both buildings at once:

INTOURIST
>again:an alarmingly ample structure, possibly a crematory? "And this is the
>Hotel Metropole." (15)

Whereas the Intourist building resembles a crematorium, the Hotel
Metropole is a splendid and luxurious building that he guesses will be more
than he can afford, as he momentarily considers the paradox of his situation.
While in Paris, he had avoided luxurious surroundings and, as he recalls, even
in America he had never stayed in such opulent accommodations:

> "the Hotel Metropole" (never,in America,has this comrade stopped at
> a really "first class" robbinghouse. Studiously,in Europe,did he avoid the
> triplestar of Herr Baedeker . . . and now?) "Change,that's all." O plutocracy,O
> socialism—gird we up our loins: forward,into paradox . . . (15)

Cummings decides for the moment to take advantage of the situation, not
having many other options, and checks into the hotel, but this interjection
("O plutocracy,O socialism . . .") reveals not only Cummings's discomfort,
but also his attempt to maintain a studied distance from participation in the
very paradoxes that his words announce and codify. In this whole opening
section, from his claustrophobia on the train, to his arrival at the station, to
his approach to the Metropole, we see Cummings falling back on the role of
the tourist, the naïve innocent abroad, as a way of not just getting by, but as
a way of adjusting his vision to take in what he sees all around him. The kind
of modernist "diagnosis" that Pound urged is often replaced with rhetorical
flourishes as Cummings himself retreats behind obscurity. He doesn't swoon
like Dante does at key moments in his progress through hell, but as he rushes
"forward into paradox" he often seems unable to reconcile what he sees with
what he knows of Russia, resulting in a disorientation that strikes the reader
as much as the narrator.

In the lobby of the Metropole, faced with the marble (or faux-marble)
staircase and the "boundlessly flowering plants," Cummings becomes even
more wary of remaining there, concerned as he is with his finances and as the
paradoxes of Soviet life continue to assert themselves. As he looks around, he
notices a Russian woman who works at the hotel, clutching an empty milk can
and descending the marble steps. This woman stands out distinctly against the
luxurious background:

> down something-or-marble vista visionary with vegetation waddles 1
> prodigiously pompous,quite supernaturally unlovely,infratrollop with
> far(far)toogolden locks;gotup rather than arrayed in ultraerstwhile

vividly various whathaveyous ; assertingly (if not pugnaciously) puffing a gigantic cigarette" (15)

The image of this woman causes Cummings to ironically recall a line from a poem by Ezra Pound, "And they talk of Swinburne's women," from "Shop Girl."[25] In this brief four-line poem, Pound celebrates the common shop girl of the title, whose delicate features, vulnerability, and implicit moral looseness recommend themselves to the poet of modern life seeking out a new kind of modern beauty. In this poem, Pound recalls also "the shepherdess meeting with Guido" and "the harlots of Baudelaire," as corresponding instances of feminine beauty. The woman Cummings sees, however, does not inspire in him any of the decadent reveries that Pound's poem conjures. Instead, these lines come to him as an ironic commentary on the pervasive contrast that he finds in Russian society, the mundane reality beneath the luxurious facades maintained for the benefit of tourists. But Cummings is clearly sympathetic to Pound's association of feminine beauty with ideal beauty, both of which the modern world threatens to subsume. Russia is, for Cummings, not merely a place of ideological failure, but a site of the erasure of conventional and sensual beauty. Cummings saw poetry as the preservation of this kind of beauty, with all of its gendered coding, and its nullification is meant to stand as a charge against the Soviet system.

During his time in Moscow, Cummings refers to the women he sees there as "non-men," implicitly suggesting that communism has erased gender distinctions just as it has obscured aesthetic beauty, and Cummings repeatedly conflates these two. This woman, who is carrying a "brutally battered skeleton of an immense milkcan" descends among an array of flowers, which symbolically possess the beauty that she lacks (15). And despite her far "toogolden locks," which only further emphasize her artificiality, she is an image of sterility. What Cummings means to signal with this image is the contradiction between the actualities of Soviet life and the version of Soviet ideology that is presented to westerners, but as he does this he positions himself as well apart from what he sees, implicitly siding with Pound's intent in "Shop Girl," even if he comes to different conclusions about the actual presence of this kind of beauty in the world. Cummings will confront this contrast time and time again, but it is at this point that he realizes the value of his role as tourist, a role that allows him to see the Soviet experiment with this double perspective, and yet remain apart, falling back on an almost naïve aestheticism in order to preserve his poetic calling.

Cummings soon understands the difficulties of seeing Russia without mediation, as the various bureaucrats that he confronts dominate his itinerary.

As he turns from the woman with the milkcans descending the stairs to the concierge's desk to check in, Cummings provides in response to questions from the desk clerk his reasons for going to Russia and states his identity. The desk clerk asks him why he is traveling to Russia, and Cummings responds in a manner that he intends to be as neutral and noncommittal as possible:

> Why do you wish to go to Russia?
> because I've never been there.
> (He slumps,recovers). You are interested in economic and sociological problems?
> no.
> Perhaps you are aware that there has been a change of government in recent years?
> yes(I say without being able to suppress a smile).
> And your sympathies are not with socialism?
> may I be perfectly frank?
> Please!
> I know almost nothing about these important matters and care even less.
> (His eyes appreciate my answer). For what do you care?
> my work.
> Which is writing?
> and painting.
> What kind of writing?
> chiefly verse;some prose.
> Then you wish to go to Russia as a writer and painter? Is that it?
> no;I wish to go as myself.
> (An almost smile). Do you realize that to go as what you call Yourself will cost a great deal?
> I've been told so. (16)

The desk clerk, whose job is to recommend the sites a tourist might want to see, is puzzled by Cummings's lack of interest in the recent and ongoing political changes of the Soviet Union. Cummings's protestations of neutrality and even lack of interest regarding "these important matters" are perhaps disingenuous and even a little defensive. And yet this story is also recounted with a degree of pride, as if Cummings is traveling independently, off the beaten track of those political writers who came before him.

As with Ezra Pound, for whom every bureaucratic encounter subsequent to his experience in Paris in 1919 or any mention of passports and visas triggered his recollection of the scene at the American consulate, so Cummings immediately recalls the application process for his visa, which also occurred in

Paris, in the Soviet consulate office. Immediately after this interview with the desk clerk and without any indication or break in the narrative, Cummings is suddenly back in Paris:

> Let me earnestly warn you(says the sandyhaired spokesman for the Soviet Embassy in Paris)that such is the case. Visiting Russia as you intend would be futile from every point of view. The best way for you to go would be as the member of some organization—
>
> but,so far as I know,I'm not a member of any organization.
>
> In that case you should go as a tourist. And I'm speaking not only from the financial standpoint : do you realize that without some sort of guidance you will not see anything,let alone understand? (16–17)

This conflation of two separate events is important for Cummings because it demonstrates that he sees his most difficult challenge when traveling through Russia not to be enduring the hardships of conveyance—the claustrophobia on the train for instance, or the cultural and linguistic barriers, which he essentially manages to neutralize through humor—but rather the persistent mediation that he is subject to, whether from fellow travelers, tourist organizations, journalists, or state propaganda. His quest for an objective, unmediated experience of Russia is, he knows, naïve, but by foregrounding as he does in these two passages this naïveté—which induces the consular officer to talk to Cummings as if he were a child—Cummings reasserts the distinction that he made in his letter regarding *ViVa*, between a prisoner who is "inhabited by formulae," here the prescribed role of the tourist who travels with Intourist, and a child who "inhabit[s] forms," in which it wanders loosely.

The Paris desk clerk remarks that Cummings "will not see anything,let alone understand," putting the emphasis on "understanding." But perhaps the more serious implication of this remark is that without guidance Cummings "will not *see* anything." The desk clerk implies that there is no unmediated knowledge, the refutation of which assumption was Cummings's chief motivation for traveling to Russia to begin with. But there is also, the man suggests, no unmediated vision. The perceptions of the individual are always directed by someone else. This is part of what it means to be a tourist, but there is the underlying assumption that this is a deeply embedded part of Soviet society as a whole, thus contributing to the stifling feeling that has haunted Cummings all along. Tourism here, from the desk clerk's point of view, is not a recreational activity, but a tool of ideology that determines not only the path of the journey and the meaning of what is seen, but what *can* be seen.

Cummings's way of countering this prescription of vision is not, however, to avoid the beaten track of tourism, beyond the simple gesture of not associating himself with any tour groups or affiliating himself with any organizations. Instead, he adheres to his role as a tourist: he allows himself to inhabit this form and wander loosely in it as he sees Moscow. He neither shuns the various guides whose company he finds himself in, nor relies too heavily on them. The only way that Cummings can travel as himself, as if in rebuttal to the desk clerk's warning, is to forge an identity that remains fluid and yet apart. In addition, although Cummings has moments of what he feels are unmediated vision, these moments usually manifest themselves against the backdrop of the conventional and over-determined tourist sites that he sees. Cummings persistently weighs what he sees against what people tell him of what he sees. We can observe this, for instance, when Cummings visits that most prominent tourist attraction and most readily identifiable image of Russia, St. Basil's Cathedral.

THE CHURCH OF PERPETUAL REVOLUTION: SIGNIFICANT TALES TOLD TO A TOURIST

Cummings's vision, like the vision of any traveler or any tourist, is mediated by the people who purport to guide him, whether physically or ideologically. We have seen the results of this mediation both in the morbid language with which he describes his arrival and in the way he presents the woman with the milkcan as a negative symbol of the damaging effects of the Soviet system. The manner in which he chose to represent these two scenes, in particular, is the result of both his own perceptions and his own secondhand ideas about Russia coming into conflict, as well as the deliberative attempt to represent them through his modern style, but it is important to recognize that even as these two scenes are saturated with the judgments that he has heard from others or the ideas about the Soviet state that he has formed for himself, they remain largely free of Soviet ideology or interpretations that are expressly in the service of the Russian state. The scene on board the train occurs before he meets his contact (who, in any event, fails to show), and the scene in the lobby of the Metropole happens just prior to the scene with the desk clerk, whose official role is in support of the state (as we see in the section immediately following). Cummings will confront this latter mediation as well, though, a mediation that occurs through the stories that are officially maintained and cultivated by the state tourist bureau, through its monuments, histories, and sacred objects. We will see Cummings variously submit to and resist these accounts as his attempts to remain detached become more urgent. His description of St. Basil's cathedral, the sixteenth-century church built by Ivan the Terrible, which stands at one end of Red Square, adjacent to the Kremlin, not far from the Hotel Metropole in which Cummings was staying (see figure 2) is one of the most significant ways in which we see Cummings attempting to balance firsthand accounts and (official) hearsay, as we see him again pondering the conditions of visibility and weighing the value of the stories that he is told.

Cummings first sees the cathedral, one of the most recognized monuments and tourist attractions in Russia, the day after he arrived in Moscow, in the company of Henry Wadsworth Longfellow Dana, who happened to be also staying at the Metropole and whom he had known from his days at Cambridge. Cummings would refer to Dana as his Virgil and he functions as such here. The two approach Red Square from the end opposite to St. Basil's. Cummings describes his approach to this huge public space and the effect that it has on him. They first see Lenin's tomb, or the mausoleum on Red Square in which it is housed, but the square and sturdy structure leaves him cold:

> L's M
> a rigid pyramidal composition of blocks;an impurely mathematical game of edges : not quite cruelly a cubic cerebration—equally glamourless and emphatic , withal childish . . . perhaps the architectural equivalent for "boo!—I scared you that time!" (25)

Here the description of the mausoleum as "childish" is entirely without the connotation of playful innocence that he described in his letter regarding *ViVa*. Instead the building is seen as mathematical and cruel, with a geometry that is foreboding and impure. As he comes upon St. Basil's, however, his senses are overwhelmed as he sees a structure that he can only refer to on the spot (in what will become the permanent shorthand name) as "Something Fabulous":

> a frenzy of writhing hues—clusteringly not possible whirls together grinding into one savage squirtlike ecstasy : a crazed Thinglike dream solemnly shouting out of timespace,a gesture fatal,acrobatic(goring tomorrow's lunge with bright beyondness of yesterday)—utterly a Self,c atastrophic;distinct,unearthly and without fear. (25)

It is no surprise that Cummings, with his love of flowers, would be attracted to this most flowery and organic structure, which stands in stark contrast to the angular buildings on the Kremlin grounds. He is fascinated in particular by the building's "crazed," unpredictable architecture.

Fig. 2. Saint Basil's Cathedral, Moscow, Russia. Photograph, David Farley.

He begins a letter to Anne Barton, who was his wife at the time, by referencing the cathedral in a way that posits it as an oasis: "Dear Anne: There is an Arabian Nights church here which you should see some day. The rest you'd hate . . ." (Kennedy 310). He does not *describe* the building in the letter to his wife; instead, he insists that she needs to see it for herself, as if its beauty was beyond his own power of description. The remainder of the letters consists of Cummings's complaints about his living conditions: from the "vile" food, to the lack of toilet paper. He does mention Lenin's tomb briefly, but only to dismiss by calling it "imposingly Pyramidical" (311).

The contrast of the "Something Fabulous" cathedral and the blockish tomb Cummings finds to be instructive. He had, for instance, similarly divided his 1922 book of poetry, *Tulips & Chimneys*, into the "lyrical renderings (tulips) in standard or free verse" and the "responses to the modern world (chimneys) in sordid urban scenes," as Kennedy puts it (238). Like *Tulips & Chimneys*, which was divided neatly into two sections, Red Square offers illuminative contrast, the difference here being that they are irreconcilably opposed. The exterior of St. Basil's is of diverting shapes, odd orthographies of architecture that give no indication of what lies inside. Cummings reveled in this incongruity between the sharp and blockish features of Lenin's tomb and the superfluity of meaning, the architectural arabesques that reminded him of the *Arabian Nights*, of other places and other times. He is so transfixed on the beauty of St Basil's that he can't leave: "The tearing of mere me and this miracle from each other demands effort on part of failing benevolence" (26). This "failing benevolence" who tears him away from his vision is Dana-Virgil, who just before he leaves Cummings urges to see the inside of the building as well, "which has been turned into a Revolutionary Museum." Cummings will return on his own to visit the inside of the cathedral several days later and will be struck by the incongruity of the transformed interior, where he sees but one roped-off icon and the remainder of the walls covered with photographs of tractors and farmers and anti-religious propaganda. The building itself, its beauty and its architecture, will continue to figure for him as an oasis, though as both a tourist attraction in the modern Soviet state and as a visible reminder of Russia's orthodox past, the cathedral will be a site for contending accounts of history and ideology.

The first anecdote that Cummings hears about St. Basil's occurs on the Monday after his arrival, May 18, when he finally meets up with Vladimir Lidin, the Russian playwright and friend of Ilya Ehrenburg who was supposed to have met him at the train station upon his arrival, but who failed to show up. Lidin is enamored of western life, dressed as he is in a slightly outdated Parisian style, "Latin Quarterishly," as Cummings refers to him, or simply "LQ" in his shorthand style (104). The two have dinner and, after, as they stroll through the city, Lidin tells Cummings a story about the original construction of St. Basil's cathedral:

> Ivan the Terrible , Emperor of Russia , commissioned a particularly famous Italian architect to build the most beautiful church in the world (LQ resumes) which when the architect had done , the emperor extinguished the architect's eyes , saying Lest you should create

something yet more beautiful. (A beggar lurched at us : LQ sidestepped
him gingerly ; frowned : spat. In a not more than whisper)and those
were the days when art was highly valued . . . (104)

This story, while almost certainly apocryphal, is customarily related to tourists
as evidence of the building's singular beauty. The clichéd nature of the story
and the perfunctory, almost obligatory way in which Lidin, an artist himself,
relates it is countered by the intrusion of the beggar whom Lidin "gingerly "
and parenthetically "sidesteps." The presence of the beggar hardly interrupts
Lidin's telling of the story or his ability to draw from it a simple moral—"those
were the days when art was highly valued." He manages to avoid the presence of
poverty before him even while he extols the aesthetic discernment of the Tsar.
Lidin's recounting of this story takes Cummings aback. It is for him another
one of these illuminative contrasts by which he sees a fundamental discrepancy
at the heart of Soviet life. The story is a proud reminder, in Lidin's view, of the
days before Communism and a testament, he seems to be suggesting, to an
anachronistic cruelty that fostered such beauty. Lidin, somewhat proudly, sees
no contradiction in the proximity of such beauty and such cruelty.

As if to underscore further Lidin's blindness to the implications of his own
story, as the two walk on, Lidin buys some flowers from a street vendor. He
asks "Isn't it Spring? Is there anything more beautiful—even a woman—than
a flower?" (104). And Cummings, whose affection for both Spring and flowers
outweighs even his affection for art, responds with words that contain a mild
rebuke to Lidin: "(K) there is an I Feel ; an actual universe or alive of which our
merely real world or thinking existence is at best a bad , at worst a murderous
, mistranslation ; flowers give me this actual universe" (104–5). Seemingly
acceding to Lidin's praise of beauty, Cummings's allusion to cruelty and his
juxtaposition of murderousness and mistranslation are a subtle reproach to
the positive conclusion that Lidin draws from his story that "those were the
days when art was highly valued." Such "real" value Cummings counterpoises
against "actual" value, which is more than simply utilitarian and does not
countenance cruelty.

As difficult as it is for Cummings to reconcile the building that he sees with
Lidin's anecdote about it, the process becomes even more complicated when
Cummings hears another story about St. Basil's Cathedral. Later that evening,
he goes to see an acquaintance whom he met the previous day, a Romanian
expatriate named Otto, who works in the Revolutionary Literature Bureau.
Otto had told Cummings previously that he would help him obtain cheaper
lodging while in Moscow, but he ultimately confesses that he is unable to do
so, since there is a shortage of available housing. This earns him the name of
"Otto Can't" from Cummings, because he can't do what he promised. When

Cummings goes to see him that night he is consoling two other people, who had similarly come to find lodging. Unable to help them either, he attempts to soothe them by praising the virtues of the Soviet system, virtues which might not be apparent to them, but which he assures them are real. Cummings watches this scene in wonder:

> What is Otto going to do ? Well, Otto's 1st going to soothe them. That's , so to speak , Ottos' business : he's in the Soviet soothing racket. He's going to sympathize and soothe and tell them everything will be all right. [. . .] And(hope springs eternal) he's going to promise them fantastic things; for that's part of the soothing. No more trouble , for instance. Trouble kapoot. (105–6)

As if in compensation for his inability to help Cummings find a cheaper place to stay, Otto takes him to a store where he can buy cheap cigarettes. On the way he praises the proletarian writers for being "active , positive , original" as opposed to the bourgeois writers who are "passive , negative , parasitic" and who remain "cowardly spectators of the greatest struggle in all human history" (107).

As they walk, Cummings's thoughts return to St. Basil's and to Lidin's story of the coexistence of beauty and cruelty. He asks Otto, who has been discussing the virtues of "permanent revolution," what he knows of the "church which makes perpetual revolution"—meaning here revolutions of form and style, "subsidary, differently timed yet perfectly intermeshing ,whirlings" (108). Otto mentions that St. Basil's is currently an antireligious museum, which Cummings had already seen for himself, and then recounts "an interesting story" about the building. Cummings pauses in anticipation that he will again hear the same story that Lidin had just told him. Instead, Otto relates a different story with a different meaning:

> during the struggle between reds and whites , the whites planted machineguns in that structure. Lenin promptly ordered his red gunners to clean out the enemy. Lunatcharsky thereupon resigned. Lenin sent for Lunatcharsky. Why have you resigned?Lenin asked. Because I cannot bear to fire on one of the greatest works of art in the world , Lunartcharsky answered. If , said Lenin , the revolution demands it ,we will knock down a thousand cathedrals. Lenin was right , of course ; Lunartcharsky , realizing that , withdrew his resignation immediately. (108)

According to Otto, this anecdote demonstrates that "a great principle has triumphed." Wanting to find some balance to the previous lesson offered by Lidin that "art was highly valued" when Ivan the Terrible was cruel, Cummings hesitatingly suggests that the moral is "the supremacy of life over art? (I hazard)." Otto responds, "The supremacy(he said , carefully and almost gently) of humanity over everything." Cummings further avers, ironically, as the conversation tugs back and forth: "except(I , eyed , murmur) principles" (108). Otto ends the conversation by falling back on the formulaic principles that he associates with Lenin: "The principles which protect humanity are an integral part of humanity 'n'est-ce pas?' (away looking , coldly affirmed Otto)" (108). Otto is yet another person who is guided by formulas and who is unable to wander loosely in forms.

The stories of Ivan the Terrible, on the one hand, who so admired the beauty of St. Basil's that he cruelly struck out the eyes of the architects who designed it in order to maintain its uniqueness (in a kind of uncanny forecast of the fears of modern mass production) and the story of Lenin, on the other hand, who was willing to destroy the building and all those in it in order to assert abstract principles of humanity, provide alternate and opposing parables, both of which are grounded in history and elaborated on in recitation, of the tensions between art and society. Cummings does not argue against or accept either of these views but rather allows them to exist in the text as alternate and contending stories as he himself remains aloof. In many ways, he saw these same tensions, as well as the tension between art and life in general, as central to his own work as he straddled the line between detached aesthetic work and polemic. In her review of *Eimi*, Marianne Moore felt that Cummings failed in his efforts to render what he saw precisely because his authorial presence in the text was hidden beneath his obscure style like the body of St. Sebastian martyred beneath the arrows of the Roman guards, to use her metaphor. And while we certainly don't wish Cummings to be more polemical, at the same time we see in many of the conversations or interactions that Cummings has with the people who guide him around or help him in various ways a refusal to engage with their words, or their ideas, or, here, their stories, which ultimately leaves them looking more like the very types that he had taken them as. Engagement is, for Cummings, a fraught enterprise, and aloofness a tempting posture that he rarely resists, but at the same time this often leaves the reader more mindful of the allegory than of the actual experience. In his expansion of the notes that he took on his trip into the book that is *Eimi*, we don't seem to see any rethinking of his original notions or any deeper understanding of what he saw, just an expansion and vegetative growth of the style, the words, the linguistic fun, all of which is deployed in order to resist experience. However, although Cummings's own deliberative assessment of what he sees remains (mostly) out of sight, his physical presence throughout *Eimi* remains central to his narrative. His decision not to expressly impose his own interpretation on events is an acknowledgement of the difficulties that occur when assessing the significance of any event, but his physical presence and his reaction to the physicality of others are particularly important, especially when he goes to view the body of Lenin.

Lenin's Tomb:
The Grave of Self

In addition to seeing St. Basil's and hearing the conflicting stories that surround it, Cummings also visits that other main tourist attraction, Lenin's Mausoleum, which he has already described from the outside as an imposing, blockish, utilitarian edifice. Adjacent to St. Basil's cathedral, it is housed on the Kremlin grounds and is, with the cathedral, one of the obligatory tourist spots in Moscow. It is almost two weeks into his trip that Cummings actually enters the Mausoleum to see the embalmed body of Vladimir Ilyich Lenin, the architect of Soviet life. This scene, located near the midpoint of the book, is often seen as central also to Cummings's vision of the Soviet Union. It is, in Kennedy's view, Cummings's descent into Hell, and his view of Lenin's body his vision of Satan.[26] However, it is not only Lenin's body that is important to this scene, but also the bodies in the crowd that go to see the former leader and Cummings's own body, as he again feels claustrophobic. This scene is important not primarily for the Satanic vision or the Dantesque allusions, although these parallels certainly do exist, but rather for the manner in which Cummings sees Lenin's body, the layers of disguise that he assumes in order to confront this vision and the device by which he simultaneously avoids the crowds.

The scene begins with Cummings among a throng of tourists, mainly Russian citizens ("tovarich," 240) who have come to wait in line to see Lenin's body. The line winds all the way to St. Basil's cathedral at the end of Red Square. As on the train that brought him to Russia in the opening pages of the book, Cummings here experiences a sense of claustrophobia from the bodies around him. Space becomes constricted and panic sets in as the mass of people is reduced to indistinguishable parts: the prose takes on a disjunctive, peristaltic movement, as can be heard in the recording that exists of Cummings reading this section aloud:[27]

> facefacefaceface
>   hand—
>   fin—
>   claw

foot—

hoof
(tovarich)

es to number of numberlessness (240)

These faces and disjointed bodies proceed in a bleak dumb-show toward Lenin's grave and, as Cummings sees it, toward death, "toward the grave of Self" (241).

In order to gaze on Lenin's body without losing his own identity that he has been so diligently maintaining throughout his journey and also simply to avoid waiting on line, Cummings assumes the identity of a reporter. He approaches the police officer at the head of the line, near the entrance to the Tomb:

> "pahjahlstah"—voice? belonging to comrade K. Said to a most tough cop. Beside shufflebudging end of beginninglessness , before the Tomb Of Tombs, standunstanding.
>
> (Voice? continues)I, American correspondent . . .
>
> (the toughest cop spun : upon all of and over smallest me staring all 1 awful moment—salutes! And very gently shoves)let the skies snow dolphins—nothing shall confound us now! (into smilelessly the entering beginning of endlessness : (242)

The guard's reaction reflects the esteem in which western journalists were held, partly because it was hoped that they would carry the news of the success of socialism back to the west. By announcing himself as an American correspondent, Cummings temporarily disclaims his identity as an independent tourist traveling unaffiliated, in possession of a "without party" visa. He descends into this identity and then into Lenin's tomb.

Nonetheless, he likens entering the tomb to entering a city, and this city seems to be death, as space again contracts ("suffocatingly envelopes"—242) and the distinction between motion and stasis fades:

> as when he enters a city(and solemnly his soul descends : every wish covers its beauty in tomorrow)so I descended and so I disguised myself ; so(towards death's deification moving)I did not move (242)

He finds himself for a moment alone in the room with Lenin's corpse, although what he sees is not what he expected to see: "Certainly it was not made of flesh," he says, but rather it was a "waxwork" statue, a "trivial idol throned in stink," that "equals just another little moral lesson" (243–44). For Cummings, Lenin's body was more than just a symbol of death; it was a mockery of life. Its waxwork appearance from the embalming made it even more dead by halting the natural process of decay. In the presence of this "trivial idol," all distinctions become erased: the distinctions between death and life, motion and stasis, ugliness and beauty, and even, most alarmingly for Cummings, that between himself and the crowd of people who stand in line to see this spectacle, as he descends to the "grave of self." Lenin's body thus both functions for the state as the focus of Soviet ideology and it acts as a symbol or spectacle of the death of the individual that Cummings so strenuously decried.

Exit

In addition to being a spectacle of Soviet ideology and representing the death of the self, Lenin's body is also for Cummings a symbol of the stasis that he saw dominating Russian life and which came to preoccupy him most forcefully as he prepared to leave Russia. Throughout *Eimi,* the ability to move about, to circulate within Russian society, is for Cummings crucial to his ability to make sense of what he sees. While in Moscow, he witnessed both Russian citizens whose movements were highly regulated through internal visas and Westerners living in Moscow who moved around and yet remained unable to accurately describe what they saw. Cummings emerges from Lenin's Tomb more convinced than ever of the futility of communism and the value and importance of movement as he continues to make plans for his departure from Russia.

Cummings's exit from the "unworld," however, is a long, complicated affair that again forces him to confront Soviet bureaucracy. Since he is leaving by a different route than he entered, he needs to make sure that he has all of the correct transit forms and has booked the proper passage. He had already begun the process of acquiring his visa before he visited Lenin's Tomb. If passports and travel documents were to Ezra Pound a nuisance that signaled a larger problem for the modern world, for Cummings in *Eimi* they represent a threat to his own identity and being. Whereas Pound registered this nuisance through an obscure outburst in the middle of a poem, for Cummings the problems of passports are a more pervasive theme throughout his book. As with all tourists, when Cummings checks in at the hotel, the desk clerk takes his passport from him. He is repeatedly concerned from that point on about getting it back and fears that if he is unable to do so he will be unable to leave the country. This fear becomes at times an obsession with Cummings, as we can see in the numerous references to passports throughout the book.

At one point, his worries about getting his passport back become real. An American couple, Charles Malamuth, a professor of Slavic languages and his wife, Joan London, the daughter of the writer Jack London, invite Cummings to live with them for the duration of his stay in Moscow, an offer he gratefully accepts. Cummings refers to the couple variously as the "Turk and Turkess," because of Malamuth's dark features, and he refers to London as Beatrice, another guide and a further reference to Dante's journey. As they attempt to move Cummings into their lodgings, however, they run into difficulties with the desk clerk at the Metropole who is holding Cummings's passport and will not return it because his Russian visa does not have the correct seal. Malamuth points out to the desk clerk that since Cummings has a foreign passport, this should not matter, a comment that suggests that this seal is some kind of internal visa for Russian citizens. Malamuth indicates that this is obviously merely a bureaucratic mix-up and tells Cummings not to worry: "The meticulous comrade is probably somewhat afraid of being shot for underzealousness or something—" (164). But Cummings becomes concerned and his concern grows into fear as he realizes that his exit depends on these documents and on the people who control them:

> "—now that I think of it : how come the Soviet Embassy in Paris delivered my visa just too late for May Day doings? And how come the socialist soviet republic granted a single month's séjour instead of the promised double? And how come—" (164)

More than simply a travel document, Cummings's passport represents to him the only means by which he will be able to leave Moscow as his fear grows into paranoia.

This concern culminates in a scene in which Cummings fears not only the loss of mobility, but the loss of identity. When Cummings arrives at the visa office in the Intourist building, he finds that in addition to filling out the necessary forms he needs to have his photograph taken. The official who takes his picture develops the film by throwing it into a pail of solution. Cummings cannot resist the urge to gaze into the pail to see how his appearance has altered while he has been in the "unworld." He wants to see himself through the eyes of the passport officials:

> . . . that pail attracts fatally myself. Fatally moving , my(feeling that am doing a deed more than dangerous , am committing a perhaps crime) self approaches the fatally attracting pail : now, over fatally it(dangerously) stooping , peers . . . & , breathless , sees(recoiling!) . . . horrific afloat images of meless , images in a dim liquid , images dreadfully themselves warping . . .
> now the latest victim arises. Whom-negative now gently micro-pastes upon a board. Me(positive)micro- fishes gently from pail's witchy broth.

> & , studying carefully atrocity, asks solemnly
>   what are you?are you Swedish?
>   American(I claim ; tottering)
>   businessman?(ruthlessly he pursues)
>   "NYET!"
>   engineer?
>   (calm, now) "peesahtel ee hoodozhnik" (227–28)

Like Narcissus who gazed into the water and fell in love with his own image, Cummings here peers into this mirror-like surface, but unlike Narcissus he recoils from this image, which is shapeless and formless from the developing solution. On one level, this is simply a case of his being appalled by a bad passport photograph, a common enough complaint among tourists; but it is also a moment when Cummings sees his identity transformed and dissolving. He sees himself nameless, faceless, and fixed, like J. Alfred Prufrock's glimpse of himself "formulated, sprawling on a pin" (483). He regains his composure as he is asked and states his occupation "peesahtel ee hoodozhnik" ("writer and artist").

Cummings resists the mediation that he finds himself continually subject to and the perceived threat to his identity in the visa office by reclaiming an image of his own as he gets ready to depart from Russia. Despite his fears, the day after he visits Lenin's tomb, his exit visa finally comes through and as a result he will be able to leave Moscow according to his schedule. He does some last minute shopping in the gift store and, among other items, buys a postcard of St. Basil's Cathedral: "& 2 comrades visit another counter,where comrade I buy some large pretty bad photographs(1 of Arabian Nights)and 12 faintly sentimental postcards and a very terrifying indeed map of the world in Russian" (248). The building that Ivan the Terrible had protected against ever being reproduced is here pictured on a postcard, mass produced for any and all to buy. Far from finding this offensive or crass, or from feeling that this image has been degraded through reproduction, Cummings purchases the postcard to remind him of his time in Moscow, an act that again marks him as a tourist. This purchase indicates that Cummings never took this role as a tourist wholly ironically, seeing in it a form in which he could wander loosely.

Although at times, Cummings was unwilling to be cast in the role of tourist—as we saw, for instance, in the scene with the desk clerk when he checked in at the Hotel Metropole—at other times he reveled in this role as it allowed him to remain aloof from the ideological debates that surrounded him. He remained content at times seeing only the surfaces of Russian life, surfaces that he found alternately repulsive and appealing. He rarely searched, as Pound did on the roads of France, for the hidden meanings that lay behind the landscape, the cultural monuments, or the literature. Nonetheless, the inconveniences of modern travel that Pound found to be not only a nuisance but a sign of the passing of an era, for Cummings were in some respects more threatening, since they not only controlled his movement but attempted to mediate his existence. Cummings purchases the postcard of St. Basil's as an oblique way of resisting the constant mediation of his own vision by the institutions of tourism and the state. In this gesture of a tourist, purchasing a souvenir, Cummings asserts the importance of his own vision on his trip. In *Eimi*, he describes St. Basil's using language that tries to re-create his view of the building's swirling forms and at the same time records the contrasting stories that have accrued to the building as a cultural landmark; but what he chooses to take with him out of the country is the image alone, on the postcard, a testimony to his own vision rather than the interpretations of his various guides.

Cummings's journey out of Russia is one of anticipation and continued frustrations over the details of his passage; but as he leaves, the nuisances of mere bureaucracy are replaced by other inconveniences, obstructions, and even outright absurdities. Once on board the ship bound for Istanbul, the departure is delayed as the result of engine trouble: "a wouldbe circular portion of our noble engine's vitals was only yesterday discovered to be imperfect" (354). As has happened so often before, Cummings is forced to wait, and as he waits, he talks with some of his fellow passengers. When he booked passage, Cummings misheard the ship's name as the "French Marine," and when he wonders aloud to a fellow passenger, who has been discussing the benefits of socialism, what this name signifies, he is met with derision: "'fraANZ' he cried with dis(pop) dain 'MERing!'" whom, he explains was "'one' (pop) 'of the great' (ping) 'est socialists who ever' (poppop) 'lived!'" (355). The boat—named after the German Socialist writer Franz Mehring (1846–1919), who was associated with Rosa Luxembourg and who wrote a biography of Karl Marx—is moored in the harbor for what seems like an eternity to Cummings, who is eager to leave Russia. He feels "marooned upon a desert island" as he waits for the ship to set sail. His impatience makes him think again of Russia as Hell, as both time and space contract: "The World of where we out of hell shall go if only something happens if/ only this/agony will not become eternal" (356). Finally, much to Cummings's relief, the ship moves, but he retires for the night only to find the next morning, much to his amazement and horror, that the ship is back in the port in Odessa: "Not 1 centimeter has Russia receded." The captain had sailed out in a circle and returned to port in order to test the newly repaired engines. This second sight of Odessa, which he had hoped to have put behind him, fills him with an uncanny dread as he feels he will never leave: "maybe we're kind of moving backward since we you know can't move sort of forward. Maybe there'll be Kiev and Moscow and N. [the Polish city through which the train passed at the very beginning of the book] and the very Paris I left at the very moment I left" (362). This futile movement made by the ship, the huge loop that goes nowhere, is, for Cummings, a further and final indication of the futility that he found in Soviet life, an existence fueled by propaganda, but going nowhere.

The image of the Soviet state as a giant modern conveyance is one that Cummings had come across before. During his stay in Moscow, Cummings had been translating Louis Aragon's socialist poem "The Red Front," a poem he clearly finds problematic in its promotion of the virtues of the Soviet state. At one point, we see Cummings in the act of translating, and he offers his running commentary on the poem:

> (and now , comrades , we come to this paean's infantile climax : now the language , fairly wetting its drawers , begins achugging and apuffing— "all aboard!" the paeaner now ecstatically cries—"everybody jump on the red train!" (alias , N.B., the bandwagon)—"nobody will be left behind!" (and of course Prosperity is just around the Corner)—U-S-S-R , choo-choo-choo-choo[.] (143)

The Soviet Union is here likened to a train whose progress into the future is assured. Aragon's poem, which Cummings's refers to later as that "hymn of hate" (175), ends with the sound of the letters U S S R mimicking the huffing and puffing of a steam engine, as word and thing merge:

> It's the train of the red star
> which burns the stations the signals the skies
> SSSR October October it's the express
> October across the universe SS
> SR SSSR SSSR
> SSSR SSSR.[28]

As if in contrast to this futuristic praise of machinery and image of inevitable progress, Cummings offers the image of the *Franz Mering*, the ship named after the "greatest socialist whoever lived," with its broken engine looping back to where it started.

Eventually, the ship does manage to leave the port, much to Cummings's relief, and they arrive the following day in Turkey, from which he will then take a train to Paris. Cummings celebrates both the train and his egress from Russia even as he mocks Aragon's poem and the ideology for which it is a vehicle. In

Istanbul he gets his train ticket for the Orient Express with comparative ease. In his relief and his glee about finally exiting Russia, Cummings identifies with the train in a manner that is clearly intended to mock the propagandistic tone of Aragon's poem: "You es es are are es vee pee pee dee kyou kyou ee dee ay men [. . .] A, train ; Is : We. We are a train are the express we are that Simplon Orient train from Stamboul to Pythian Transit" (411). The sounds that comprise USSR and that mimic the sound of the train also playfully elide into R.S.V.P, P.D.Q, and Q.E.D. and end with "Amen."

When the train stops briefly at a switching station in the Balkans, Cummings gets off and offers a prayer to aliveness of which even the train itself is a part: "metal steed ,very treacherously wherefrom descending the promiscuous urbans plundered rus!through you I greet all itgods" (418). Clearly meant to be a counter-hymn to Aragon's "hymn of hate," Cummings here also prophesizes the ultimate demise of the Soviet Union, even as he recalls those moments of beauty that he saw, especially St. Basil's:

> I prophecy to faultless them a moving within feelfully Himself Artist, Whose will is dream , only Whose language is silence—heartily to most heartless them I say that their immaculate circles are mere warped reflections of one selfinventingly unmitigated Spiral(of selfdestroyingly how strict untranslatable swooping doomlessly selfcontradicting imperfection or To Be). (418)

Cummings counters the immaculate circles, which represent the enclosed space of Moscow, the circles of Hell in Dante's *Inferno*, the circular, futile journey of the *Franz Mering*, against the "unmitigated Spirals," which represent both the fluid forms of the self traveling in and out of Russia and the spiral-shaped onion domes of St. Basil's cathedral. By seeing Russia for himself, Cummings has seen the "warped reflections" of what life could be like in Russia and at the same time the distorted image of his own self that is always in the process of becoming.

When Cummings had earlier woken to find that the *Franz Mering* had returned to the port in Odessa, he briefly felt that he was going back in time to his original point of departure in Paris, a feeling that filled him with an unnamable dread and a sense of frustration. But on board the train, as Cummings realizes that he is finally heading home, his experiences of the past several weeks come rushing back to him. His mind opens as these memories flow together in a joyous, exuberant vision:

> Something Fabulous L's M a filthy big baby stealthily WHAT'S—a tension?that pill!Bolshoy means : it's the cap—And time moans

in(that serious disease)of marble—or—something INTOURIST
of wonderful one hoss ; for both of us haven't the train's. Deer in
Sir Ladybug's world of Was hammer and a sickle and sonofabitch—
over nearly everything a mirror has been bandaged you smoke mystic
Thelike change , that's something in people are writing's as funny . . .
but life , life! Enlivened by si je me vous ne ça(lower of gent : Verb
The be to seems (430)

His memories rush over recent events—from St. Basil's ("Something
Fabulous"), to Lenin's Mausoleum, to Intourist, to the opening scene on board
the train. His recollection stops just short of reiterating the first word of the
book, "SHUT." As the train moves forward toward Paris, Cummings's mind
returns to Moscow and his time there; but unlike the dread that he feels on
board the *Franz Mering* when he also felt as if he were returning to Moscow,
here he has a sense of relief and openness. The language is again difficult, with
the words oddly spaced and weirdly punctuated, more so than usual, but it is
not obscure in the way that other passages of the book are obscure. There is a
sense of familiarity to all of the words that Cummings places before us, as if he
is inventorying his memory or clicking rapidly through a slide show of places
that we have come to know deeply, through Cummings, having riddled out
his originally obscure presentation of them.

Eimi ends with the word *OPEN*, but more importantly it ends with a sense
of movement. The words seem to cascade off the page. There is no final vision
of a terminal point or destination city, as there was at the end of *The Enormous
Room*, but only the perpetual spiraling movement of Cummings's mind that
ranges between his earliest memories, his recent trip, his immediate present,
and the unknown future. This kind of fluid movement that Cummings had
associated with children wandering loosely in forms in his letter regarding
ViVa, is, for him, more valuable than the images of unidirectional travel and
progress that constitute Aragon's poem or the pointless circles described by
the *Franz Mering* that represented the Russian revolution as a whole. The
various roles in which Cummings traveled and the various ways of seeing that
were associated with this role all return to Cummings as we witness his journey
taking form in his mind at the same time that it takes form on the page.

3

WYNDHAM LEWIS IN MOROCCO

"A Satiric Enterprise"

It is we who have the air of barbarians in the midst of barbarians.

—Louis Hubert Gonzalve Lyautey

R EBECCA WEST BEGINS HER 1932 *DAILY TELEGRAPH* REVIEW OF
Wyndham Lewis's *Filibusters in Barbary* with an important clarification
for the benefit of the London book-buying public. She points out
what might not be immediately apparent to the casual reader, that there are
in fact "two Mr. Wyndham Lewises, each of a critical turn of mind and able
to dispense disapproval with the force and definiteness of a mule, and only
in eternity, when opposites shall be reconciled, can anyone imagine pleasing
them both."[1] The two Lewises that West is referring to, both of whom were
writing in the nineteen twenties and thirties, are D. B. (Dominic Bevans)
Wyndham Lewis, humorist, author of a biography of Francois Villon, and the
editor of *The Stuffed Owl: An Anthology of Bad Verse,* and Percy Wyndham
Lewis, author of *Filibusters,* as well as the novel *Tarr* and the philosophical
tract *Time and Western Man.* Percy Wyndham Lewis himself often confessed
to frustration over the confusion that at times arose over their similar names,
and the feeling must certainly have been mutual, as both authors were
attempting to create niches for themselves in an already saturated London
literary marketplace.[2]

According to West, the potential for confusion was as much the result of
these writers' similar views as it was of their similar names. Both were critics
of interwar English society in particular and of the modern world in general,

97

although West acknowledges that their respective antidotes for modernity are antithetical: D. B. Wyndham Lewis, West writes, has "a distaste for the present because it is not the past," while Percy Wyndham Lewis has a "distaste for the present because it is not the sturdier future." If these opposites could not be reconciled until the hereafter, neither could they be fully disentangled in the present moment:

> One or the other each of us must be offending; and yet none of us can rely on the converse of this proposition, and feel confident that if we offend one we must be pleasing the other. For even as their definitions of heterodoxy are wide, so are their doctrines of orthodoxy narrow. (n.p.)

In distinguishing between them, West thus wryly figures "these two Lewises" as twin emanations of the Zeitgeist, or uncanny reflections of one another, suggesting a relationship less accidental than that afforded by their similar names. The review must have been particularly disconcerting to Percy Lewis, who had always reserved the right to mint his own doppelgangers, assuming throughout his career a variety of thinly veiled personas, such as the Enemy or the Tyro, when venting his displeasure.[3]

West was not being entirely innocent in linking the two, as she touches on what was perhaps Percy Wyndham Lewis's most abiding anxiety during the post–World War I period: the fear of the dissolution of the self amidst the proliferation of Bloomsbury aesthetes, parlor-room nihilists, and "revolutionary simpletons" that Lewis saw around him.[4] Lewis had spent much of the twenties bemoaning the death of the individual and the murkiness of a modernity that couldn't distinguish mind from matter, subject from object, let alone one modern writer from another since, according to him, they all seemed to be caught up in the uninterrupted flow of the stream of consciousness or to have affected a stuttering style, whether writing poetry, prose, novels, or philosophy.[5] By probing the indeterminacy of Lewis's authorship and identity, West plays on Lewis's fears about the modern world, especially on his fears about his role as an artist in this world.

The travel book, as we have seen, was a common way for writers to express similarly generalized fears regarding the relationship between the individual and society in the years between the wars.[6] For Lewis, it was an unusual although not unprecedented genre for him to employ, a genre that in its reliance on descriptive prose and desultory commentary gave room to his talents both as a visual artist and as a writer. West detected both of these features in *Filibusters*, praising how the book was "brilliant with verbal sketches of people drawn not with the intellectual understanding of the writer, but with the pervasive physical sympathy of the painter." In a 1934 letter to his publisher, while acknowledging the painterly aspects of *Filibusters*, Lewis emphasized the ideas that lay behind it. He describes the reasons for his trip to Morocco as being highly serious:

> The picturesque ridicule that I called upon, in the pages of *Filibusters in Barbary*, to assist me in my antiseptic mission—throwing into the most comic, unromantic and unattractive light possible—the least flattering language I could command—the types selected, in this cosmopolitan colony of France, to show the unsatisfactory operation at a distance of a crooked political system—this picturesque ridicule was, that I should have thought is obvious enough, a *satiric* enterprise, and not the mere horseplay of a fun-maker.[7]

In *Filibusters*, Lewis utilizes the conventions of the travel genre in order to advance his "satiric enterprise" and to sketch out this "picturesque ridicule." He visits 1931 Morocco, a North African country with a pervasive European colonial presence, to examine the mechanisms of a society striated by opposing notions of governance, by rival political structures, and by a variety of ethnic and cultural groups (see figure 3). The satire of his "satiric enterprise" was directed for the first time beyond the boundaries of the closed London literary and artistic scene.

Satire is a complex term for Lewis, directed as it is just as much at individuals as at groups or governments. In *Filibusters*, where one of the targets of Lewis's satire is the French colonial set that he sees as a microcosm of the West in general (the "types selected" from the above quotation), Lewis navigates a complicated course between cultural critique, polemic, and parody as he attempts to find a perspective from which to view, and therefore judge, the wider modern world. The satire of *Filibusters in Barbary* ranges from sarcasm to outright mockery and is intended as a double-pronged critique of both home and abroad. Although in a later essay Lewis writes, "Satire in reality often is nothing else but *the truth*—the truth, in fact, of Natural Science,"[8] this truth, filtered through the "satiric enterprise" of a travel book, must take into consideration the role and perspective of an observer who is author, a narrator who is a character, as well as the narrative conventions used to render these.

In Lewis's fictional works during this period, such as *The Apes of God*, he satirizes the modern world by focusing on individuals devoid of a genuine interiority and who were engaged in what he saw as various art rackets. In his polemical works from the same period (and, in fact, from the same artistic effort) he satirizes this same modern world by focusing on the external social and political scene that he saw as similarly devoid of any meaning at all. In *Filibusters*, we see an attempt to wed these two different approaches as Lewis organizes his satire against the west by turning his satirist's eye on the foreign inhabitants of a country that was a victim to social and political intervention by the West. However, in this travel book, the satire is less uniformly applied as Lewis also finds moments of authenticity, not only in the foreign culture he confronts, but in certain Western figures who operated in this culture as well. Always engaged, like any satirist, in a struggle between the authentic and the false, Lewis uses the travel genre to advance the theories about the West that he had formulated throughout the twenties.

In his discussion of *The Apes of God*, Mark Perrino describes what makes Lewis's satire distinct from traditional satire: "The traditional conception of satire . . . assumes a relatively stable homogeneous society with a generally accepted standard of conduct and assumes deviance to be the satiric target. In the absence of such a consensus in the twentieth century, the basis of judgment is unclear" (13). Throughout Lewis's fictional works and as his notion of satire developed, his judgments became more urgent and his perspective more seemingly enthroned precisely because the stability of society between the wars, he felt, could no longer be taken for granted. In the absence of such stability, Lewis posited various examples of stable societies that he gleaned from his travels both to Berlin and Morocco in the early thirties. In his accounts of these milieus, Lewis imaginatively projected his own desire for stability and order onto these foreign locales. Unlike in Berlin, however, where Lewis examines the single political phenomenon of National Socialism, in Morocco he travels to a number of cities, each with its distinctive system of accommodating its varied populations and all of which achieve varying degrees of the order and stability that Lewis sought for the West in the post-war years. The picturesque ridicule is directed mostly at the intruding outsider whose presence undermines the health and traditions of society, though the satire itself is more far ranging, encompassing the entire interwar west.

Lewis's progress through Morocco is simultaneously a progression through a political landscape with its shifting zones of power and influence. His representation of this space and of the various people he meets are oblique commentaries both on the nature of France's presence in the region and on the impact of any outside influence on a region, whether this is a colonial government, the film crew that he encounters, or any of the various foreigners who have taken up residence in Morocco. According to Lewis, "Everyone is a *filibuster* of some sort who is installed upon the territory of a race that his not his own" (121). Though the term *filibuster* is one that Lewis generally assigns to all outside presence, throughout his book there are exceptions to this rule, as

Fig. 3. Division of Morocco 1912–1956. Courtesy of the University Libraries, The University of Texas at Austin.

the forthrightly polemical text often unravels in the face of the inductive travel narrative. By traveling through this space, but not claiming to be a part of it, Lewis feels he is able to assess the dynamic of the colonial presence accurately.

Although he claims to employ his satirist's eye in Morocco in order to expose the "crooked political system" of French colonialism as a whole and of individual colonialists in particular, Lewis does not completely dismiss all aspects of colonialism. While this is an unpleasant aspect of Lewis's political thought, it is nevertheless a reminder of the complex ways in which Lewis's reactions against modernity were formed and operated. Lewis's satire is directed as much against the intellectual and cultural climate of the west during these years, when both colonialism and the romanticizing of foreign cultures flourished, as it was an exposé of the crooked aspects of the French colonial government. Lewis holds up for censure, for example, both the postwar gloom that was associated with Oswald Spengler's *Decline of the West* and the related sentimental portrayals of the exotic east that were prevalent in popular novels and films at the time. In *Filibusters in Barbary*, Lewis sees these as related issues in that they, like the crooked aspects of French colonialism, contributed to the further destabilization of interwar society.

Lewis had most famously critiqued Spengler's fatalistic views in *Time and Western Man* (1927), where he accuses the German historian of being part of what he dismissively referred to as the "Time School," an umbrella term that Lewis used to designate philosophers such as Henri Bergson and Alfred North Whitehead; authors such as James Joyce, Ezra Pound, and Gertrude Stein; and scientists such as Albert Einstein. For these thinkers, according to Lewis, "time and change are the ultimate reality" as opposed to the reality of the intellect that perceived things spatially (*Time and Western Man*, 160). Lewis continued his attack on the "Time School" in the 1929 *Paleface*, where he critiqued the idealization and commodification of the Negro and the Native American, which in his view were related issues. Again discussing Spengler and his followers in *Paleface*, Lewis wrote:

> "The West" is for almost all of those a *finished* thing, either over whose decay they gloat, or whose corpse they frantically "defend." It never seems to occur to them that the exceedingly novel conditions of life today demand an entirely new conception: in that respect they are firmly on the side of those people who would thrust us back into the medieval chaos and barbarity; at whose hypnotic "historical" suggestion we would fight all the old european wars over again[.][9]

For Lewis, the idealization of "barbarity" and the glorification of history were similarly retrogressive as they refused to acknowledge the current "novel conditions" of Western society that in his mind demanded attention because they were once again leading society toward war. Like Ezra Pound, who felt that the modern world demanded unconventional forms to portray its "accelerated grimace," Lewis here demands a "new conception" of the modern world, one free from the corporeal metaphors of an anthropomorphized West. This new conception would, Lewis hoped, privilege the spatially oriented intellect over the temporally oriented emotion.

In her review, West claims that Lewis's critique of the modern world possessed a "savage resistance puzzling in our insular literature but healthy enough if one considers the rest of Europe." While West is referring here to

Lewis's polemical work as a whole, she perhaps found this resistance especially puzzling in *Filibusters in Barbary*, not because she found such resistance to be unwarranted, but rather because it manifested itself in the unusual form of a travel book. If *Filibusters* contravened the "insularity" of current literature, it did so by tapping into a readership that saw in travel writing merely an escape from unpleasant social conditions. During the interwar years, Morocco and other "Eastern" lands were frequently portrayed in novels and film in a Romantic and exotic light, as if these lands offered a remedy to postwar malaise. One example of this is L. Noels's *Kasbah*, a popular novel that was advertised on the same page of *The Daily Telegraph* on which appeared West's review of *Filibusters*. The advertisement reads: "A romance of Morocco by an author who made himself world famous with those popular stories 'The Caid' and 'The Veil of Islam.'" Such advertisements testify to the public appetite for both romance and the exotic as a way of countering the mundanity of the domestic situation. Romantic portrayals of Arabic lands appeared in the cinema as well, in films such as *The Arab* (1924) and *Love in Morocco*, Rex Ingram's 1931 movie about a Bedouin tribesman who falls in love with a Christian missionary woman. Ingram's film was shot on location in Morocco in 1930, a major selling point to an audience enamored of things Eastern. During his journey, Lewis was in Marrakech as Ingram was filming *Love in Morocco*, and in *Filibusters* he describes his encounter with the actors and crew. Lewis's satire, couched in the innocuous form of a travel book, is directed as much against these Romantic portrayals of the East and the packaging of exotic experience as it is against the crooked operation of the French colonial government. Announced as it was to an audience who had to be told who the author was and advertised along with books such as *Kasbah*, it is no wonder that Lewis's book was passed over in virtual silence.

Before examining Lewis's "satiric enterprise" in Morocco and showing some of the ways in which his "picturesque ridicule" is called down, I first look at selected critical appraisals of Lewis's body of work that focus in particular on the connections between his fiction and his polemical writing and between his aesthetic practices and his political thinking, in order to show how in his travel writing, Lewis blends aspects of these different modes. I then examine several earlier works by Lewis to show the development of Lewis's narrative method from the early travel stories set in Brittany to his more complex satire in works such as *The Apes of God*. In all these works, and in his 1930 book *Hitler*, traveling or moving about within a foreign milieu is an essential component of the narrative. As Lewis's narrative technique develops, so does his satire expand to take in those larger cultural and social realities of the modern world. This expansion does not always make for a coherent narrative, as the polemic becomes at times diluted in the satiric machinery. Lewis's anxieties about the modern world, anxieties that West touches on in her review, are particularly on display in *Filibusters in Barbary* as Lewis visits and inventories a country in whose features he sees the outlines of a revivified West as it continues to struggle with the political and economical consequences of the First World War. At times, as we will see, Lewis cast his journey as a relief from the stifling atmosphere of post-war Britain, but traveling was also a means by which he could measure his own proscriptions for the modern world against the realities of a foreign land.

THE CRITICAL CONTEXT

Lewis's status in the canon of modern literature has always been a point of contention. From the beginning of his career before the war, he deliberately set himself against all that was modern even as he strove to be stylistically avant-garde and innovative. As a result, he is frequently seen merely as a figure of opposition, a role that was largely self-constructed. In one of the first critical accounts of his work, Hugh Kenner describes Lewis emerging from the void, self-incarnated on the London literary and artistic scene, a "mystery man without a past."[10] This account, with its eschewal of both personal and literary history, fits well with Lewis's own subsequent self-fashioning, especially in his two autobiographies, *Blasting and Bombardiering* (1937) and *Rude Assignment* (1950). In both of these works, Lewis suppressed many of the conventional elements of autobiography in favor of a critique of the modern world that came in the guise of a heavily bracketed account of his professional and intellectual development.

Lewis's oppositional stance began most energetically after the First World War, as he strategically set himself against all of the trends of modernity. During the twenties, in works such as *Time and Western Man* and *The Art of Being Ruled*, Lewis was highly critical of mass movements, popular culture, and what he saw as the intellectual and artistic fraud perpetrated by the London literary elite against authentic artists such as himself. This critique operated both by unmasking larger cultural trends and through personal attacks on both friends and contemporaries. He often portrayed people in both his polemical works and in his novels at the mercy of these cultural forces, as puppets unaware of the powers controlling their existence. Using Lewis's own terminology, Kenner calls those fictional works where Lewis illustrates the theories he expounded in his critical works the "puppet-fictions" or "automata-fictions" (91). The most prominent example that Kenner cites of this genre is the 1932 *Snooty Baronet*, a novel set partly in the deserts of Persia, for which Lewis used material from his trip to Morocco. The narrative of the "automata fictions," according to Kenner, eschewed the subjective aspects of stream of consciousness in favor of the cold and detached processing of information. Thus, in *Snooty Baronet*, for example, the automaton was both a character and the narrator.

At the heart of Lewis's theory of satire, of which the automata fictions were an extreme example, and his related though not identical theory of comedy was a belief in the inherent dichotomy between mind and matter. This dichotomy, Lewis felt, was one that most people were ill equipped to recognize let alone negotiate. As he writes in *Men Without Art*, "Men are sometimes so palpably machines, their machination is so transparent, that they are *comic*" (95). This comedy, however, and the laughter that ensues from it, are neither tonic nor cathartic; rather, the radical division between mind and matter was to Lewis essentially tragic. Lewis's satire was a way for him to portray this duality while remaining above it, recognizing its absurdity but detached from its implications. The lessons of Lewis's satirical portrayals are that the modern world is suffering at the hands of the pseudo artists and intellectuals. These pseudo artists were simultaneously flourishing during this period of economic crisis, political uncertainty, and cultural decline. It is often difficult to distinguish in Lewis's satire symptom from cause, but what is clear in his work from the period is the unique challenges he sees facing the modern world. Despite ridiculing Spengler for his defeatist subscription to the "time school," Lewis's descriptions of what he sees (and as we have seen, satire for Lewis is primarily descriptive) would lead us to the same stark conclusions, that society and the West itself are in decline. Such contradictions beleaguered Lewis throughout his career as an oppositionist, and they are manifest especially throughout the text of *Filibusters*. Even if the purpose of Lewis's satire, fiction, and polemic was to diagnose such ills for the sake of a cultural and artistic reawakening, there remains a hint of the very doom that he disparaged in Spengler beneath the cultural critique.

As a result of the stark dichotomies that fueled Lewis's fiction and nonfiction alike, Lewis himself is frequently seen as trapped within the binaries that he sets up in his texts. Bonnie Kime Scott in *Refiguring Modernism*, for example, while grudgingly bestowing on Lewis the laurels of postmodernism, cannot see past these structures of thought, structures that she sees as indicative of a not-so-latent misogyny: "I do think it appropriate to see Lewis as far closer to a postmodern, deconstructionist, fragmented, demystifying sensibility than, for example, Eliot. Yet Lewis's binaries always favor the masculinist pole, and his art always proceeds from it."[11] Other critics have seen in Lewis's impulse toward such binary thinking a predisposition for fascism, with its clearly demarcated ideology, masculinist code, and love of order. Vincent Sherry, as we have seen in the Introduction to the present study, suggests that Lewis's penchant for clear outlines in art, as well as a writing style that privileges the visual, had its counterpart in the visual aesthetic of fascist propaganda.[12] Few critics, however, have recognized the underlying self-critique that such reactionary positions at times entailed and which was such an important element of his satire. This self-critique manifested itself most powerfully when Lewis considered the role of the audience as well as his own role as author/ narrator, and we see this most clearly in the travel genre, where considerations of audience were paramount.

The most useful critical approaches to Lewis's writing have employed the methods of poststructuralism, providing a way out of these binaristic binds. Fredric Jameson in *Fables of Aggression: Wyndham Lewis, The Modernist as Fascist,* for example, while remaining convinced that Lewis's work "could be invoked to legitimize the most mindless forms of brutality and institutional lynching,"[13] nevertheless argues that Lewis's harsh style and narrative voice undermine the conventions of the novel that have since become the dominant aesthetic of what we call "modernism," and that, further, the "repudiation of the hegemonic naturalist and representational conventions which he shares with other modernisms is in Lewis reduplicated by a prophetic assault on the very conventions of the emergent modernisms themselves, which will become hegemonic in their turn only after World War II" (19). Ultimately for Jameson, however, as for Scott, Lewis simultaneously forecasts postmodernist concerns while remaining trapped within the ideological binds of his texts.

Unlike Jameson and Scott, SueEllen Campbell, in *The Enemy Opposite: The Outlaw Criticism of Wyndham Lewis,* while similarly employing poststructuralist methods, sees the binaries that shaped Lewis's thought and writing not as an inexorable ideological bind, but rather as "deliberate patterns of organization and strategy."[14] Campbell detects in the highly structured makeup of Lewis's critical writing—what she calls "one of the most important but also most difficult characteristics of Lewis's work" (xiii)—an attendant, though not always explicit desire to deconstruct the political tendencies of the day as well as the tendencies that guided his own thinking. Campbell focuses in particular on the various and complex ways in which Lewis conceived of his audience. The structures of opposition that she detects are located not solely *within* Lewis's texts (as Scott might suggest), nor are they psychologically generated (as Jameson might suggest); rather they operate primarily during the reception of the work, in the crucial space between audience and writer. As Campbell notes, Lewis, in his persona of the Enemy, is always in a double bind that is persistently anti-ideological: "He must try to keep his readers' interest and engage their sympathy; on the other hand, he must maintain his position as an enemy to everyone and everything" (34). The outcome of this strategy, according to Campbell, is that "in each of Lewis's major statements of belief we can also see traces of the opposite belief—in what adds up to a pervasive structure of half-hidden self-criticism" (xv).

This same critical undertow applies as well to Lewis's fiction, his satirical works in particular, where the voyeuristic pleasure of seeing others exposed as charlatans is turned back on the author as well as on the reader. In her review of *Filibusters in Barbary*, in which she detected both large-scale cultural critique and the descriptive prose of the painter, Rebecca West also saw beyond Lewis's binaries, detecting in his project of polemic for polemic's sake an important touchstone for the modern world and a useful rhetorical strategy for gauging the unspoken tendencies of the time. While Campbell's structuralist approach can certainly help us understand some of the features of Lewis's satire in general and his narrative structure in *Filibusters* in particular, at the same time it should be said that in Lewis's attempt to discover or create in the landscape of Morocco a unifying principle that would halt the decline of the West that he saw as imminent if not inevitable, Lewis still adheres to the tenets of modernism. Although the travel book would seem to offer numerous opportunities for local fragmented "histories" that would counter the grand narrative of a Spengler, Lewis's tendency is always toward a kind of unity that would lay the groundwork for a resurgent and at the same time more global west.

Although different in kind from both Lewis's polemical works and his imaginative writing, *Filibusters in Barbary* can best be read keeping Campbell's analysis of Lewis's texts in mind. Lewis's travel book is driven by the same tensions that arise in Lewis's polemical works and that operate in his satirical works. In *Filibusters*, Lewis confronts a transformed post–World War I environment and attempts to find in colonial Morocco a political structure that would mitigate the chances of future world wars. Lewis's traveling persona is related to his fictional narrator and to his polemical stance in important ways. To understand this connection in greater detail, we first need to understand the development of Lewis's narrative voice, since it is there where his satire is most expressly deployed.

FILIBUSTERS IN LEWIS'S OEUVRE

Lewis's narrative persona and his satire developed alongside one another throughout his career. His first literary efforts, what he later called "those hasty notes of very early travel" appeared before World War I.[15] Two stories in particular forecast the later style of Lewis's narrative: "Some Innkeepers and Bestre," which appeared in Ford Madox Hueffer's *The English Review* in 1909, and "Les Saltimbanques," which appeared in Douglas Goldring's *The Tramp: An Open Air Magazine*, the following year. These stories emerged from Lewis's experiences traveling in Spain and Brittany in 1907 and 1908 after he left the Slade School in London. Both his early travels and these early travel stories were formative for Lewis. In his 1950 autobiography *Rude Assignment*, Lewis acknowledged the importance of these stories: "What I started to do in Brittany I have been developing ever since" (121). What Lewis was doing in Brittany and in these stories was reconfiguring the relationship between author, narrator, and audience, in a way that would give room to both his polemical attitude and to his satirical predispositions.

These early travel sketches owe a great deal to a genre of pre-war adventure tales and travel narratives exemplified in the work of George Borrow, whose novels of gypsy life and wanderlust, such as *Lavengro: The Scholar, The Gypsy*, and *The Romany Rye*, were much in vogue.[16] However, they go beyond the mere adventurous and romantic to show the interactions of different cultures. In these stories, Lewis describes the effects that an outsider has on the local inhabitants of a small town in Brittany. The outsider in these stories, usually the narrator, is frequently a traveling art student who goes to Brittany after the intense incubation period of university life and to paint in a more authentic environment. In "Some Innkeepers and Bestre," Lewis describes these nomadic bohemians as they take up residence in the inns of Brest in Brittany, insinuating themselves into the local community as soon as they arrive in town, and the economic interdependence between them and the townspeople.

The local inhabitants have become used to the incursions of these wandering students and have, over time, developed a system for interacting with them. When the students' funds run out, as inevitably happens, according to Lewis, the landlord accepts their paintings in place of the rent. They do this strictly for the economic benefit, not for the artistic value of the students' work. According to the narrator, the landlords first became aware of the potential market value of these student's paintings when years before a painting that had been left behind by a student fetched a significant amount of money from a London art dealer who was visiting the region in search of "authentic" local art. Like their later avatars in *The Apes of God*, the innkeepers feed off the artists while contributing nothing to art themselves.

The narrator's feeling toward the innkeepers, however, is mixed, despite the fact that he himself is one of these students. When Lewis revised "Some

Innkeepers and Bestre" for a 1927 collection, *The Wild Body*, an unexpected admiration for, even affiliation with, these ambiguous figures emerged. In the later version of "Some Innkeepers and Bestre," Lewis expands the section that focuses on one of the innkeepers, in particular, whose name is Bestre. Bestre functions according to a simple code: "[His] great principle . . . is that of provocation" (229). He outrages both his fellow innkeepers and his tenants alike by remaining contrary on every point, by always playing the enemy. This provocative behavior, however, is as much an affectation as it is a character flaw, since "the subtle notoriety of his person is dear to him" (230). Bestre is part scheming speculator and part shrewd artist. Like the artists he houses, he has a talent for a "wonderful empirical expertness in reality, without being altogether home in it" (231). The boundaries of his character are not fixed: "He never seems quite entering into reality, but observing it; he is looking at the reality with a professional eye, so to speak, with a professional liar's" (483). Lewis sees in the ambiguous and mercurial figure of Bestre—something between provocateur and patron, enemy and artist—an externalization of his own interests as an artist. Whereas in the original story the narrator identifies primarily with the wandering artists, in the revision he identifies more with the scheming innkeeper.

In "Les Saltimbanques" and its subsequent revision as "The Cornac and His Wife," Lewis focuses not on the relationship between artist and innkeeper, but on the sometimes antagonistic one between artist and audience. "Les Saltimbanques" describes a strolling circus troupe in Arles, among which are two characters known only as the Cornac and his wife, two Breton peasants who "had a standing grudge against their audience" (237). Their performance consists of a kind of Punch and Judy show, in which they dress in bright colors and knock each other about. What fascinates the unnamed narrator is the way their performance for the crowd upsets the bond with their audience, on whom they depend both for their patronage and for their physical response to their comedy: "The merriment of the public that their unhappy fate compelled them to provoke, was nevertheless a constant source of irritation to these people" (76). This couple, doomed by fate to please a public that they simultaneously hold in contempt, fascinates the narrator. Like Bestre, these circus performers are provocateurs even while they are artists. The Cornac and his wife refer to the crowd as a "vast beast" and complain of the responses to their performance as being different in kind than the reactions of an individual. "For what man," they complain, "would ever go *alone* to see their circus[?]" (77).

In his revision of "Les Saltimbanques," Lewis highlights the essayistic and empirical aspects of the scene rather than its fictiveness. As Bernard Lafourcade points out, the revision of "Les Saltimbanques" as "The Cornac and His Wife," "remains much more a semi-fictional essay than a real story."[17] As he further suggests, in "The Cornac and His Wife," "the aesthetic (on the whole impressionistic) of the fragmentary vision and the realistic detail, which together are typical marks of the travelogue, gave way to a fictional dramatized concentration of effects characterized by the introduction of a narrator and dialogue." This narrator, whom Lewis calls Ker-Orr in the revised story, frees Lewis from being directly implicated in the narrator's views, as he would be in a nonfiction essay or in a straightforward travel account. Ker-Orr articulates much of the lengthy theoretical, essayistic "semi-fiction" that makes up the revised story. However, the introduction of a narrator to this essayistic vignette does not lessen the impulse to attribute the narrator's statements to Lewis. The result is an uneasy narrative structure in which Lewis realigns the distance between author, narrator, characters, and reader, a strategy that he developed in other of his fictional works as well.

After these early travel stories, Lewis left behind the theme of the wandering artist and focused more on the figure of the provocateur exemplified in their respective ways by Bestre and the Cornac and his wife. Lewis's narrators at the same time increasingly resembled Ker-Orr in the way they voiced ideas and recited lengthy essayistic points that could easily be attributed to Lewis.

TARR AND THE APES OF GOD: THE NOVEL PERSONA

First published in 1918 and heavily revised in 1928, Lewis began *Tarr* as early as 1911, as he was composing the early travel stories. Like these early stories, *Tarr* shows the interactions, both professional and personal, of various nationalities and artistic personalities thrown together on the artistic scene in Paris. The title character, Frederick Tarr, like Ker-Orr, resembles Lewis—a point that has been commented on by many of Lewis's contemporaries and later critics alike—although he is not necessarily meant to be identical to him. Tarr punctuates his conversations with lengthy theories on aesthetics, polemical interludes that seem out of place in a fictional work.

Lewis's narrative methods left many readers confused, including Lewis's friend, the poet T. Sturge Moore. In a letter of September 1918, after having first read *Tarr*, Moore wrote to Lewis to express his admiration for the book. This admiration, however, was tinged with unease as he could not quite determine to what degree Frederick Tarr was voicing the opinions of his creator. Moore found this indeterminacy unsettling: "I wish he had either been more frankly you or more wholly distinct from his creator."[18] At times, Moore suggests, we feel sure that it is Lewis broadcasting his ideas through Tarr. At other times, Tarr's stilted speech comes off almost as self-parody, as if Bestre had suddenly lapsed into theorizing his role as an innkeeper. If in the early stories the narrator merely shared Lewis's experiences traveling through Brittany, in *Tarr*, Lewis created a mediating character through whom he could broadcast his ideas. Rather than resolve these uncertainties (and Moore's doubts) in subsequent works, Lewis instead capitalized on the uneasiness generated in the mind of the reader as he increasingly assumed the role of provocateur. Lewis's relationship to his audience thus became as provocative as that of Bestre and, at times, as contemptuous of his audience as the Cornac and his wife were to theirs.

In *Wyndham Lewis: Fiction and Satire*, Robert Chapman articulates the differences between the early travel stories and the post-war work such as *Tarr*. Chapman writes: "In *The Wild Body*, Lewis had focused upon primitive—if complex—individuals in primitive environments; in the war stories he looks at the effects of complex—if, ultimately, uncivilized—environments upon the individual" (59). One of the complex though uncivilized environments that Lewis would treat next was that of Bloomsbury, in his 1930 novel *The Apes of God*, the work that Pound saw as an important diagnosis of the London literary and artistic scene between the wars.[19] Although *The Apes of God* is not properly speaking a war novel, it does mention specific crises that Lewis saw as characteristic of the postwar period, such as the 1925 General Strike in Britain. As Chapman's comments suggest, the relationship between the individual and their milieu was never one of mutual exclusivity but rather one of interdependence. It is worthwhile examining this book briefly for the further transformations that Lewis's narrative style underwent, as we see him once again disrupting the bond between narrator, subject, and reader, in his most sustained effort at satire.

In *The Apes of God*, Horace Zagreus, artist and impresario, circulates among the denizens of an intellectual and artistic community that is clearly modeled on Bloomsbury of the nineteen twenties, the circle that included such eminent moderns as Clive and Vanessa Bell, Virginia Woolf, Lytton Strachey, and Edith and Osbert Sitwell. All of these figures have their counterparts in *The Apes of God*. Zagreus's "mission" in the novel is to introduce into this society Daniel Boleyn, a young poet and "genius" whom he has claimed as his latest discovery. Zagreus, however, is at the same time a double agent, working undercover as a kind of intellectual agent provocateur. His real goal is to show to Daniel the "apes" in their natural habitat and to reveal their crooked operations and their stranglehold of the London art scene. Horace is given this mission by the mysterious Pierpoint, a character we never see but whose presence is constantly felt. These instructions, which Zagreus faithfully follows, are clearly and programmatically detailed in an "encyclical" that Pierpoint gives to Zagreus. This document is presented in the text and makes up most of Part 4 of the novel as Zagreus reveals the contents of the encyclical to Daniel. The dissemination of this information reveals a kind of vertical chain of command, with Pierpoint being both the most removed and the most authoritative.

Like Frederick Tarr's aesthetic disquisitions, Pierpoint's encyclical reads like a lengthy authorial intrusion, and it seems out of place in a work of fiction. Chapman describes the contents of the encyclical, these "broadcasts" of Pierpoint that shape our readerly expectations, as follows: "The 'broadcasts' in *The Apes* point the reader away from the fictional world towards the everyday world, and the effects of these reality interpolations may be compared to the use of newsreel in an imaginary film" (106). In this encyclical, Pierpoint describes the new "Bohemia" in which Horace and Daniel move, a bohemia inhabited not by the true tramps of George Borrow's day, but by the idle wealthy who play the role of the bohemian artist. Pierpoint defines these "apes of god" as "*those preposterous mountebanks who alternately imitate and mock at and traduce those figures they at once admire and hate*" (123, Lewis's emphasis). Pierpoint concludes the encyclical by delineating the boundaries of his own authority in the plot, and reveals, if not his intentions as the author of this plot, at least his own involvement:

> I am not a judge but a party. All I can claim is that my cause is not an idle one—that I appeal less to passion than to reason. The flourishing and bombastic rôle that you may sometimes see me in, that is an effect of chance. Or it is a caricature of some constant figure in the audience, rather than what I am (in any sense) myself. Or, to make myself clearer, it is my opposite. (125)

Whereas the "apes" mock and traduce the artists they admire, Pierpoint caricatures and mocks a "figure in the audience" in order to provoke his desired response. It is difficult not to take this statement and more generally Pierpoint's shadowy presence overall as some version of Lewis himself, although this identification is foreclosed even as it is asserted. The various roles that Pierpoint assumes, for instance, are a deliberate screening of the self behind what he calls the "not self." The strained and complex relationship among author, narrator, and reader that results is a recasting and amplification of the role of artist as provocateur that we have seen in the early travel stories. It is furthermore similar to the tension that Campbell has shown among reader, text, and author in Lewis's polemical works.

In *Filibusters in Barbary*, Lewis himself is author, agent, and character in an odd replication of the triadic structure of Pierpoint, Zagreus, and Bolelyn. Such a narrative arrangement raises obvious problems regarding authorial intent, similar to those recognized by T. Sturge Moore when trying to discern Lewis's own presence in the text of *Tarr*. Traces of such an arrangement can be detected as well in Lewis's 1931 book on Adolph Hitler, a work based on his travels to Berlin and an odd mixture of travel writing and polemic. Though not a travel book per se, *Hitler* is an important pre-text for *Filibusters in Barbary* because it demonstrates the difficulties that Lewis had when assessing empirical evidence in a foreign country and when broadcasting these ideas without the detached assurance of the polemical works or the screen of characters in his fiction and satire. In *Hitler*, Lewis also introduces and critiques what he calls the "exotic sense" for its role in clouding travelers' perceptions.

The Thirties and *Hitler*

In *Hitler*, as in the early travel stories, Lewis describes a foreign milieu, here 1930 Berlin. Lewis traveled to Berlin to report on the phenomenon of National Socialism. These reports were originally published as a series of articles for *Time and Tide* in 1931 and appeared as a book that same year. Lewis felt that this book provided an accurate assessment of the political scene in Germany in general and of the character of Adolph Hitler in particular, whom he notoriously described as a "Man of Peace."[20] Lewis supported his account by providing authentic local color and by describing events that he witnessed, such as the youth rallies that he saw and Berlin's nightlife. As Paul O'Keefe points out, however, according to one reviewer in *The Spectator*, "The worst fault of the book is the inescapable feeling that Mr. Wyndham Lewis has thrown it all together in a few hectic afternoons of work. It is slapdash and often confused" (qtd. in O'Keefe, 301). Unlike the satirical, pseudo-anthropological portraits in *The Apes of God*, *Hitler* was closer to propaganda in the eagerness with which Lewis described the nascent political movement with little supporting evidence.[21] In *Hitler* Lewis as narrator is always visible, as is apparent in his eagerness to find a political remedy for the post-war period in the orderly and masculinist ideology of Nazism. It is, however, precisely this transparency of the narrative that makes *Hitler* empty of the self-critique that was such an important element of both his polemical work and his satiric fiction. In *Hitler*, Lewis, like Zagreus in *The Apes of God*, naively broadcasts the beliefs of another and confidently guides the reader, like Dan Boleyn, through this foreign scene. This hurried account of National Socialism led one reviewer, Cecil Frank Melville, a critic of Oswald Moseley and British Fascism, to call Lewis an "Intellectual Innocent Abroad."[22]

Hitler is nevertheless an important pre-text for *Filibusters in Barbary* because it was written just prior to his trip to more "exotic" Morocco and because in both works Lewis is attempting to find some political or social structure that would prevent a recurrence of the events that led to the First World War. Unlike in *Filibusters*, where Lewis sees a variety of government and social structures in the various cities he visits, in Berlin there was only the single phenomenon of National Socialism for him to report on. However, more relevant to a discussion of Lewis's Morocco book is Lewis's discussion in *Hitler* of what he calls the "exotic sense," the romanticized view of foreign countries and peoples that was cultivated by authors such as L. Noel in *Kasbah* and directors such as Ingram, but also in Lewis's mind by writers such as D. H. Lawrence. Lewis had attacked Lawrence in the 1929 *Paleface* for his primitivism, an issue that Lewis saw as related to exoticism. In *Hitler*, Lewis continues this line of argument:

> The Exotic sense, in the nature of things, is a direction taken by the mind that implies a decadence. For it is a flight from the Self, is it not—a yearning for violent change? No very active man could experience it—he would be too absorbed with the satisfactions of his own personal activity to wish to transfer his attentions so far away from his vital and effective centre—his own creative principle of life. (115–16)

Opposed here to both decadence and to the "violent change" of revolution, Lewis privileges a vital and active center, one that is both personal and political. Neither this vitality nor this activity calls for an expansion beyond these boundaries of self or nation.

Moreover, idolization of the exotic is for Lewis essentially a component of western imperialism and colonization that comes cloaked in sentimental good will. He sees it above all as a way to enact and naturalize certain power relations that, in his view, contributed to the decadence of modernity:

> All indulgence in the Exotic Sense postulates a state of affairs in which the person indulging in it belongs to a social system still powerful and superior in its resources to the system to which the object of the exoticist's infatuation belongs. That is essential. It is an aristocratic, or a plutocratic, indulgence—of the same order as Globe-trotting, or Big-game-hunting, or Foreign Missionary Work. . . . What after all is the Exoticist but the White Conqueror turned literary and sentimental? (116–17)

It is important that Lewis's critique of the "exoticist's" infatuation appears in *Hitler*, a book that bridges Lewis's defense of the West—articulated throughout the twenties in works such as *Time and Western Man* and *Paleface*—and his critique of France's colonial presence in Morocco articulated in *Filibusters in Barbary*. In Lewis's elaboration of the exoticist's infatuations, there is an underlying self-consciousness of his own previous travels in foreign countries and an anxiety that seems to forecast his travels to Morocco.

In *Filibusters in Barbary*, the seductions of the exotic are more expressly an issue as Lewis travels throughout North Africa, a region, as we have seen, that had a certain romantic allure in the public mind in Britain at the time. How Lewis construes Morocco as an example of a stable though heterogeneous society worthy of admiration—perhaps even emulation—can be seen in the way he praises both the local native government structures as well as aspects of the French colonial government. If Lewis intended in *Filibusters* to reveal the "unsatisfactory operation at a distance of a crooked political system," then this could only be accomplished by bridging this physical distance, by circulating within the foreign milieu. In *Filibusters*, however, unlike in *Hitler*, Lewis employs satire to maintain the narrative distance and more effectively to contain the exoticist's infatuation, which he felt would hinder his empirical methods. To recall Marina MacKay's comments regarding the literature of late modernism more generally, Lewis was to struggle mightily, and not always successfully perhaps, with "experimental form and political impurity."

FILIBUSTERS IN BARBARY

Since at least 1912, the year that the French established the Protectorate, the European imperial presence was the dominant fact in much of the North African region, especially in Algeria and Morocco. Prior to this date, according to Douglas Porch in *The Conquest of Morocco*, Morocco was not strictly speaking a separate geo-political entity, comprised as it was of separate regions controlled by local caids or lords:

> Morocco in 1900 was a country because the Sultan said it was. For Europeans who knew anything about the place, this claim appeared preposterous. Morocco was a land of tremendous contrasts—geographical, racial, linguistic. . . . What gave it unity, at least on a map, was that it was virtually the only patch of Africa which had yet to be absorbed into one of those sweeping areas of pink, or yellow, or whatever color a European country used to delineate its empire. Morocco remained a cartographic anomaly, an untidy splash of noncolonial independence.[23]

By 1905, the sultan's claims to statehood for Morocco had gained enough credence that the European imperial powers, which had established a significant presence in the region throughout the nineteenth century, had begun quarreling over its division. Morocco had a strategic importance for Europe because of its location on the straits of Gibraltar. Control of the country became a point of contention among the European powers that were expanding their colonial and imperial reach. Their urgent negotiations over Morocco's division formed an important backdrop to the First World War.

The French Protectorate thus established, two years prior to the outbreak of the First World War, operated by means of "indirect rule." Under this system—which in its general structure is possibly what Lewis had in mind when he referred to the "unsatisfactory operation at *a distance* of a crooked political system"—the administration of the colony was under the aegis of the resident general, who from 1912–1925 was Marshall Louis Hubert Gonzalve Lyautey. Lyautey's method of ruling was not to conquer and subdue the native populations, but to placate them by establishing a joint rule with the local lords and caids. By this means, France could assert the "civilizing influences" of European culture through the structures of the native government and through the progressive ventures of city planning and expanded commerce rather than through outright conquest. According to Paul Rabinow in *French Modern: Norms and Forms of the Social Environment*, "The protectorate form (like paternalism) employs a rhetoric of cooperation, progress, and mutual accommodation."[24] By 1925, however, Lyautey's control of the Protectorate had weakened as a result of the combination of the agitation of Abd el Krim, the Moroccan nationalist who occupied the Spanish controlled Riff, and the increased presence in the region of European freebooters, or as Lewis calls them "filibusters," who sought profit and gain in various legal and illegal activities and undermined the spirit of "mutual accommodation" sponsored by the French by exploiting both the native population and Europeans alike.

As a result of this complex political scene and the competing interests involved, Lyautey's method of indirect rule was increasingly suspect to the impatient military elite back in Paris who were facing their own problems on the European continent and who were less and less willing to devote either time or resources to Lyautey's slow process of pacification. In 1925, Lyautey was summarily and, in Lewis's mind, ignominiously removed as resident general. By 1931, the year of Lewis's visit, Abd el Krim had since surrendered and the French were still in control of much of the region. The international presence continued to be strong in Morocco, and the specter of nationalist uprisings continued to hover.

These historical events form an important historical backdrop to Lewis's trip. How Lewis records these events—to the degree that he does—how he sees and portrays the various cities he visits, and how he asserts his own presence on the scene as a traveler and as narrator, reveal both Lewis's desire to seek a political remedy for the troubled West and his role as an artist/provocateur in the modern world. Coming soon after his hasty travel account of 1930 Berlin, *Filibusters in Barbary* represents a further attempt by Lewis to seek out a system of government and a model of society that would prevent the West from having to fight "all the old European wars over again," as he said in *Paleface*. Lewis's self-portrayal in the opening pages of *Filibusters in Barbary* is important for understanding his satire and his larger narrative strategy. In the description of his leave-taking, Lewis establishes the parameters of his traveler's persona and his narrative voice as he prepares the ground for his "satiric enterprise."

Leave-Taking

Lewis embarked on his journey in the spring of 1931, traveling for several months throughout northwest Africa and seeing Algeria, Morocco, and the border of the region known as the Rio de Oro in Mauretania. His description of his departure from England is replete with the conventions of the travel genre, beginning with his dramatic leave-taking:

> I sold my goods, "liquidated" my belongings, sold my barrels, upon which stood my lamps, put in store my books. The "Luther of Ossington Street" (as the naughty, naughty post-Ninetyish old and young kittens call him) left that ultra-Lutheran spot, he kicked the dust of moralist and immoralist England off his un-Lutheran feet, determined for a while to exchange it against the red dust of the Sand—Wind of the Rio de Oro! (24)

Fresh from the publication of *The Apes of God* and the controversy that surrounded it, Lewis here seems fatigued by the London literary scene and its petty squabbles, although at the same time this self-presentation is tinged with the paranoia that was such an important element of his self-fashioning. He accuses his detractors—here abstracted to England as a whole—of being both "moralist and immoralist," as he attempts to remain above the fray that he largely caused. The narrative voice shifts from first person to third person precisely at the moment when he recalls his enemies fixing him with a label. The traces of ill will and mutual recriminations that Lewis obliquely records give us some indication of his feelings about the literary environment in

London, feelings that seem not to have been fully purged by the rebarbative satire of *The Apes of God*.

Having unmoored himself from the London milieu and articulated in part his motivations for traveling, Lewis next describes both his psychic and material preparations for travel:

> Thoroughly unanchored, all trim in the rear, ready for anything (even slander after demise) with a *loupe*, water and oil colours, wood and clay palettes, razors for pencils, inks, insecticide, an *Arabic Without Tears*, a *Berber for the British*, and a *Fool-proof Tifinar*, a map of the Sahara and one of the High, Middle and Anti-Atlas—*Stovarsel* against dysentery, a Kodak (an unfortunate purchase)—unaccompanied, I set out. (24)

Other than these items, Lewis gives no indication here of any other preparations, despite the fact that, as Cy Fox points out and as will become clear later in the book, Lewis did a considerable amount of background reading on the history of Morocco in preparation for his trip.[25] This fact casts this initial description in a different light and demands that we read this self-presentation more closely. Lewis first steels his mind against those enemies whom he is leaving behind, who will now have free rein to slander his name, and then he describes those items that will facilitate his travels through Northern Africa. In the description of the latter, Lewis emerges as a naïve traveler, a kind of innocent abroad, who has casually prepared at the last minute for a difficult journey. As in much of Lewis's fiction, which as he said was concerned primarily with "the outside of things," the objects that he describes are crucial signifiers. The loupe and the Kodak offer alternative ways of seeing, of augmenting his traveler's eye. As an artist, he will use the tools of his trade to portray what he sees with that "pervasive physical sympathy of the painter" that West described; but the inclusion of the camera suggests a more casual approach to travel. The parenthetical comment about the "unfortunate purchase" of the Kodak foreshadows the difficulty that Lewis will have later on in his trip procuring film, since the film supply is controlled by one of the local "filibusters"; but it is also unfortunate for Lewis because in his mind it marks him as a tourist, a role that he holds in disdain. In this opening scene, the casual traveler and the "enemy" artist are both present, existing in an uneasy tension.

Like Lear, "more sinned against than sinning," Lewis casts himself in the role of victim for the purpose of his melodramatic "Hail and Farewell!" His claim that he traveled "unaccompanied" is false, as his wife Gladys Anne was with him for the entire trip. Lewis conceals this fact in order to highlight the dramatic gesture of solitary leave-taking. His departure, he claims, was "in the heroic style," although this heroism and the previous drama are inflected with a tone of sarcasm as he caricatures both the romantic conventions of travel and his own clandestine impulses: "shrouded in anonymity I 'stole silently away'" (24). As he leaves, the petty bickering of Bloomsbury merges into the global conflicts of the European powers:

> The sedentary habits of six years of work had begun, I confess, to weary me. Then the atmosphere of our dying European society is to me profoundly depressing. Some relief is necessary from the daily spectacle of those expiring Lions and Eagles, who obviously will never recover from the death-blows they dealt each other (foolish beasts and birds) from 1914 to 1918[.] (24)

In these opening pages, the local milieu of the London literary and artistic scene of the 1920s is abstracted to stand for the interwar West as a whole. The "profoundly depressing" sight of "our dying society" alludes to Spengler's notion of a dying European and American society.

Airing his grievances against the West here, Lewis makes it seem as if his decision to travel to Morocco was the result of fatigue and made on the spur of the moment. He deliberately avoids the traditional travel spots, such as "the beaten track to Russia," and instead chooses what he says is a "less controversial spot": "I said to myself that I would go to the highest mountains in Africa and look down upon the mirages of the great electric desert" (24). Lewis extricates himself from the claustrophobic environment of postwar London ostensibly to gain a perspective on the modern world from a vantage point free from the entanglements that characterized interwar England. This freedom will be gained as much from his "anonymity" as from his greater perspective. However, as we have seen briefly, the complicated national, ethnic, and colonial makeup of Morocco in 1931 was by no means "less controversial" than that of Stalinist Russia. Therefore, just as in his letter to his publisher in which he discourages us from seeing mere horseplay in his portrayals, we should be wary of seeing Lewis's desire to travel to Morocco as simple escapism or as an infatuation with the exotic.

The conventions of the travel genre that Lewis employs in these opening pages, the "Author's Foreword," are amplified and further satirized in the following chapter, entitled "A Conventional Farewell," as he describes his progress to Marseilles, and as his role as traveler and weary intellectual becomes more "bombastic" (to recall Pierpoint's term from the encyclical in *The Apes of God*):

> England, my England! I gasped, my face streaming with rain. Shall I
> return: or, like so many of your sons, become from henceforth an exile?
> I wished frankly to escape for ever from this expiring Octopus, that held
> me to it by my mother-tongue (unless America can be said to share, with
> England, that advantage over me.) (26)

In the opening lines of this passage Lewis's role is that of the enervated
and long-suffering intellectual. His feverish exhortation to his native land
recalls the romantic posturing of Stephen Dedalus, for whom going abroad
into exile was the only way to escape the nets of church and state cast by
Ireland. However, as "conventional" as the opening lines of this farewell are,
the latter part of this passage is more casual in its tone, which shifts from one
of long suffering to confiding frankness, suggesting that this "escape" was not
merely a Romantic posturing but a deliberate act. This is born out in the
following passages where he describes in great (and comic) detail the amount
of preparatory reading he has done on his destination, regarding everything
from the climate to the classifications of the wild goats of the region.

Lewis ends his brief farewell chapter to England in particular and to Europe
in general not by cutting all ties and abandoning it altogether, but rather
by recognizing that what he will see on his journey will most likely be to
some degree prescribed by his nationality as an Englishman. In this scene of
departure, Lewis carves out an identity that allows him to remain a "judge, not
a party," a detached observer, although not one without his own biases. Lewis
links the unpredictable climate of Europe to its shifts in political power and
influence:

> The climate of Europe is changing. Indeed the climate of the world is
> doing so. . . . But in Morocco they say, on the other hand, the climate has
> become European (European in the old, superseded sense of seasonal)—
> "Now we have your European seasons," as one *Vieux Morocain* said to me,
> with some pride, as if it were the result of the French Protectorate. (27)

Here he also recognizes as he departs that the divisions between home and
abroad are no longer viable as a means of defining identity, either personal or
national. Thus, even as Lewis scripts his journey as an escape from a "dying
European society," he at the same time seeks out the remains of a "superseded"
idea of European unity, one that he hopes to find in some form in French
Morocco.

In these opening pages, Lewis reserves most of his satire for the figure of
the weary intellectual and the modern tourist, figures that he both holds in
contempt and embodies in his narrative persona. Although seeming to offer

precisely the detachment that Lewis was seeking for his narrator, the tourist is an object of scorn for him. Lewis had expressed his scorn for the modern tourist prior to this, in his 1926 work *The Art of Being Ruled*, where he sees the recreational practice of international travel as a needless "displacement" that was nothing more than a dilution of modern life:

> The real approach to the question of "foreign travel" and cheap tourism is that the mass of people *do not want it*. . . . It is only the perpetual thrusting under their noses of advertisements recommending cheap foreign travel that ever induces some of them to take this disagreeable step. It is, in short, an excellent example of how the precious liberty of free movement is not a "liberty" at all. (99)

Travel and tourism are thus for Lewis another manifestation of modern consumer culture. Unlike Pound, who bemoaned the difficulty of travel after World War I, Lewis points out that in the postwar years despite the inconvenience of modern bureaucracy, "there is a complete *liberty of circulation* everywhere for everybody" (*Art of Being Ruled* 96). Such unrestricted freedom of movement, Lewis suggests, because of its simultaneous lack of authenticity, has had the unfortunate effect of homogenizing the experience of foreign countries.

Liberal Democracy and Authoritarian Rule: Scaling the Heights of Modernity

Lewis's comments on international tourism come in the context of his analysis of the "physical liberty" of the European and the rise of Liberal Democracy. Earlier in *The Art of Being Ruled*, Lewis juxtaposes "Liberal Democracy" and "Authority" as two opposing categories for regulating modern life. He suggests that throughout the nineteenth and early twentieth centuries authority was in decline as the promise of post-enlightenment rationalism asserted itself, but he also suggests that the resulting democratic principles, which he always connected to the rise of mass culture, would ultimately be the undoing of European identity or unity without which the larger and more vital internationalism that he hoped for would not materialize. While Lewis does not explicitly mention colonialism in *The Art of Being Ruled* as one of the ways in which this eclipsed authority would reassert itself, there is an implicit suggestion that the mechanisms of such "indirect rule" could counter the homogenizing effects that foreign travel and international tourism promote:

The white man has not in his imagination been able to look all round the world and see it as one large mud-ball with certain possibilities. Its possibilities of unification have escaped him, in spite of all his mechanical opportunities for becoming himself a unifier. He has only been able to propel his body laboriously round it, not his mind. So he made a better globe-trotter and buccaneer than an organizer, or civilizer. (69)

Foreshadowing his interest both in the French colonial government of Lyautey and his own travel account in which he records the propulsion of his body through the space of Morocco, Lewis here is highly critical of the rise of Liberal Democracy, which, he feels, has drained travel of any serious purpose.

We can see the beginnings of this concern about the problems of Liberal Democracy in Lewis's focus on race in the above passage, a focus which also forecasts his later concerns in *Paleface,* where, in arguing for the vitality of a new internationalist order, he dismisses the social problems associated with race both in Europe and in America as being distracting to the political goals of a larger internationalism. He offers a lengthy analysis of W. E. B. DuBois's novel *Dark Princess,* seeing its agitation for racial pride in African Americans as an attempt to merely replace one kind of superiority with another, and thus as suffering from the same illusions that whites have been suffering from under capitalism. Lewis saw such artificial divides as race and gender as distracting from the greater and more immanent threat of another global conflict, and while his ideas about race, even in the context of a critique of capitalism, fail to convince, they do offer insight into Lewis's thoughts about the almost utopian internationalism that would be a bulwark against future global conflict.

In his critique of modern Liberal Democracy, Lewis frequently talked in terms of scale, as if the homogenizing effects of Liberal Democracy was some-how diminishing. Lewis's comments on "physical liberty," for example, appear in a section of *The Art of Being Ruled* called "The Small Man." In Lewis's view, in the name of individual freedoms offered by Liberal Democracy, people had reverted to a childlike state, both mentally and physically. We see a similar focus on scale of a much more literal kind towards the beginning of *Filibusters.* Whereas, in his dramatic leave taking Lewis cast himself, as we have seen, as a Lear, "more sinned against than sinning," at this moment, we see Lewis as a Lemuel Gulliver, for whose creator, Jonathan Swift such shifts in scale was the essence of his satire, as Gulliver towers over the Liliputians in his first adventure far away from home.

As Lewis leaves Europe for Northern Africa, the question of scale evoked by the concept of the "small man" of modern Democratic society ceases to be merely metaphorical as his argument becomes grounded in the empirical account of his travels. Lewis travels from London to Marseilles where he sees the French port city buzzing with international activity. He notices in particular the presence of Japanese warships in the harbor with their sailors who "looked like the merest children. . . . . They pervaded the town like an army of phantom dolls" (29). These soldiers represent for Lewis a more general tendency toward infantilism that, he felt, had also gripped the West in the wake of the First World War, and also the consequences that contact with democracy and internationalism could have even on a country such as Japan: "Before this I had not realized how youthful in the mass a great nation could remain—or was it become?" (29). Upon seeing these Japanese soldiers, Lewis offers another reason for his desire to leave England as he sees in them an analogous situation to that of England:

> In England we exist so much in the midst of the reverse of all that is satisfyingly life-size, naked and simple, so much in fact in contact with what is undersized and so *everymanishly* mean (far too *menschlich*, in the German of Nietzsche) that one might cease to believe in its existence if one did not go and resume contact with natural things from time to time, to forget how men have dwarfed it to their own stature, especially under the guidance of the Democratic Idea. (30)

In this passage, Lewis scripts his journey as an escape from a society that is as degenerate as that described by Spengler in *The Decline of the West*. But unlike Spengler, who attributed this decline to the inevitable laws of history, Lewis here sees it as the result of the "Democratic Idea" and manifest in the loss of a sense of scale. Democracy has, for Lewis, reduced the West to something less than "life-size." This concept of scale preoccupies Lewis throughout his trip, as he constantly compares England, Europe, and Northern Africa.

Lewis's critique of the Democratic principle also emerges in his satiric portrayals both of the colonial population and of individuals he meets on his journey. While on board the packet from Marseilles to Oran, Lewis mixes with the French colonial officers and their families, circulating within their society and yet remaining apart from it. He proudly asserts that he is not a tourist—"No international tourists ever go by this packet"—but neither is he a colonialist or even a French citizen (31). This detached identity gives him a privileged perspective when recording the scene aboard the packet. The ship's progress is impeded as it gets caught in a dense fog. As a result, the foghorn sounds throughout the night, disturbing the passengers' dinner. This already noisy scene is further disrupted as both a radio and a gramophone are blaring throughout, creating a scene of "surprising pandemonium," as Lewis puts it (31). This pandemonium affects the colonial passengers differently from the way it affects Lewis:

> At moments the discord became so startling that even the colonial passengers seemed to notice it slightly. For my own part I was seized upon once or twice by an indescribable panic. There was something frantic and deliberate in the cacophonous attack, taken in conjunction with the stolidity of the ship's guests—the decorous colonialism of them. (31)

The racket is an ominous sign of the discordant worlds of Europe and North Africa. However, whereas this discord brings Lewis to the brink of panic, it barely ruffles the "decorous" surface of the colonialists' dinner. It is as if Lewis alone were cognizant of this dissonance, taking it as evidence of the futility and fakery of these glorified international tourists.

The packet itself is a microcosm of the French colonial class. This society embodies an odd mixture of Liberal Democratic principles and aristocratic tendencies, a mixture reflected in Lewis's description of the scene on board the packet the first night. Lewis then speculates on what this discord might signify as he probes the character of a typical colonialist. During the dinner on board the packet, Lewis describes in particular the wife of a colonial official, an unflappable woman who dresses in the "most surprising costumes" of the Second Empire and who remains especially impervious to the din around her. This woman embodies for Lewis the French aristocracy of the *Ancien Régime*. Lewis speculates that despite her pretensions of being a "queen among colonial women," she was most likely the wife of some functionary or minor official (34). In his caustic description of this woman, Lewis also refers for the first time to the former resident general of the French Protectorate in Morocco, Marshall Lyautey, and sets his achievement apart from the colonial class that is on board the ship. The wife of the official is for Lewis a parasite who feeds off the gains of colonialism, while paying lip service to Liberal Democracy. Lewis captures this woman in a verbal snapshot and, in what will become a familiar strategy, elicits from his empirical description a larger political point:

> This obese groceress wallowing in the profitable squalors of the Third Republic became symbolic, perched up in that way upon the *passerelle* of the Algerian Packet. It was a Stature of Liberty. A century and a half after the tumbrels and the guillotine, here stood this bogus butter-and-egg marchioness—this enthroned charlady—being borne in triumph towards a land won for the Third Republic by the great Lyautey—a Christmas present for a régime which could find no better way to thank him for his gift than to dismiss him at last, with an insulting recall, allowing him to leave the shores of Africa anonymously, in the first Packet at hand, much like the one we traveled in—less honoured than the inflated daughter of the democratic bureaucracy.(36)

In his 1935 letter to his publisher where he mentions *Filibusters* as a "satiric enterprise," Lewis cites this passage as evidence of his picturesque ridicule and his high seriousness. He further states in this letter that "[i]n general the Moroccan scene as described in *Filibusters in Barbary* reveals the existence of a conflict between the colonizing, the Roman, impulses of the French Nation— of which impulses Lyautey is the archetype—and the irresponsible, commercial and capitalistic, interests" (xvi). This particular portrait makes the dichotomy especially clear. In both this letter and throughout *Filibusters in Barbary*, Lewis clearly aligns himself with the "Roman" virtues of Lyautey, not with either the diminishing effects of Liberal Democracy or the authoritarian nature of fascism.

THE BERBER WORLD

Upon arriving in Oran in Algeria, the contrast between the colonialist and native cultures becomes apparent to Lewis, although without the sense of pandemonium and discord that the scene on the boat seemed to presage. Lewis is struck by the degree to which an entire city can be subject to the homogenizing tendencies of colonization. "Oran is a stereotypical French city," he claims upon seeing the Boulevard Galliéni and the Boulevard Séguin, two main thoroughfares, named after famous French colonialists, which bisect the city (41). Even more so than Marseilles, which was characterized by a pervasive internationalism, Oran is a simulacrum of a French city. Wherever the French influence is apparent, according to Lewis, there is a corresponding reduction in scale. The city is a "little model of French Civilization," although interspersed with the French city is the "native town," populated by the Berbers. Thus, the French have not completely succeeded in absorbing the indigenous population.

In fact, these two groups exist alongside one another in stark contrast. He sees the French section of Oran and then, "[t]here at once is the Berber world" (41). This Berber world, which exists alongside the French settlement, has maintained a certain integrity in Lewis's view, an integrity that he finds praiseworthy: "The people who fill it are as they have always been. Is not that enough?" When describing the native Berber population, Lewis again refers to scale: "Their archaic nobility sticks out in stark elevation, like a grand black forest above the depressed levellings of our Western life" (41). Here, the layout of the city allows the various groups to coexist, although in describing this coexistence, Lewis clearly admires the Berbers' ability to maintain a certain degree of ethnic and geographic independence despite the infiltration of French and other foreign imperial outsiders.

For Lewis, Oran is of interest for the way that the various ethnic and religious groups coexist, and he praises the Berbers in particular for the manner in which they set the terms for this coexistence. As Cy Fox points out, Lewis's admiration for the Berbers—or for any particular group or individual for that matter—was unusual. As further evidence of the sincerity of his admiration for the Berbers, Lewis had planned a second book based on his Moroccan journey that he intended to call *Kasbahs and Souks*, although he never completed it aside from a few articles. In these articles, Lewis speculates on the origins of the Berbers. He argues that since their population is diffused over much of the region, it is difficult to posit any single origin. This realization leads Lewis to another important question: "to what extent [the Berbers] are nomadic or the reverse: and if nomadic, what that may signify exactly" (190). The Berbers, Lewis explains, are possibly the only indigenous population in the area, and their continued existence is remarkable because of their resistance both to Arab and European invaders who throughout history attempted to subdue them either through conquest or colonization. Their survival in Oran, alongside the French, is a testament to their adaptability. At the end of a chapter fragment from *Kasbahs and Souks* entitled "The Berber Bug," Lewis writes: "[W]hat is most interesting politically about Morocco at the present moment derives from this hereditary disposition of the extra-Moroccan, the Saharan 'Berbery,' to take the lead, and to supply (or threaten to supply) the great religious chiefs, for the liberation of Berbery from the successive yokes of the civilized world" (200). Whether or not Berber independence was accomplished by virtue of their nomadic nature remains to Lewis unclear, but their ambiguous, permeable relationship to the numerous other groups that installed themselves in the region is certainly instrumental, in Lewis's view, for their survival and is an indication to him of their "noble dignity."

The contrasts Lewis sets up operate both locally and globally as he again considers what lesson the coexistence of Berbers and Europeans offers Europe, suffering as it was from the aftermath of war. The description of the Berber's relation to the land they occupy and to the foreign occupiers can be compared in particular to Lewis's description of postwar Europe in *The Art of Being Ruled*. Here, Lewis argues that the First World War led to a recrudescence of nationalism in the twenties as the European nation states drew their borders more sharply. They amplified their differences to those around them in order to maintain stability and national identity rather than adapting to the changing conditions of modern life. Lewis saw the European nations assuming a bunker mentality in the postwar years—a false stability. As we have seen, Lewis criticized international travel and tourism for encouraging this bunker mentality by emphasizing the differences between nations through the highlighting of "exotic" features, even as these activities purported to offer increased opportunities for cultural interaction. Tourism, for Lewis, was simply another way for people to highlight differences that would otherwise be inconsequential:

> These *differences* are primitive things, that in future will be of interest to the curious student while they last. But they are, as it were, a sign of backwardness. They no longer represent either a living culture or political power. The nations of Europe are helplessly laid out side by side, each talking 'its own language' like so many indian tribes in reservations or reductions. . . . All the European nations have recently suffered great losses and their privacy should be respected. If they retain their local customs and speech, it will be on sufferance and as a concession to a colony. (98–99)

These two instances of the adaptable, seminomadic Berber and the entrenched, traumatized European nation states represented for Lewis the political poles of modern life. Lewis sees in the latter the elimination of that sense of scale and the "life size" that he hopes to find in Morocco and that he sees in the Berber sections of Oran.

However, as if mindful of the potential for his remarks on the Berbers to be taken as mere Romanticizing of a "primitive" race—a charge that he had leveled against Sherwood Anderson and D. H. Lawrence in *Paleface*—Lewis encourages us to take his comments in the context of his critique of the West:

> There is no inalienable, inherent "mysterious" dignity about Berbers. Need I say that? It is the *time* or "period" they represent. That is better than ours—*better* if you mean by that adjective possessed of more dignity, possessing all the grand attitudes and habits impossible to that "hurried man" of transatlantic pattern.(42)

Lewis urges us here to see his racial portraits as an allegory of the "time," a time—here the post-war period—in which these peoples have not abrogated their dignity for the pseudo-individualism offered by modern liberal democracy. He claims that his portrayal is not an essentialist one, but one based on his perceptions and on a comparison with the "hurried man" of the West. It is here where Lewis's disparagement of the time school begins to have its effects on his ability to assess what it is that he sees. In the quotation above Lewis sees the European nations all existing spatially "laid out side by side," and how they got to where they are now, in this interwar landscape, is not to be looked for in history, which seems in Lewis's estimation to be nothing more than the codification of grievances, but rather in the clash of differences in the present moment that make communication so difficult. Similarly, in the following quotation above, in order to dispel the "mystery" of a "primitive" race and the accompanying infatuation of the exoticist, he resorts to an erasure of their history: "It is the time or 'period' they represent." Lewis will continue to confront the problems of history as he moves through various cities in Morocco, though his pronouncements will become more contradictory in this regard as the inductive nature of the travel narrative challenges the polemical pronouncements that he seems unwilling to give up or rethink.

"A Good Smattering of History"

As we have seen in the introduction and in the previous chapters, history and historiography pervade the modernist travel narrative, as both what is seen and how it is represented pose unique challenges in the interwar world. For Cummings, the difficulty of representing a society so firmly under the sway of official ideology resulted in a like difficulty on the surface of the text, as Cummings himself retreated behind a veneer of impressionistic prose. For Pound, the only way to record certain ills of the modern world was to encode them in a poetry that was obscure in its particulars but curative in its large-scale structure. In both cases, these writers were more concerned with how to write history than with understanding the impact that history had on individuals in the milieu in which they traveled. For both Lewis and for Rebecca West, as we will see in the next chapter, history becomes more of a problem not just in its recording and rendering, but also because of the way history so deeply shapes people's lives. Lewis, who had come out strongly against the historically minded "time school" in *Time and Western Man*, suddenly finds himself contending firsthand with populations and cities for whom "history" is a much less academic affair. In attempting to distinguish among the various cities he visits and in the interest of driving his polemic home, Lewis finds himself struggling to contain the very notion of history that has been let loose in the modern world. In his journey from Tlemcen to Casablanca to Marrakech to Agadir to the coast of the Rio de Oro, we see Lewis struggling to accommodate the picturesque and the historical, as the experimental form of his modernist satire comes into conflict with the political impurity of his polemic, to paraphrase Marina MacKay's description of the contending features of late modernism.

After leaving Oran, Lewis's next stop is the Algerian city of Tlemcen, which borders Morocco. As he approaches this city by train from Oran, he is struck by the mountains that act as a natural gateway to the land of the Great Lords of the Atlas, the "Cherifian Empire": "For a traveler entering Morocco by this route the Massif of Tlemcen is indeed a worthy gate to Barbary" (52). Tlemcen is, according to Lewis, the "first Moroccan town." It is also, according to E. F. Gautier, whom Lewis cites here, "the first *city*" (51 Lewis's emphasis) that the westerner comes across that has not been demolished by the repeated incursions of outside groups. In addition to admiring Tlemcen for maintaining its integrity throughout its troubled history, Lewis finds the architecture and city planning to be well adapted to its geography: "The enormous, rufous battlements of nature thrown up about this entrance gallery to the Cherifian Empire are of course vaster than the works of man, but, because they have a regularity reclaiming chaos, these cliffs should be classed with the tremendous Kasbahs that the chieftains of the High Atlas have built" (52). The geometric arrangement of the mountains, which the founder of the city took advantage of when building Tlemcen, is for Lewis a sign of technical achievement, and he likens the intermingling of geography and city planning to both modern machinery and modern art.

While marveling at the aesthetic splendor of Tlemcen, Lewis also insists that the traveler must be "historically-minded" in order to be able to appreciate the beauty of the city and its political and sociological importance: "You must have a good smattering of the history of Morocco, or more properly of Maghreb, to be able to breathe its balmy citron-scented air intelligently—in addition to staring at its storks' nest at the top of all its minarets, and remaining open-mouthed in front of its Fondouks and Synagogues" (53). Lewis stresses the importance of history as a way of adding depth to what he sees, though he does so in language reminiscent of the globe-trotter. He compares the uninformed, non–historically minded view of this city in particular to the uninformed view of modern industrialism:

> Often in the past I have stared stupidly at vast systems of machinery— in factories and power-houses—for many minutes, until it got too hot or I was moved on, without having the least idea what these monstrous concatinations [sic] of steel might be for. A city and its history are the same as that. Wherever you get people you get this: it is all meaningless and really rather silly unless you know what it's all about. (53)

This scene ironically conjures the moment in *The Education of Henry Adams* when Adams finds himself on the brink of modernity, standing in front of a dynamo in almost religious awe, unable to understand its workings but seeing in its novelty and mystery a useful lesson for the historian. After Adams considers the unseen forces with which the modern physicist must contend, he goes on to apply this new science to the study of history:

> Historians undertake to arrange sequences,—called stories, or histories,— assuming in silence a relation of cause and effect. These assumptions, hidden in the depths of dusty libraries, have been astounding, but commonly unconscious and childlike; so much so, that if any captious critic were to drag them to light, historians would probably reply, with one voice, that they had never supposed themselves required to know what they were talking about.[26]

In alluding to this scene before the dynamo, Lewis underscores the skepticism he feels that history in its traditional chronicle of cause and effect can help us to understand our present moment. However, as is typical of the internal tensions that drive Lewis's work, he insists on the "smattering of history" that one must have to make sense of Tlemcen. Lewis characteristically draws back from insisting on history as a way of guiding what he sees and instead accuses the overly "historically-minded" accounts that he has read of ignoring the importance of firsthand observation: "There is an opposite difficulty of course: namely that when people know what a thing signifies *historically* (just as they might be informed of the uses of a complicated machine) often they see too much, and much that is not there at all" (53). He describes the "lyrical flights of fancy" employed by certain historians and travel writers—with his eye at this moment again perhaps on Spengler as well as on Gautier—as "aberrations" that are "a triumph of history over the eyes in the head" (57). Lewis corrects both the uninformed view of the tourist, which takes only casual aesthetic interest in what it sees, and the overly determined view of the historian by asserting the prominence of his artist's eye.

While in Tlemcen, Lewis visits the Moroccan marketplace and bazaars in which he sees a combination of "lethargy and incessant movement" (54). This incessant movement, Lewis claims, the Moroccans have learned from Western Europeans who have traversed the region whether for adventure, trade, or conquest: "[T]hese are people who have learnt restlessness from the European, who is their main customer" (55). Like the innkeeper and provocateur Bestre from Lewis's early short story, the Moroccans have learned to deal with the incursions of outsiders in their own way and to their own economic benefit. They have adopted European habits in order to engage them in trade, which suggests a deceptive and strictly economic relationship. Despite assuming certain features of European mercantile existence, the inhabitants of Tlemcen nevertheless retain their own traditions. Lewis sees in the factories and in the architecture of Tlemcen in general an arrangement less oppressive than that of the industrial West:

> At a period when man has not been powerful enough to transform the accidental dispositions of nature—with no dynamite to blast, or rock-drills to disintegrate—and is compelled to build the streets of his cities in and out and up and down, inventing, as he goes along, untried architectural devices, delightful deformities and structural freaks, then, it is too plain, the result is more agreeable and stimulating to the eye. (57)

The necessity to comply with nature and with natural boundaries provides the restrictions that can be beneficial to society, and he takes this as a lesson to the artist: "By following the vast, non-human, lines of nature, our human arts score their best successes" (57). The architecture in Tlemcen further draws its geometry from both the demands of nature and from the demands of society. In *Filibusters* he admires Tlemcen for the way the city and its people have adapted to their surroundings:

> Projecting his tortuous, not yet oppressive, geometry, out upon the chaotic superstructures—being methodic where he can, in the teeth of natural disorder—man is seen at his best. He then produces something of intellectual as well as emotional value, which the unadulterated stark geometry of the Machine-Age precludes. (57)

This sounds like the Vorticist Lewis of *Blast*, for whom a more rigid, though not oppressively industrial, geometry was required to contain the disorder of modern life. Lewis alludes to this earlier period perhaps because the Vorticist campaign was likewise positioned firmly against the history that had been handed down to it as it strove to "make it new." Lewis's contradictory pronouncements on history in this section, and his ambiguous call for the need of a "smattering" of it, reveal the fissures in *Filibusters* that emerge from the conjoining of modernist style and politically engaged travel book. Lewis's modernist style, as revealed in his satire in particular, would have us question the authority of history and historiography, for example; but the inductive nature of the travel book and the polemical intent of seeking stability in the modern world would require us to rediscover this authority in the firsthand account of the narrator. Such contradictions will continue to score Lewis's text as he explores this colonial space further.

Casablanca and the Erasure of History

As Lewis enters Morocco proper the question of history will take on a new valence and it will be a more crucial element of the thesis that he is advancing about the state of the west and his political remedies for it. The first city Lewis visits in Morocco is Casablanca, a city he describes as the "city that Lyautey built," invoking the city's "founder" in the convention of the historical chronicle or epic. At the same time, fixing this originary moment in this way erases any history of the indigenous peoples. Lewis further erases the city's native identity as he describes it as a "huge marine outpost of Europe" (65). Casablanca is for Lewis "emblematic of the precarious post-war power of France. It is perhaps the place that holds the secret of the destiny of this astonishing latter-day colonial conquest." Whereas for Lewis the history of Tlemcen itself was important for understanding its present, here "[t]he history of Casablanca, or Dar el Beida, is not important" (65). History is unimportant here for Lewis because the population is composed either of nomads or of European settlers who have no claim to the city. In other words, history is not just unimportant, it doesn't exist. It is, Lewis acknowledges, an ancient city, and yet it is a city peculiarly without continuity or traditions implying that Casablanca itself is a kind of blank slate, devoid of history.

Despite finding history to be unimportant in Casablanca, Lewis refers to various books on the city that describe the history of its peculiar racial and ethnic complexion. He refers, for example, to a book by Arthur Leared who visited the city in the nineteenth century and who claimed that Casa was "the dirtiest, most tumble-down place ever seen" (qtd. in Lewis, 66). He cites other sources as well that similarly describe the city as dirty and that note the preponderance of beggars and indigents. Casablanca, for Lewis, is similar to these nineteenth-century descriptions in that it is made up primarily of what he calls "an auxiliary population of nomads" (67). However, on the other hand, since the nineteenth century, the Europeans, especially the French, brought to Casablanca an infrastructure that provided hygiene through the construction of sewage systems: "Europe has brought its drains and lavatories with it, all stinks are banished and middens frowned upon" (67). Thus the colonial presence was in part beneficial to Casablanca, although it remains for Lewis a city of nomads without its own history. This "smattering of history" that Lewis consults thus serves to further underscore the lack of history of the region that Lewis described above. Such erasure of history is not without its polemical purpose in *Filibusters*, as Lewis will continue to advance his theory about the dire situation of the west in his search for a new viable form of governance.

While in Casablanca, Lewis notes various makeshift settlements—miles and miles of rundown shacks—and he describes the population of these settlements as either nomadic or seminomadic. He first sees the various "Arab villages," or "nouala" villages, that are "an important nomad or semi-nomad settlement composed of many hundreds of families, come there to work" (69–70). The populations of these cities fluctuate as the availability of work demands. The lives of these people Lewis sees ultimately as too "fluid" to describe with any certainty, however: "In this country where the day-labourer is a nomad, who pitches his tent against the field or mine he is to work in, the question that presents itself to the statistician is no doubt whether these people are 'transhumant,' 'nomads,' or, on the other hand, uprooted 'sedentaries,' in search of work" (70–71). Lewis sees these settlements throughout Morocco, but their existence in Casablanca in particular suggests to him the peculiar uprootedness of Western life. They are for him symptomatic of both the benefit of the French colonial government (the stability that he sees it bringing to the region) and of the drawbacks of capitalism: "In Casablanca, for instance, there is a vast settlement that the French have named 'Bidonville.' It is a city within the city, in fact. It consists of small huts mainly composed of petrol-tins" (71). In order for a region to have a "history" in Lewis's mind it must have a degree of stability, either a growing stability as engineered by city planners and colonialists or a declining stability like that of Europe which had ceded its vitality for the dubious permanence of Liberal Democracy. What is odd here is how this implicit paradigm mirrors Spenglerian notions of history with its cycles, its rise and fall of civilizations, and its reliance on the stability of postenlightenment notions of governance. Lewis's portrayal of Casablanca figures as a warning to the West, and its "lack of history" is for Lewis the ultimate cost of uprootedness.

There is, however, a glimmer of hope along with the implicit warning to the West as Lewis draws one of the closest parallels between Morocco and the West, in this case America. Whereas the nomadic existence of the Berbers that Lewis had seen outside of Tlemcen was to him a sign of their nobility and evidence of their ability to adapt to the infiltration by outsiders, the more sedentary existences of the residents of Casablanca are less stable, recalling to Lewis the shantytowns of America:

> By the Petrol-tin Town, or Bidonville, of Casablanca, one is irresistibly reminded of another excrescence of the same sort, recently described in the English newspapers, namely the sub-city, or shack-town, growing up outside Chicago. *Capitalism and Barbary breed the same forms*—but how odd! The world-slump that hit America with the velocity of a tornado,

> spewed out onto the streets millions of decent people, not necessarily
> passionately nomad. (71)

The difference for Lewis between the situations in Casablanca and America, however, is that whereas the denizens of the Chicago shantytowns were forced into their conditions by the crisis of capitalism, the inhabitants of the Petrol-tin towns outside of Casablanca are "the creation of born nomads, who are, by choice, the inhabitants of a tent or a caboose" (71). Even though the "fluidity" of the nomads who inhabit Casablanca foreclosed for Lewis any sense of history, there is a way in which these born nomads are privileged over those in Chicago who were expelled from the body politic by the economic crisis facing the West at this time.

Lewis ultimately sees the mainly black populations of these Petrol-tin towns and the white populations of the Chicago shantytowns as on opposite paths, whereas the desired common ground for both these populations would be a common European way of life: Americans are, Lewis claims, "being thrown back into Barbary—not invited to issue out of Barbary into the advantageous plane of the civilized European life" (73). Complicating this argument still further, Lewis concludes his impressions of Casablanca by arguing that despite the French presence, Casablanca is "a city upon the American model. . . . An impression of kaleidoscopic unreality of the same order as that that disengages from the 'canyons' of Manhattan, assails you as you enter it for the first time." He further argues that "from both emanate the same unmistakable sensations of violent impermanence" (73–74). Such impermanence and such unreality were for Lewis the result of a loss of the stability that existed before the war and that the French, especially in the person of Lyautey, were trying to reclaim in Morocco through the civilizing influences of colonialism.

Lewis's conclusions about Casablanca are ambiguous since by 1931 the city had been further overrun by foreign, European freebooters and filibusters, a subject to which his book turns with more frequency and greater vituperation from this point on. He admires the seminomadic nature of the towns that paradoxically indicate to him a tendency toward stability rather than a decline. These makeshift cities reveal the wide gap between capitalism and Barbary, even as they indicate some common ground: "The gamut of human advance," Lewis argues, "is to the stable from the unstable," and for Lewis, Lyautey's impulses were distinctly toward stability. Lewis admired Lyautey because he controlled as best he could the European freebooters who exploited the lack of stability of Casablanca, but this stability was also helped along by the born nomads who were trending towards stability anyway. This leads Lewis to his most explicit praise of French colonialism, which sought to limit the claims of these outsiders:

French Morocco is the last great European enterprise of that order, magnificently carried through by a great soldier—one of the last of the great European military figures. It shows the French at their best—as the humane, civilizing, most genially—acquisitive, of all powers, able and good-humoured—something like what the Normans must have been, when mellowed a little by the benefits of conquest. But their protectorate is built upon sand, in every conceivable sense. The type of "European" who is running it is as unfixed, restless and incalculable in everything as is the nomad, semi-nomad, "transhumant" or only technically "sedentary" population he is invited to boss. All that is essentially stable is the military. (76)

For Lewis, Casablanca does not make a good impression overall, but he does see an important connection between "Barbary" and the West, as the divergent paths temporarily converge in a society that has been dramatically riven by competing claims and a diverse population. In stripping these populations of their histories, however, even as he manages to admire them for rather peripheral reasons, Lewis is complicit in the colonial project that he so admires.

Lewis continues to describe the cities he visits in terms of their relative stability or their resistance to various forces of dissolution. After Casablanca, Lewis proceeds to Marrakech, which he finds similar in its urban development: "All that can be said, upon the lines laid down in the last chapter, of Casa, can be said . . . of the Capital of the south, Marrakech" (79). The city is "a vast rendezvous rather than a capital. It is a walled-in converging point of nomads or of extremely restless peasants" (79). Marrakech, according to Lewis, is nevertheless "more real" than Casa (80), in that it shows a greater resistance to European influence in certain aspects of its buildings: "The desolation of cracked mud and sand, endless fine upstanding palms, loaded with dates, miles of these plumed plants—everywhere, wall within wall . . . of which earlier travellers speak, is still perfectly intact" (83). The city has managed to resist the overweening influence of the European presence. Why this resistance would suddenly be a good thing is not quite clear until we recognize the particular "overwhelming influence" that the residents of Agadir resisted was precisely that of the Germans, whose presence presaged the onset of the First World War.

AGADIR AND THE RETURN OF HISTORY

Where the history of Casablanca was relatively unimportant when assessing its present, as soon as Lewis arrives in Agadir, the next city on his itinerary, history of a sort becomes an important factor both in what and how he sees. But the history that confronts Lewis in Agadir has an artificial, almost nightmarish quality to it, and as with Casablanca, the only history to speak of is that of the European presence. The section on Agadir begins with Lewis's claim that the history of this city and the history of the West are inextricably linked: "Agadir has its name in our European history books. For us *Agadir* is a word that consorts, in a rather cheap and sinister fashion, with *Kaiser*" (100). "Agadir" conjures various other names and phrases for Lewis, such as "a gunboat of the name of *Panther*," the "Exile of Doorn," names that while they sound exotic and romantic, refer to names and events that were in the news in the run up to the First World War. In 1911, Kaiser Wilhelm II ordered the gunboat *Panther* to make a show of force off of the coast of French controlled Agadir, a move that was a part of the prewar posturing of the great powers, in a showdown that was eventually quelled by a treaty that paved the way to the formation of the Protectorate. These phrases that assault Lewis vaguely recall these events: "Agadir will stand for a dream-town in the old *Welt-politik* world, whose horizons were swept with clattering imperial eagles, a vanished breed" (100). Lewis implies that these phrases are laden with historical significance and, against his advice when he was in Tlemcen, he becomes for a moment distinctly "historically-minded" when recounting these pre-war ventures, intrigues, and diplomatic missions. Lewis presents these images in a manner that suggests that the worldview that they conjure is passé, out of date, as he once again mocks an aspect of historical knowledge.

Lewis's impressions of this city, however, are not influenced solely by history: "For me, who stayed for some time upon that black spot, which is all the map gives of it, Agadir has a quite different significance. At *Agadir* I see a crowd of images that compete with the imperial pre-war fustian" (100). His "empirical description" also has its nightmarish qualities, qualities which border on satire: "At the word 'Agadir' I see (metaphorically) the wild-eyed maraboutic figure, gesticulating above the serpent, and the no-less-wild-eyed physician, rushing down the field after the barefooted Berber" (101). The images of "pre-war fustian" of Kaisers and gunboats and the exotic, barbaric images of the barefooted Berber stand in striking contrast as Lewis tries to weigh historical evidence and firsthand impressions in order to determine what Agadir connotes to readers in the West in the present political context of interwar Europe. But this is not so much a rendering of competing histories, but rather a contrast between the historically minded European and the blank slate of barbarism, whose rituals and exoticism exist in an inscrutable present, conjuring up perhaps the novels of Conrad, who similarly projected the problems of the West onto the blank slate and dark heart of Africa. Even when Lewis explores a more distant and darker past, it is one that involves the arrival of westerners as a marker of historical chronology.

According to the sources that Lewis refers to, Agadir, as a port city, had always been attractive to filibusters and pirates. Lewis returns to a more distant past—one before that of the Kaiser and the gunboat *Panther*, to a past that is nevertheless uncannily familiar and in keeping with the dreamlike quality of his descriptions of Agadir thus far. He recalls the first outsider who came to Agadir: "In the year 1551 Captain Wyndham sailed into the beautiful bay of Agadir, in a 'tall ship called *The Lion*, of London.' Captain Wyndham was the first European trader to get his foot upon these shores. . . . But how shall we name the 'trade' Captain Wyndham . . . 'invented?' I fear his 'trade' was that of a *filibuster*" (101). For Lewis, the accidental resemblance of his name to that of this first filibuster causes him to think about his own role as an outsider in Morocco. It also leads him, however, to consider the various kinds of filibusters that exist in Morocco. Lewis does not take this opportunity to condemn all outsiders, only those who came to Agadir solely for profit or exploitation. Lewis cites one author who salvages the name and reputation of Captain Wyndham, the original freebooter and pirate: "A certain Mr. Scott O'Connor gives it as his opinion, in a travel book, that this coast 'has always attracted filibusters and adventurers.' But its filibusters have formerly come in 'tall ships called *The Lion*' and done the thing in style" (102). Thus, Lewis here, through O'Connor's testimony, excuses Captain Wyndham, the original filibuster and namesake. This historical snapshot of the first filibuster—which Lewis takes out of *Hakluyt's Voyages*—is for him a kind of originary moment of the whole colonial enterprise.

In Agadir, Lewis's satire becomes particularly pointed as he distinguishes among the different kinds of filibusters and as he describes the effects that "opening Agadir" to outside influences had on the city. The history of Agadir from Captain Wyndham's arrival was one of continued and, for the most part, successful resistance to exploitation by Europeans, at least until the late nineteenth and early twentieth centuries when the French military established control of the city. The military presence in Agadir, according to Lewis, served as a further source of stability and protected the city, in Lewis's view, from foreign exploitation that had destabilized other regions of Morocco. Lewis again praises Marshal Lyautey for his policy of keeping Agadir closed against rogue adventurers and international speculators. He cites approvingly the Resident General's pronouncement, "*We must never open Agadir!*" (103, Lewis's emphasis). Despite Lyautey's efforts, however, and soon after he was removed from power by the "Paris politicians," the city was opened to foreign interests other than the French, and a civilian government was established.

The only significant result of this move, according to Lewis, was that the civilian government was much less efficient than the military leaders in running the city and that everyone cursed the day when the military had ceased to administer it" (104).

The opening of Agadir gave license to the numerous foreign speculators who had built up connections in the region surrounding Agadir over the years and who were waiting for the French to leave the city. Lewis mentions, for example, the Mannesmann brothers, German industrialists who had entered into various agreements with the local caids in the region since before the First World War. When the French ceded control of Agadir and after the Germans left, many British bought up the rights to the city that the Germans had formerly possessed. The various foreign groups, who subsequently installed themselves on the land, were compelled to interact through a series of "capitulations," by which each foreign government asserted its own rights on the city without establishing a rule of law that took into consideration the native population. The result of these capitulations, according to Lewis, was a kind of lawlessness that destabilized the entire region. This history fostered the rise of the kind of filibuster for whom Lewis reserves his most concentrated satire.

Lewis understands what he see before him only insofar as what he sees has been shaped by history, by western intercession in particular; which is ironically just the kind of historical mindedness that he disparaged in everyone from Spengler to Whitehead to Joyce and other followers of the "time school." Lewis had attempted to rectify this kind of "historical mindedness" by shining the light of his satire on certain representative figures (Stein, the Sitwell's, Joyce, Alexander) who, while claiming to be individuals, were in fact unwitting contributors to the debased *Zeitgeist*. This was perhaps his intent when setting out, as we see in the ludicrously satirical "leave-taking" and as Lewis's satire had always formed itself tightly to the body of the text that he was satirizing. But as *Filibusters* goes on and Lewis moves through this space, the satire takes an almost secondary role, being deployed mainly for the isolated portraits of those individuals who could have been characters in one of his automata fictions; or rather, these portraits compete with the large scale sociological essays or cultural critiques of the cities and regions. The former, the individual portraits, seems to be what he means by the "picturesque ridicule" that he boasted of in his letter to his publisher quoted above. It is this focus on the individual where we see the remnants, the vestiges of his satiric enterprise, and it is here as well where we can perhaps see a momentary failure of satire itself as Lewis moves from the local satiric portrait of the individual to the exalted view of the mountain tops and the postal fliers. Lewis has stopped moving about among the people, the apes, the filibusters, and abstracted himself to a more exalted view. Such movement signals not the failure of the travel genre or the modernist concern with history and representation (though this representation is clearly lacking in important ways) but it does perhaps signal the failure of Lewis's brand of satire as a way of facing the growing problems of late modernism.

While in Agadir, Lewis visits one of the British filibusters who, he claims, had bought up land in the region from one of the local lords or caids. This filibuster, or "British Bulldog," as Lewis refers to him, is never named, although Lewis is fairly specific about certain details regarding the man. He lived, for instance, "outside Agadir in a smug white 'Arab' house he [had] built for himself" (107). He is, according to Lewis, a distinct British type: "the good, solid, pink, fetch-and-carry order of faithful dog-Toby of a man" (107). For Lewis it was these types, this class of Briton who, by engaging in the illegal purchase of land and by exploiting the lack of order in the region, were immobilizing "the march of progress upon the sea-front" (107).

As we saw when Lewis described the wife of the colonial official aboard the packet to Oran, Lewis again condemns a type by way of description of an individual, as his satire ranges between personal slander and a kind of sociological critique. In the description of his meeting with the British filibuster, Lewis himself is the detached, innocent observer who remains completely objective in a manner reminiscent of the opening pages when he described his departure from England. In this scene, Lewis remains for the most part silent, playing the role of the detached observer. The "British Bulldog," however, is on guard and defensive: "Me he regarded immediately with hostility and suspicion to my very great surprise" (107). Lewis asks some innocuous questions about wanting to travel into the area of the Ikounka, outside of Agadir, to which the man reacts defensively, discouraging Lewis from traveling any further, and suggesting that the French had established a security zone around the area that only he could penetrate. Lewis is skeptical of the "British Bulldog's" characterization of the French security zone, seeing it as an unnecessary mystification of the few remnants of French rule. The British filibuster says to Lewis that traveling into the French zone is risky and that "you have to have *guts*" (108), a statement that Lewis takes as self-aggrandizing. Lewis, instead of responding to these claims, resorts to his satirist's eye, as he looks the man over in a detached though derisive manner:

> I cast my eyes down, and stopped them upon his waist-line, and saw that he had guts; but he looked very fierce and chewed his pipe in true bulldog fashion, and I wondered what order of risks these were, that this prosperous

unofficial British Beadle and perfect picture of a Special Constable who
had taken the wrong turning, might conceivably run: instinctively I knew
that it must be one of those bogus-risks and cheaply earned thrills, so dear
to the romantic soul of that particular fresh-coloured off-shoot of some
well-policed Tooting Bec[.] (108)

Lewis's accusations here are purely speculative, and while his eye runs over
the man's ample belly, his insinuations run to the whole class of filibuster that
he has been describing throughout. As it turns out, Lewis visits the French
authorities the next day and is immediately granted permission to travel:
"The Colonel made no difficulty at all about giving me permission to visit
the Ikounka" (109). Thus for Lewis, the result of the "opening of Agadir"
to people such as this "British Bulldog" counterintuitively had the effect of
keeping the region even more closed than it had been, due to the personal
intrigues and the general lawlessness.

Superior Altitudes

Lewis does manage to travel into the territory of the Ikounka as the question
of stability once again asserts itself. His account of his journey to Morocco
ends with him approaching the edge of the Rio de Oro, a region that is a
vast desert, "an enormous nothingness" (170). The only outsiders who have
managed to circulate within this region regularly are the pilots of the French
aero-postal service. After having traveled from the "expiring octopus" that
was "over-moist" England, through the numerous cities of Northern Africa
that were in various states of stability, Lewis is suddenly faced with a land
that, metaphorically, is so unstable as to be ephemeral, through which the
only way to travel is by air: "For the first time in the Earth's history we have to
take into count a new territory—namely the upper atmosphere" (170). At the
beginning of his journey, Lewis had expressed an interest in going to the top
of the Atlas mountains and looking down on interwar Europe from an exalted
perspective, but here he finds that there is an even higher, more detached
view than that:

But now, higher even than the mountains, we have to take into our
conspectus that new, very solitary, not by any means numerous, people,
who for all practical purposes live in those superior altitudes. So, when we
are speaking of the nomads of the Rio de Oro, the fact that there are *other*
nomads higher up cannot be ignored. (170)

Ironically, in this case, Lewis appears to admire the Romantic nomads of the sky who "have lived amongst clouds and storms" (171). Whereas, for the most part, Lewis decries the fake Romantic views of the "exoticists," preferring, for example, the "noble dignity" of the Berbers to the "globe-trotting buccaneers," here he sees these pilots as heroic figures, pioneers, who possess a nobility of their own. It was perhaps for their exalted perspective as much as any Romantic trappings for which Lewis admired these pilots. But we again see the strain in Lewis's "argument" here, an argument that has been largely against the filibuster and the exoticist, figures who have their analogues in interwar London art circles in the pseudo artists and art racketeers. While in Morocco Lewis finds himself swayed by a certain kind of authenticity that is often hard to distinguish from the very fakes that he is castigating. Unlike *The Apes of God*, which catalogued and taxonomized all the ills of the art world that he had seen and experienced, *Filibusters in Barbary* moves uneasily back and forth between the travel genre, a genre born of the physical circulation within a place, and an abstracted historical-minded-assessment. We see this especially in the final image of the book.

Lewis draws especially on the work of Antoine de Saint-Exupéry for his description of the pilots, whose book *Vol de Nuit* describes the life of these Romantic figures. He ends his description of the Rio de Oro with an image of absolute instability and yet one that has a dreamlike quality of detached nobility and exalted agency. Basing his description on Saint-Exupéry's account, Lewis describes this odd "landscape":

> On occasion *the desert itself* levitates, It rises bodily into the air for thousands of feet—what is its maximum I do not know—and provides an almost solid surface, far above the inferior plain, as though to afford an absurdly physical basis for this mere metaphor of mine. It is the *Sand-Wind*—that is what this agency is called. (173)

Lewis continues in *Filibusters in Barbary* to examine the character of the filibuster in general and other "nomadic Berbers" who travel throughout this region, but this image of the pilots flying through the Sand-Wind "without any point of reference, in an abstract world of fluid sand" (175) is for Lewis an important climax to his "satiric project." He posits this most otherworldly phenomenon of a floating desert as a satiric and imaginative remedy for interwar society. It is an unattainable, unreal space, one that does not admit the fake filibusters and those who would exploit the land. At the same time, it is as if space itself had achieved agency, exercising a kind of revenge on all but the most intrepid of travelers. It is also a space that has no history, and thus for Lewis is free from the complications of historical perspective and representation, as Lewis in this final moment cedes the picturesque for the almost purely speculative. The landscape of the country through which he traveled gives way to that most blank of slates, the sky.

THE CONSEQUENCES OF SATIRE

Travel was important for Lewis throughout his career because he felt it gave his own perspective on the arts and his criticism of the West more substance by providing him firsthand with alternate models of society and alternate traditions of art. He also hoped that by escaping the claustrophobic environment of the London literary scene he would be able to better focus his imaginative work. In 1930, he had promised two further installments of *The Childermass* to his publishers Chatto and Windus. While in Agadir, he wrote to them about his progress: "The country is most remarkable and the desert-cities, humped antelopes, Berber brothels etc. abound in suggestions of a sort favourable to the production of the major book."[27] As with his early travels to Brittany where Lewis went after his studies in order to live the life of the authentic artist, traveling to "Barbary" in the early thirties was a form of both escape and rejuvenation; however, as in Brittany, Lewis finds that in Morocco such escape is impossible, as the Western world and its habits had spread even to these remote locales. As the letter to his publisher makes clear, the travel genre was for Lewis a subsidiary one, one that he worked in only while the "major work" was fermenting. Travel was only important insofar as it provided him with the materials for his imaginative work. Nevertheless, as we have seen in *Filibusters in Barbary*, the descriptions and portraits that emerge are, as West pointed out, among his most engaging, and it was this fidelity to the visual that also shaped Lewis's notion of satire.

For Lewis, satire was closely tied to the real. It was both what he saw and a way of seeing. In the 1934 letter to his publisher quoted above, where he described *Filibusters* as an antiseptic mission and a "satiric enterprise," Lewis insists that there is a high seriousness to his project that is more than mere horseplay. This satire was at times too close to the truth. Lewis began *Filibusters* by casting himself in the role of the weary intellectual. Not too far below the surface of this self-portrait were the personal and legal difficulties that had arisen as the result of *The Apes of God*, difficulties that Lewis had brought on himself, despite the fact that he casts himself in the role of victim in the opening pages of the book. While the controversy that surrounded *The Apes of God* did not extend to legal action being taken by the objects of Lewis's at times cruel satire—objects who were clearly recognizable—there did ensue a flurry of bitter exchanges in the press that resulted in Lewis's decision to publish a pamphlet defending his book and further detailing what he meant by satire.[28] It is almost as if Lewis really did not understand that his "antiseptic" satire, so close, he claimed, to the natural sciences, had any effect on the real people that he attacked. In December of 1933, however, after *Filibusters* had already been published, one Major Thomas Girdwood Macfie came forward, having recognized himself in Lewis's portrait of the British Bulldog of Agadir. Macfie "complained through his attorneys that *Filibusters* contained 'false and malicious matter of the most serious character [about Macfie]'" (Morrow, 67). The letter cited passages from "The Filibuster of Tooting Bec." According to Bernard Lafourcade and Bradford Morrow, Macfie claimed that he "was libeled by passages in *Filibusters* 'which are capable of being understood to refer to [Macfie] . . . [accusing him] of defying the French Authorities [in Morocco] and . . . engaging in contraband traffic and smuggling of arms'" (Morrow, 67). Despite Lewis's protestations that he had not "intentionally referred to Macfie anywhere in the text of the book," his publisher, Grayson and Grayson, took the British edition of *Filibusters in Barbary* off the shelves and paid Macfie compensatory fees.[29] It is with some irony that the person whom Lewis had accused of evading all French and British law while in Agadir exercised his legal rights by bringing charges against Lewis for libel.

Through an oversight on the part of the lawyers representing Macfie, the initial notice of the claim against Lewis was sent to the address of "D.B. Wyndham Lewis," a mistake that was corrected by the time the final action was brought. The final letter from Macfie's attorneys Soames, Edwards & Jones, which quoted the libelous passages from *Filibusters*, was eventually sent to the correct address and reached the correct person, although, as Paul O'Keefe points out, it still bore the name "D.B. Wyndham Lewis."

REBECCA WEST'S
BLACK LAMB AND GREY FALCON
The Quality of Visibility in Yugoslavia

Methinks with all this loss I were content,

If the mad Past, on which my foot is based,

Were firm, or might be blotted: but the whole

Of life is mixed: the mocking Past will stay:

And if I drink oblivion of a day,

So shorten I the stature of my soul.

—George Meredith, "Modern Love" XII

A YEAR AFTER HIS TRIP TO MOROCCO AND BEFORE THE LEGAL wrangle that arose over his portrayal of Major T. G. Macfie in *Filibusters in Barbary*, Wyndham Lewis exhibited a series of comparatively naturalistic portrait drawings of notable contemporaries that were later published as a portfolio entitled *Thirty Personalities and a Self-Portrait*.[1] The sitters included, among others: the Roman-Catholic writer G. K. Chesterton; the editor of *Time and Tide*, Margaret Haig Viscountess Rhondda; the artist Augustus John; and the famous British aviator Augustus Henry Orlebar, this last being a further testimony to the admiration for pilots that Lewis had expressed toward the end of *Filibusters*. After the cool reception of *The Apes of God* in 1930 and the appearance of Lewis's book on Hitler in 1931, it is perhaps worth noting that there were still thirty personalities willing to subject themselves to the eye of the "Enemy," the self-styled "Luther of Ossington Street."[2] The exhibition, held in October of 1932 at the Lefevre

Fig. 4. Drawing of Rebecca West, by Wyndham Lewis (1932),
pencil. Courtesy, The National Portrait Gallery, London.

Galleries in London, though, was a critical success, reestablishing Lewis's
career as a visual artist at a time when his literary reputation was undergoing,
in Hugh Kenner's words, the "occultation from which it has never recovered."[3]

One of the finest of these portraits is a 13" x 10" chalk drawing of Rebecca
West, rendered in a naturalistic but stylized manner (see figure 4). West's
slightly turned head, disheveled hair, and averted glance convey a weary
composure. Her hand, pivoting from the cylinder of her forearm, is partly
supporting her head and partly caressing both her throat and the base of her
neck. The scalloped collar of her dress and the fringe of her sleeve are semi-
circles echoing the more natural disarray of the curls of her hair. Unlike the

mask-like renderings of Chesterton, Desmond Harmsworth, or Augustus John, or that of Orlebar, whose pilot uniform and goggles resemble the carapace of an insect, Lewis portrays West in the act of contemplation with a minimum of accoutrement. With the exception of the smudge that makes up her ear, details are rendered with breathtaking accuracy, from West's firmly set jaw and broken brow line, to the wedding ring visible on her left hand from her marriage the previous November to Henry Andrews, an English banker. The inclusion of the ring is perhaps Lewis's silent acknowledgment that West was now, like Evadne Silverton in the story that West had contributed to *Blast* many years before, indissolubly married. The drawing strikes a harmonious balance between fidelity to nature and the geometric pull of Vorticism, between the demands of structure and the strange necessity of design. West greatly admired Lewis's drawing and owned it until her death in 1983, at which point it was moved to the National Portrait Gallery in London, where it is currently housed.

I begin with this view of West through the eyes of Lewis in part because it was West's complicated portrayal of "the Enemy" that began my chapter on Lewis, but also because the mixture of unease and confidence that he captures in West's pose speaks to the way that we have come to see Rebecca West as uneasily poised in the modern world. Despite their importance to understanding modernism in particular and the literature of the first half of the twentieth century in general, neither Lewis nor West has traditionally been afforded the central place in modernism proper given to such figures as Pound, Joyce, Woolf, Eliot, or Lawrence. This is partly because although they were at the center of the creative swirl that characterized literary modernism at its most experimental, neither writer fits neatly into early definitions of modernism that put a premium on aesthetic integrity and wholeness, their respective bodies of work being too diverse in scope and genre. If Lewis was, as Yeats referred to him, an "entangled Absalom,"[4] a wayward son of the modern world whose lack of prodigality was his doom, then West was a Cassandra whose vatic warnings of the impending war were rarely heeded by her contemporaries as she became increasingly involved in Balkan politics and history. Frozen in Lewis's portrait at a moment between the wars and prior to her travels, West seems preoccupied by the difficulties of rendering the past and speculating on the future.

Like the prose of *Filibusters in Barbary*, Lewis's portraits are more consistently representational than anything Lewis had done previously, but also like *Filibusters* they were not solely naturalistic. In the introduction to the catalogue for the exhibit, Lewis wrote rather defensively about the style of the drawings:

Coming from the workshop of an extreme experimentalist, they may at first be regarded rather as a demonstration of traditional draughtsmanship. They are not that. I have always practiced side by side the arts of experiment and the arts of tradition. To an artist there seems no contradiction in this—it only seems contradictory to the outsider, or the person imperfectly acquainted with the aims of the artist.[5]

The relationship between tradition and experimentation, whether the complementary one of Lewis's view here or the agonistic one of T. S. Eliot's "tradition and the individual talent," is a hallmark of modernist writers as they attempted to find a language with which to represent the modern world, especially the tumultuous period between the wars.[6] We have seen this with E. E. Cummings as he structured his personal account of the First World War in *The Enormous Room* on John Bunyan's *Pilgrim's Progress* and his travels to the Soviet Union in 1931 on Dante's *Divine Comedy*. Rebecca West certainly understood these seemingly contradictory, simultaneous impulses as she attempted to render what was before her eyes during her several trips to Yugoslavia in the nineteen thirties, an effort that culminated in her lengthy travel book *Black Lamb and Grey Falcon*. Armed with a host of historical studies, travel accounts, and a guide provided by the Yugoslavian government, and traveling at the encouragement of the British Council, West's lecture tour did not seem to offer much opportunity for literary experimentation. However, by employing strategies that she had utilized throughout her career, both in her novels and in her essays, West manages to create a work unique in its ability to harness tradition and experimentation for the purpose of recording the history and culture of a country about which many in England had little knowledge, while at the same time making manifest the crisis facing the West of the prospect of another war.

Lewis's point about the intertwined but not always discernible relationship between tradition and experimentation can help us better understand West's complex narrative, as can the relationship between Lewis and West in general. West praised Lewis for more than his skills as a visual artist, claiming late in life that he was "a writer of the greatest importance."[7] Having known each other since before the First World War at South Lodge, the home of Ford Madox Hueffer and Violet Hunt, the two met only infrequently over the years, so it is difficult to talk of mutual influence; nevertheless, their interests in the cultural and political well-being of the modern world in the wake of the Great War kept them attuned to one another's work. West favorably reviewed many of Lewis's books in addition to *Filibusters in Barbary*, most famously his 1918 novel Tarr, where she compared Lewis to Dostoevsky.[8] She also thought highly of *The Childermass*, Lewis's 1928 novel in which the slaughtered men of World War I gather outside the gates of heaven to await their final judgment. In a review of Lewis's 1930 *Paleface*, his attack on D. H. Lawrence and Sherwood Anderson and on the glorification of the primitive in contemporary art—a review in which she is mostly critical of Lewis—West praised the diagnostic function of the book and Lewis's polemic in general and regrets that his brand of cultural criticism had not been more influential: "There is no one who has had a greater acumen in detecting the trends of contemporary thought that are not candid, that are merely rationalizations of a desire to flee towards death. There is no one whose dialectic style is more sparkling."[9] Throughout *Black Lamb and Grey Falcon*, this language resurfaces as West repeatedly castigates British intellectuals for "fleeing towards death" by remaining pacifist in the face of Hitler's increasingly imperialistic policies and the growing threat of Nazi Germany.

It is her praise of Lewis's "dialectic style," however, that is most revealing of West's procedures in *Black Lamb and Grey Falcon*, a work in which she attempts to elucidate the "not candid" thoughts of her British—and to a lesser degree American—contemporaries. That West singles out this aspect of Lewis's thought before embarking on the journey that would lead to what is by most accounts her major work is important to recognize because it is difficult to see West entertaining opposing arguments in her book. Both West's narrative voice, which is at times as unyieldingly polemical as Lewis's, and the conditions under which she traveled seem to belie my argument that in her travel book West remains open to the opposing arguments of history, to the contradictory messages of political reality, and to the polysemous nature of cultural artifacts. But it is precisely this dialectic movement that she identified in Lewis's style and polemic that shapes West's own narrative style. We have seen various ways in which aspects of modernist style have been employed by writers who were facing a transformed and transforming world. We saw it with Pound, whose understanding of the role of obscurity in his verse was behind his modernist preoccupation with difficulty and allusion, prompted as it was by a very real partition. We saw it with Cummings, for whom travel was a means to explore and reconfigure the relationship between subjectivity and objectivity and for whom style was a defense mechanism against a political reality that he loathed as an artist and as an individual. And we saw it in the way that Lewis relied on the picturesque scenes that he confronted on his travels in order to structure his modernist satire. West's modernist style can be seen in this dialectic, which is revealed through her use of symbol and myth and in the reliance on certain images that emerge from what she sees and that present themselves as "dramatic renderings." These visual images or renderings allow West to rethink the role and purpose of history in all its complexity as she travels through the Balkans.[10]

POTENT SYMBOLS AND DRAMATIC RENDERINGS

In this chapter, I examine West's gradual reception into the canons of modernist and late modernist literature and I examine the wider reception of *Black Lamb and Grey Falcon* in political and diplomatic circles. This latter reception and the way that the book was variously read in these circles—even entering into the wider political discourse of the 1990s—I offer as evidence of the book's affiliations with late modernism, where the representation of historical particularity and political thought is one of the chief features. I discuss the ways that West's political thesis draws as well on earlier modernist precepts. In particular, I focus on an early travel story, "Trees of Gold," in order to show the way that the potent symbol that she employs in *Black Lamb and Grey Falcon* had its roots in the social interests and literary techniques of a writer familiar with modernist tropes. I examine *Black Lamb and Grey Falcon* for the ways in which West probes the quality of visibility in her quest for comprehension through another set of symbols or scenes that she confronts on her travels—the assassination of King Alexander, the iconostasis, the Sheep's Field, the plain of Kossovo—but which become for her a way to read the modern world as she struggles to convey her findings to an audience back home. How she witnesses or otherwise "sees" these scenes and objects and places; how she transforms them into the powerful symbols that comprise the argument of her larger political thesis is the main purpose of this chapter. In making this argument, I want to recall again François Hartog's view of the importance of the travel account as a means of highlighting the question, not "*what* have I seen? but *what is it* that I have seen?"—a question appropriate not only to the travel genre but to historiography as well, a question that demands a certain abstracting from experience to the potent symbol, a movement from impression to intellection.[11]

History was important to West primarily because of the way it intruded on the present moment. She wrote *Black Lamb and Grey Falcon* on the eve of the Second World War and saw her book as a call to arms, a manifesto against what she considered the falsity of disengagement as was being preached and practiced by the intellectuals of England who in 1935 signed the Peace Pledge Union.[12] England's appeasement of Hitler in the face of the manifest horror of the Nazi regime was to West a form of madness akin to suicide. Her position evolved gradually as she saw firsthand the effects of imperialism on the peoples of Yugoslavia, although to some degree West's position had been developing prior to her travels. A year before going to the Balkans for the first time, West had traveled to Finland on a series of lecture tours sponsored and arranged by the British Council, the cultural arm of the British Foreign Office. West agreed to go to Finland because it seemed to her "a beautiful example of a small nation threatened by the great powers."[13] Soon after traveling to Yugoslavia, however, West felt that she had found "a more picturesque and convenient example of the political thesis I wanted to expound" (148). Like the "picturesque ridicule" that Lewis calls down on the French colonial set in *Filibusters in Barbary*, West relies on this picturesque quality to help expound her thesis.

West's "political thesis" developed throughout the course of *Black Lamb and Grey Falcon* to encompass two main ideas: first, that it was necessary for England to resist the imperialistic expansion of Nazi Germany, the possibility of which was demonstrated by Serbia's continued resistance to the Turks and the Austrians throughout history; and second, that it was necessary to resist the corresponding inner desire to "flee towards death," a desire, West felt, possessed by many intellectuals in her day, but which she also discovered in the course of writing her book, at times possessed her. The narrative of *Black Lamb and Grey Falcon*, while ostensibly dictated by what West saw on her journey, is subterraneously dictated by this twofold controlling thesis, an apparently paradoxical situation for a travel narrative, a genre usually more inductive and exploratory in its methods. However, it is this paradox that makes West's travel book such an important contribution to the modernist literature written between the wars, a time when writers were faced with the very real problems of how to "include history" in their works and how to address the complex political reality of the day.[14]

As West's work grew in length and detail words continued to prove insufficient for convincing West of the verity of what she had seen before and what she sees again, and these symbols become more and more important. While in Dalmatia, early on her trip, West makes her most explicit statement regarding the relationship between ideas and sensory impressions and between secondhand accounts and firsthand sight. Having stopped over in the port of Korchula on the Dalmatian coast, West is reading a guidebook on the region. She complains to her husband about the inaccuracies in the book and suspects that the author "could have seen no scenery at all" (200). In response, her husband urges her away from the book: "There is no need for you to keep your eyes down on any guide-book, you might just as well be looking at the islands" (200). Looking up from the book and toward the town, West sees a young girl who "had wholly lost the will to live" being carried by a crowd on a stretcher

(201). Immediately thereafter, also in the town square as if in response, she sees an old woman, withered by age and by illness, being borne triumphantly on a chair toward a ship in the harbor. West takes these two public displays as emblematic of life in the Balkans, as a kind of *tableaux vivant*. These scenes enacted a struggle, in West's view, in the ongoing argument for life against death and provided a picturesque example of the process of life. For West, it was this process of abstraction that was of utmost importance: "Here in Yugoslavia I did not have to poke about among the detritus of commonplace life to find allusions to this process: an old woman and a young girl came out into the street and gave a dramatic rendering of it in the presence of the people. It is that *quality of visibility* that makes the Balkans so specially enchanting" (202, my emphasis). In eschewing one of the traditional functions of the travel book, to go "[poking] about among the detritus of life," West is likewise eschewing the notion that it is her experience as a traveler alone that gives her the authority to draw parallels between Yugoslavia and the West. Instead it is, for West, the combination of material reality and the abstracting impulse of the artist that is the unique essence of her book.

As West sees Yugoslavia again, talks with the people there, hears from her guides, reads historical accounts, and discusses all these with her husband—in other words, as "the quality of visibility" continued to impress her senses and her memory—she finds that what she sees yields not a single meaning but numerous and at times contradictory meanings. While traveling to a monastery in Sveti Naum in Macedonia, for instance, a land that West particularly cherishes, she finds that "even here truth does not grow on every bush" (748). What she admires above all in the tomb and environs of Sveti Naum is the way the monastery and the surrounding landscape demonstrate that "life, painful as it is, is not too painful for the endurance of the mind, and is indeed essentially delightful." For West, this delight is manifest throughout Sveti Naum, which "presents that argument in a series of symbols" (747). These symbols—the lakes, the rocks of the mountains, the "squat, dark, strong buildings" of the monastery—impress West's senses and demand to be read as a "picture of man's life," a picture that doesn't offer full revelation, but a limited readability. In words that are to be a refrain throughout the book, West says: "Nor is it pretended in any part of Sveti Naum that the revelation is complete, that all is now known" (748). Throughout *Black Lamb and Grey Falcon,* West ponders the conditions of visibility but repeatedly stops short of claiming, "all is now known." She does not take the limits of her ability to know, however, as an excuse for inaction; rather, she traces the complex ways in which the contested meanings of what she sees shape the political and social realities of the Yugoslavian people and, by extension, the impact that these meanings have on the British people.

Discussing Herodotus, François Hartog suggests that the Greek historian and traveler was creating in his Histories a mirror into which "[he] never ceased to peer as he pondered his own identity" (xxiii). Hartog's book provides a model for my approach to West in particular in the way he casts Herodotus as more than just a historian or just a traveler, but as embodying these roles and more. In the first lines of the *Histories*, Herodotus says that what he

> has learnt by enquiry [*historie*] is here set forth: in order that the memory of the past may not be blotted out from among men by time, and that great and marvellous things [*erga*] done by the Greeks and Barbarians and especially the reason why they warred against each other may not cease to be recounted. (qtd. in Hartog, xvii)

Like West and the other writers that I discuss in this book, Herodotus was writing between two wars—the Persian wars before his time and the Peloponnesian wars, the beginning of which he lived long enough to witness for himself. His statement here, in its anxiety to prevent the past from being blotted, for the good of an interwar community, strangely forecasts West's intentions in *Black Lamb and Grey Falcon* as well as the lines from George Meredith's "Modern Love" that I use as an epigraph to this chapter.[15] Meredith's sonnet sequence articulates the corresponding anxiety of recording the past and reading the present within the private, domestic space of a marriage, a space that also shapes the narrative of West's book. For both Herodotus and Meredith, the historian and the poet, the only recourse when recalling the past is to recount it again and again, to resist the urge to fix it forever or to blot it entirely, both tempting alternatives to living in perplexity and doubt.

Recent Critical Reception

With the appearance of Carly Rollyson's biography of West in the mid-nineties, the numerous critical studies of West's work in recent years, as well as the publication of a volume of West's letters and previously unpublished works such as *Survivors in Mexico*, a later travel book, and *The Sentinel*, an earlier novel, West studies have largely moved from a focus on recovery and recuperation to a focus on assessment and even reassessment.[16] This assessment is one of the more vital areas of West studies as her reception has been, and continues to be, an uneasy one, and her place in the literature of the twentieth century remains to some contended. Bernard Schweizer has also been instrumental in the more widespread reassessment of West's body of work, editing *Survivors in Mexico* as well as an essay collection that appraises West from a variety of critical perspectives and in a variety of contexts.

But the interest in West's writing grew somewhat slowly and haltingly before this recent renaissance, beginning in the nineteen eighties when Jane Marcus published a collection of West's early feminist and socialist writings from *The Freewoman, The New Freewoman,* and *The Clarion,* along with the early short story "Indissoluble Matrimony."[17] In these early essays and reviews, the wit and savage bite of West the social and literary critic emerges most forcefully, as does West the feminist, a West with which many feminist critics in the eighties were either unfamiliar or scornful. Marcus claims that her volume was intended in part to correct the incomplete view of West by those who were familiar only with her later work: "Many socialists remember Rebecca West only for her sharp anti-communist polemics in the 50s. It is for this reason particularly that I wanted to reprint these early essays" (89). Despite Marcus's assertions, recent studies of West have struggled to place her work within either a modernist or a feminist tradition, a doubly vexed project made more difficult by the sometimes intractable nature of West's writing, which at times seems resistant to either approach.

Much of this unease has centered on West's feminism and on *Black Lamb and Grey Falcon* in particular, as some critics feel that West's early feminist impulses were forgotten or, worse, abandoned in her sweeping account of the history and politics of the Balkans.[18] As Bonnie Kime Scott notes in *Refiguring Modernism, Black Lamb and Grey Falcon* does not readily fit into recent feminist readings, and she cites Mary Ellmann, who "found a stereotyped polarizing of male and female qualities in West's work that she considered the very opposite of radical thinking."[19] Loretta Stec, in "Female Sacrifice: Gender and Nostalgic Nationalism in Rebecca West's *Black Lamb and Grey Falcon,*" suggests that in her book, "West wished to mitigate the subjection of the woman to the man but not abolish it" and that West "participates in a nostalgic logic of gender discrimination."[20] Many critics are similarly nostalgic for the early Rebecca West, as views of her vacillate between the progressive feminist and the reactionary conservative.

Margaret Diane Stetz, for instance, in her essay, "Rebecca West and the Visual Arts," argues that West rejected the influence of both her immediate male predecessors and her male contemporaries and returned instead to a more distant tradition of male painters as a way of resolving what Sandra Gilbert and Susan Gubar elsewhere call the "female affiliation complex," whereby women writers must choose among a variety of predecessors, both male and female.[21] In Gilbert and Gubar's view, the choice of the female predecessor is precluded by Freud's Oedipal theory, which sees the choice of literary father and the rejection of literary mothers as the "ultimate normal feminine attitude" (qtd. in Gilbert and Gubar, 168). Choosing male painters rather than male writers, according to Stetz, was West's way of redressing this inferiority complex: the visual arts "sheltered [West], validated her, and invested her with an authority of her own much as a god parent would" (44). For Stetz, the visual arts allowed West to see herself in relation to the canon of English literature from the outside: "Perspective meant, for her, an angle from which to contemplate such seemingly paralyzing contradictions and oppositions as speech and silence, motion and stillness, argument and appreciation, masculine aesthetics and female aesthetics" (60). However, while showing how disinclined West was to assume the mantle of "authority" and "validity" with which male writers, such as Wells, John Galsworthy, and Arnold Bennett would have invested her, Stetz fails to acknowledge that this anxiety of authority was a common preoccupation for many modern writers.[22] In fact, West's deliberate restructuring of her intellectual debts is one of the attributes that bind her most closely to her peers, to other modernist writers such as Pound, Woolf, and Lewis.

Scott addresses West's "female affiliation complex" in another way, by arguing that we need to see West as one of the "women of 1928," a phrase anxiously attuned to Wyndham Lewis's "men of 1914," which he used to describe himself along with Ezra Pound, T. S. Eliot, and James Joyce.[23] For Scott, placing West in the company of writers such as Virginia Woolf and Djuna Barnes allows us to see West both as a modernist writer and as a writer who brings a social awareness and praxis to her work that many of her male contemporaries lacked. West figures in Scott's book as modernism's "most deliberate political thinker and its most outspoken polemicist—qualities that set her at odds with traditional, aesthetic definitions of modernism" (123). Scott's West thus looks forward to postmodernism with as much urgency as Stetz's West looks back to an alternative tradition, in both cases in order that West avoid the implications of her surroundings—the "aesthetic" taint of modernism—and of her immediate historical moment. West's relation to her contemporaries is deliberately absent from Stetz's argument just as it is deliberately foreground in Scott's. By having West look back to tradition or forward to postmodernism, however, these critics fail to account for the persistence with which West looked around her, an essential feature in any travel writer.

It is precisely in the way that West scripts her travel journey as well as the way in which she engages the political issues of her day that we can see West as an important feminist figure. Bernard Schweizer, in his introduction to *Rebecca West Today*, concludes that the strength of West's feminism lies precisely in the "ardent struggle" we see "of a new consciousness trying to overcome older, socially ingrained ideas about gender and sexuality.[24] And we can see this struggle as well in the way she rethinks the nature and rewrites the conventions of the travel journey. In her study *Thinking Fascism: Sapphic Modernism and Fascist Modernity*, Erin Carlston argues for a more complicated view of the relationship between political thought and gender during these politically and ideologically charged years. Responding in part to Reed Way Dasenbrock's claim that fascist tendencies were the exclusive domain of the male modernists, Carlston argues that the "systematic division of political tendency along gender lines is inadequate as a description of the complex effects of what Dasenbrock terms the 'fascist imagination' in writing by both men and women" (5).[25] In her study, Carlston attempts to expand the purview of modernist criticism by examining the particular historical arena in which fascism arose and the particular responses to it by certain women writers. Her intention is "to articulate descriptions of gender and gender relations in modernism that steer between the relentless sexism of masculinist versions of modernism on the one hand and an overemphasis on separate spheres on the other" (3). Although Carlston does not discuss Rebecca West in any detail, in *Black Lamb and Grey Falcon*, West, as we will see, navigates just such a perilous course between traditionally male travel experience and separate female spheres of experience. One way she does this is by invoking the figure of Ulysses at the beginning of *Black Lamb and Grey Falcon*, a move that ostensibly aligns her with many of the male modernists.

As evidence of the sweep of her narrative, West begins *Black Lamb and Grey Falcon* in a manner reminiscent of other works of high modernism—works such as Joyce's *Ulysses* and Pound's *Cantos*, whose authors were very deliberately creating modernist epics—with an invocation of Ulysses, the paradigmatic modern traveler.[26] Unlike Joyce or Pound, West does not identify with the heroic Ulysses who returns to Ithaca and restores order within his home; rather, she identifies with the numerous travelers who may never find their ways home. West's Ulysses is imaged through the French of Joachim Du Bellay's sonnet, "*Heureux qui, comme Ulysse, a fait un beau voyage*," "Happy the Ulysses who gets back home," which she quotes at the very beginning (*Black Lamb*, 1).[27] The narrator of Du Bellay's sonnet is envious of those who return to a familiar environment from a foreign clime: "The little place built by my ancestors/ Pleases me more than Roman palaces,/ And all this marble is nothing to my slate" (49). Like Du Bellay's Ulysses, West can only imagine the happiness of a traveler who completes a journey, recognizing that such closure is on some level denied to her. The nostalgia for home expressed in these lines, in West's case, is directed simultaneously toward England, where she lived at the time, and toward Yugoslavia, a country that always had figured prominently in her imagination. As she says near the end of the book about one region in particular: "Macedonia is the country I have always seen between sleeping and waking" (1088). West's nostalgia is directed toward an imaginary home, and in this nostalgia we see not the "separate sphere" of female experience but the collapsing of Ulysses and Penelope, the domestic and the foreign, as West co-opts Ulysses, the icon of male modernism for her own purposes.

West's use of the figure of Ulysses calls to mind another way in which the experiences of women have been under erasure during the period, one that has to do more directly with the issue of travel.[28] Joyce and Pound, among many other male modernist writers, use the figure and persona of Ulysses to order the disparate materials of their seemingly anarchic work. Even in *The Waste Land*, despite the fact that Eliot claimed that Tiresias "although a mere spectator . . . is yet the most important personage in the poem," it is in the guise of a wandering Ulysses that the reader, released from the moorings of narrative sense and wandering through the poem, heeds Tiresias's instructions.[29] In *Penelope Voyages*, Karen Lawrence argues that the Ulysses myth excludes women's experience in that it scripts the role of the female not as an active agent but rather as both poles of a male journey—the domestic and the foreign, Penelope and Circe, the safety of home but also the alluring enticement of the far away and exotic: "Women are generally excluded, their absence establishing the world of the journey as a realm in which man confronts the 'foreign.'"[30] Lawrence goes on to say that this "mapping of the female body underwrites not only travel literature per se, but the more general trope of the journey as well" (1). Lawrence quotes Lillian Robinson, who suggests "the Ulysses myth has . . . remain[ed] essentially external to any central female project" (qtd. in Lawrence, 17). Most travel studies, concludes Lawrence, "fail to theorize a place for woman as traveling subject" (2). To counter the predominance of Ulysses, Lawrence offers the image of a traveling Penelope, Ulysses' faithful wife and traditional embodiment of the domestic. Lawrence sets Penelope in motion, in order to explore "the way travel writing by women creates a permeable membrane between home and the foreign, domestic confinement and freedom on the road" (19). Rebecca West's invocation at the beginning of *Black Lamb and Grey Falcon* incorporates Ulysses' restless wandering and nostalgic yearning into her own narrative; however, this Ulysses is, as we shall see, a figure closer to Lawrence's Penelope than to the Ulysses of Joyce or Pound, as West struggles with the tension between home and abroad as well as with her own agency as she travels throughout the Balkans.

Initial Reception of *Black Lamb and Grey Falcon*

Black Lamb and Grey Falcon was greeted at the time of its release with high praise both for its portrayal of the complicated situation in the Balkans and as a high water mark of the travel genre. Writing in the *New York Times* to an American audience, Katherine Woods proclaims the book to be not only the "magnification and intensification of the travel book," but also its "apotheosis."[31] The transcendence that Woods alludes to in her use of the word "apotheosis" results from the intensification of the historical analysis as much as from the immediate empirical description, as "the travels are most significant for their observation of history." And yet at the same time, since this history also had such clear analogues with West's own historical moment and since the book revealed various and vested interests from different parties, West has been criticized for the naiveté with which she believed the information that was provided to her by her local guides. And in fact, throughout *Black Lamb and Grey Falcon* West tends to create straw villains out of either individuals or nationalities, as we see for instance in her portrayal of the despicable Gerda, the German wife of her Serbian guide Constantine, or in her vilification of the Turks and the Habsburgs, who are portrayed as cartoonish conquerors and inefficient administrators in what seems to be very base propaganda.[32] And in fact, these at times reductive portrayals of complex histories and groups make it difficult to determine whether *Black Lamb and Grey Falcon* is a conventional travel book sometimes burdened, as were so many literary works in the thirties, with the political freight of its time, or a work of propaganda that used the travel form to promulgate its message more effectively. In *Radicals on the Road*, Bernard Schweizer makes this very point about *Black Lamb and Grey Falcon*, noting the "questionable historical premises of her argument" as it relates to Serbian history. According to Schweizer, historians have challenged the views that West puts forward throughout the book, such as the "centrality of the Kossovo myth in Serbian history as well as the wholesale condemnation of Turkish rule" (137). In detailing some of the liberties that West takes with Serbian history in her attempt to cast a "liberationist" message onto her travel book, Schweizer highlights the ways that the "deductive thesis" of West's book threatens the inductive methods of the travel book.[33]

Subsequent early reactions to West's book were split precisely along these lines of a naïve aestheticism and an engaged politics. Praised by Clifton Fadiman, who called it "one of the great books of spiritual revolt against the twentieth century," *Black Lamb and Grey Falcon* was just as strongly criticized for being less revolt than capitulation (Rollyson, 180). Writing in *The Nation*, one reviewer, Stoyan Pribichevich, felt that "[West] had become a stooge for the government press bureau in Belgrade and had naively transmitted its propaganda for a unified and centralized Yugoslav state" (180). The substance of Pribichevich's accusation derives in part from the fact that West's guide throughout the trip, whom she calls Constantine in the book, was in real life Stanislav Vinaver, a Serbian poet and nationalist who was, at the time of West's visit, the press bureau chief for the Yugoslav government.[34]

West vehemently denied the charge that her book was intended or could be construed as propaganda. In a letter in response to the charges that the Yugoslav Press Bureau was funneling information to her, West angrily rebukes Pribichevich:

> About the political aspects of your review: please cut out that stuff about the Belgrade Press Bureau, which is an obsession among you émigrés. It had no influence on my views of Yugoslav politics. My connection with that body was formed after I had decided to write a book on Yugoslavia on roughly the same lines as I wrote it, and it was a straightforward and unimportant connection.[35]

West does not deny in the course of her letter that she traveled with a preconceived idea of what she wanted to say; she merely challenges Pribichevich's accusation that she was a mouthpiece for the Yugoslav government with whose views she clearly sympathized. She goes on to recount in this letter her original intention of writing about Finland and gives some clues as to the formation of her political thought:

> I went with some experience of Nazi Germany and Fascist Italy and a supreme loathing of both, and a great distaste for Austria. . . . I had also thirty years of experience as a journalist behind me, and this had given me something quite other than the naiveté that you have so naively ascribed to me. . . .
>
> I went back to London and worked on Yugoslavia, and found out a great deal about the country and the part it played in the dream of other countries. I may tell you that while your friends were chattering about the Belgrade Press Bureau there were forces at work against them which were much more deserving of their attention. . . . There were in Belgrade a number of people who posed as sympathisers with the enemies of the regime and spread over Europe stories against the regime—but not because they were friends of liberty. Their aim was to discredit Yugoslavia and make it seem an uncivilised country, which deserved to be partitioned between Italy, Hungary, and Nazified Austria. It was partly to defend your country against this propaganda that I wrote my book. (189–91)

West here casts *Black Lamb and Grey Falcon* not as a work of propaganda but more as a kind of counter-propaganda, as a book that by means of a detailed inventory of local customs and historical records gives a more accurate portrait of the region than was currently available in the West, despite the prominence of discussions on Yugoslavia in the newspapers.

Although compelled by a thesis that to some degree circumscribed her ability to see things freshly and judge historical and political reality objectively, and guided by people who were heavily invested in her interpretation of what she saw, West's narrative is not simply a monologic tract that espouses a single ideology or promulgates propaganda; rather, *Black Lamb and Grey Falcon* is, as we shall see, propelled by the refusal of the seen to always comport with the known, and it reveals in its fissures a deeper engagement with the ideas that had led West to travel in the first place.

West traveled to a country deeply imbued with the issues of modernity and not free from the taint of war in order to refine her argument about the need to resist imperialism, a thesis she was not alone in adopting during these years. Yugoslavia, for her, in addition to being at the geographical heart of Europe was also at the heart of the modern world. At the beginning of *Black Lamb and Grey Falcon*, West writes:

> I had to admit that I quite simply and flatly knew nothing at all about the south-eastern corner of Europe; and since there proceeds steadily from that place a stream of events which are a source of danger to me, which indeed for four years threatened my safety and during that time deprived me for ever of many benefits, that is to say I know nothing of my own destiny. (21)

Whereas in her letter to Pribichevich, West unambiguously states that she traveled with a preconceived idea in mind, here she suggests, in a moment that links public awareness and private knowledge, that her journey was primarily inductive. In writing *Black Lamb and Grey Falcon*, which she at one point confesses seemed "at times an unendurably horrible book to have to write," West stresses the dynamic interconnectedness of events as well as their internal tensions and contradictions (1126). She refines her ideas through a process that precludes either the priority of the eye or the mind, of either the concrete or the abstract, of either the deductive or the inductive. Although expounding a thesis that emerged from a particular political context, West's exposition became increasingly unwieldy as her narrative grew; and while she at times maintains the tone and urgency of a manifesto, especially, as we will see, in the epilogue, written as Germany invaded Yugoslavia, the length of her book she felt—with some anxiety, it should be noted—would undermine any immediately useful purpose it might serve, let alone any propagandistic purpose.

Nevertheless, the view of *Black Lamb and Grey Falcon* as a work of propaganda has persisted over the years, much to West's dismay, who saw her work as a testimony to a world that she had come to know recently but deeply through her trips there and through the numerous people she had met and the extensive reading that she had done both prior to her journey and as she prepared her manuscript. The answers to many of the questions that she asks she finds to be "too long, as long indeed, as this book, which hardly anybody will read by reason of its length" (773). How the answers to these questions and the judgments she forms have been transmitted and received over the years has been complicated both by the shifting modernist canon and by the fact that West's book has in recent years become part of the dialogue on the Balkans, as events in the former Yugoslavia once again entered the political arena.

BLACK LAMB AND GREY FALCON IN THE NINETEEN NINETIES

In sharp contrast to the hesitant and at times conflicting ways in which West has been revisited by literary critics and feminist scholars, she has been more frequently cited in recent years by journalists, diplomats, and politicians, although with just as much disagreement over how she should be read. In these instances, it is always *Black Lamb and Grey Falcon* that is referred to, as events in the countries of the former Yugoslavia were again in the public mind throughout the nineteen nineties. Since its initial publication, *Black Lamb and Grey Falcon* has frequently been returned to as a source for information on the Balkans, both as a work that records the complicated history of the region and a work that details the fractious political situation between the wars. West's presence on the scene as a traveler and the way she highlights her own difficulties when ascribing meaning to any historical event free her book from being either a straightforward work of propaganda, as has sometimes been the charge, or a simple travel narrative devoid of political or social meaning. Vesna Goldsworthy claims that *Black Lamb and Grey Falcon* "plays a major part in the move to establish a new role for travel writing in a more specialized and compartmentalized world," and an important feature of this new role is the ability to create these "dramatic renderings" and tableaux. (2).[36] But like Eliot's objective correlative and the "formula" it provided to the senses, the "formula" of West's symbols don't reduce and simplify the historical material they are meant to convey, but rather attempt to re-create their complexity for an audience that doesn't have the same experiential access to them that West did on her travels.

Most famously, the journalist Robert Kaplan claimed West as the presiding spirit of his 1993 book *Balkan Ghosts: A Journey through History*, one of the first works to draw attention to the ethnic and religious crisis of the former Yugoslavia in the early nineties.[37] Kaplan's book, written as war in Bosnia and Herzogovina was at its fiercest and as, for the first time, pictures of atrocities were appearing in the Western media, was read widely in certain circles. In part as a result of Kaplan's invocation of West, it became commonplace, almost obligatory, for political writers and journalists covering the region to return to West's book.[38]

West's influence does indeed pervade *Balkan Ghosts*. Kaplan records his debt to West at the beginning of his book: "I would rather have lost my passport and money than my heavily thumbed and annotated copy of *Black Lamb and Grey Falcon*" (8). Kaplan begins his journey in a monastery in Pec, in what he calls, following West, "Old Serbia," also known as Kossovo.[39] His description of what he sees is pervaded by West's influence, predominantly in the way he invokes the Manichaean categories of darkness and light, of which West was enamored, and her love for Dostoevsky, which she proclaims throughout her book and her career. Kaplan writes of the monastery at Pec:

> The workings of my eyes taught me the first canon of national survival: that an entire world can be created out of very little light. It took only another minute or so for the faces to emerge out of the gloom—haunted and hunger-ravaged faces from a preconscious, Serb past, evincing a spirituality and primitivism that the West knows best through the characters of Dostoyevsky. I felt as though I were inside a skull into which the collective memories of a people had been burned. (xvi)

Despite Kaplan's claim that he is relying on the "workings of his eyes," this is not empirical description so much as gripping narrative that evinces the dire situation of the victims of the extreme nationalism that pervaded and continues to pervade the region. Kaplan's primary purpose is to make this suffering manifest, and he clearly learns from West how to "reel in the thoughts, passions, and national histories of Europe and Asia, and to remake them into a coherent, morally focused tapestry" (8). Kaplan saw his book as more than mere journalism.

Balkan Ghosts had, in fact, an audience beyond the journalistic community. According to diplomat Richard Holbrooke in his 1998 book *To End a War*, in which he records the diplomatic background to the events in the former

Yugoslavia leading up to the 1995 Dayton Peace Accord, Kaplan's book had a significant influence on President Clinton and his cabinet at a moment when the administration was still framing its policy on the Balkans.[40] In Holbrooke's view, this influence was unfortunate because *Balkan Ghosts* "left most of its readers with the sense that nothing could be done by outsiders in a region so steeped in ancient hatreds" (22), thus presenting a true nightmare of history and delaying the military intervention that he felt was necessary to avoid further conflict. Holbrooke, along with others, further suggests that Kaplan's fatalistic account of the Balkans had its source in *Black Lamb and Grey Falcon*, and he calls the "Rebecca West factor" the view that the history of the region was "either too complicated (or trivial) for outsiders to master," thus "making it impossible (or pointless) for anyone outside the region to try to prevent the conflict" (22).

Kaplan has objected to the use of his book by policy makers in Washington, saying on numerous occasions that he never intended to write a political book, but simply a travel journal. In a *New York Times* editorial on June 13, 1999, published during NATO's military campaign against Serbia, Kaplan suggests that, as the result of what David Remnick elsewhere calls "President Clinton's learning curve,"[41] Washington had decided to intervene in the Balkans, and he felt that his book was again being consulted in the matter, although he gives no evidence that such was the case. In this editorial, Kaplan attempts to mitigate the impact of his book, suggesting that any negative consequences resulting from his book were due to the lack of responsibility on the part of the reader, not to the ambiguity or intention of the author. He claims that, in any case, a travel book should not be used in this way, whether it be by "a President searching for an excuse to do nothing in 1993, or for inspiration to do something in 1999." Kaplan further abstracts his argument, which is directed toward those with the "tendency to politicize every book," by suggesting that the "real questions" to be asked of a travel book are "do the characters and descriptions come alive, is the reader engaged enough to care about what happens on the next page," and "does the author's account quicken the reader's interest sufficiently to want him [sic] to read other books on the subject," concluding that "travel books are narratives, not policy guides."

In this claim, however, Kaplan seems far from Rebecca West, who from the beginning saw *Black Lamb and Grey Falcon* as explicitly bound up with issues of statecraft. As already mentioned, West traveled to the Balkans under the auspices of the British Council, which provided her with an itinerary and to whom she reported regularly. While the British Council was primarily a venue for cultural exchange, it was also a branch of the Foreign Office, and both the Council and West felt that her journey had the potential for a broader significance beyond that of cultural exchange. West was encouraged by the Serbian Press Bureau to deliver a radio talk when back in London on "The Beauties of Yugoslavia," a project that the British Council endorsed. Officials at the BBC, however, rejected the idea, seeing in it the potential for propaganda and fearing that it would set a dangerous precedent. The BBC's position provoked West's wrath. In a letter to her liaison at the British Council, Lt. Colonel Charles Bridge, West suggested that the BBC should defer to the Council in this matter since, she argued, it was not equipped to make such decisions on its own:

> It is quite impossible that the BBC should be allowed to decide whether or not it is advisable to give radio talks regarding foreign countries, for obviously, it has no machinery for judging whether it is advisable that these should be given. In these matters it must submit to the advice of such bodies as the British Council, otherwise the situation is completely anarchical.[42]

West further suggests that it would be better if the BBC were to operate under the auspices of the Civil Service.

West's position in this matter, fueled by her ire, reveals the kind of reception that she envisioned for her book, one that would take into consideration both its political and its literary merits. Of the idea of radio broadcasts in general, West wrote again to Colonel Bridge: "May I ask if there is any purpose for which the radio can be used which is more important than the improvement of our relations with foreign powers? If it is desired to keep the radioforce from propaganda, this desire, though lofty, seems unwise at this juncture in our history."[43]

Far from disavowing the notion that *Black Lamb and Grey Falcon* might have an impact on Britain's foreign policy, West felt that although what she had written might be misconstrued, it should not be ignored, either by leaders in the government or by citizens. West intended her book to be a mirror for rulers and ruled alike.

Thus, just as literary critics were returning to West as an example of a woman writer who did not shrink from political praxis, a new generation of political journalists was, somewhat counterintuitively, reclaiming West as a writer who lived up to Paul Fussell's claim about the "secret of the travel book," which was "to make essayistic points seem to emerge empirically from material data intimately experienced." Kaplan, who recalls these lines from Fussell, elaborates on the function of travel writing: "At its very best, travel writing should be a *technique* to explore history, art, and politics in the liveliest fashion possible," and he cites West's book as the "best example of this I can think of" (Kaplan, ix, my emphasis). However, as MacKay points out regarding West's "mythic method" in *Black Lamb and Grey Falcon*, West "refuses to invoke recurrence as a way to diminish the significance of present political action: purporting to be universals, the black lamb and grey falcon have pressing and particular implications" (66). Kaplan's view of West as a paragon of *techne* rather than of *praxis*, however, is as misrepresentative as the view expressed by Pribichevich earlier that West was writing propaganda.[44] The fact that *Black Lamb and Grey Falcon* contains both of these elements and that West was as comfortable with praxis as she was fluent in technique, has made it difficult to assess her book, a problem we also encounter—and that West acknowledged—when we look at her career as a whole.

West's reception in the canon of modernist literature in general and the reception of *Black Lamb and Grey Falcon* in particular show the care with which we have to negotiate the "experimental form and political impurity" (to recall Marina MacKay's distinctions from the introduction) of her travel book, reading the experimental form in the context of other modernists and reading the "political impurity" in the context of the more widespread politically engaged traveling during the thirties as described especially by Schweizer. In this way we can better assess, or re-assess, West's achievement.

Late in *Black Lamb and Grey Falcon*, as West is considering the length and complexity of her narrative, she admits that her body of work is difficult to grasp as a whole and that its parts tend to be exploratory, not conclusive:

> I had never used my writing to make a continuous disclosure of my own personality to others, but to discover for my own edification what I knew about various subjects which I found to be important to me; and that in consequence I had written a novel about London to find out why I loved it, a life of St. Augustine to find out why every phrase I read of his sounds in my ears like the sentence of my own doom and the doom of my age, and a novel about rich people to find out why they seemed to me as dangerous as wild boars and pythons, and that considerations of these might severally play a part in theses on London or St. Augustine or the rich, but could not fuse to make a picture of a writer, since the interstices were too wide. (1084)

Unlike many modern writers, West was less concerned with creating a well-wrought masterwork than a series of inquiries into the modern world. She did not feel that it was her charge to forge in the smithy of her soul the uncreated conscience of her race, nor did she feel that this conscience needed forging so much as it needed to be lured out from the dark recesses of history and memory. Her earlier works are tentative gestures in this direction, as we can see in the case of the early travel essay "Trees of Gold," where considerations of the foreign helped West put into perspective her developing social and political views. This pre–World War I travel account forecasts some of the issues and methods that West was to treat more comprehensively in *Black Lamb and Grey Falcon*. It is worth examining this account in some detail as we consider the importance of travel and the conditions of visibility for West in the years leading up to the Second World War.

WEST'S EARLY TRAVELS:
"TREES OF GOLD"

West published "Trees of Gold" in *The New Freewoman* in 1913. This brief, impressionistic travel essay is the account of her trip from England through the Pyrenees Mountains to Spain. According to West, her journey was motivated by frustration over the complacency that gripped England in the early years of the century regarding issues such as labor and women's rights, issues that West had been writing in support of for several years. Her frustration, for so long channeled through the columns of periodicals, eventually manifested itself in the impetuous gesture of travel: "When I find myself consumed by any passion (which is usually rage) I fling myself out of London into some little place."[45] Motivated by anger to leave the stagnant London environment, West at the same time concedes that her journey was prompted by a kind of escapism, an escapism that she associates with death: "That was what I really liked: dying a little death and dropping my life behind me, and giving to pleasant little plans when I could contemplate the innocent activities of the natives as a virgin martyr new to Heaven might survey the gambols of the Cherubim" (570). In this image, West acknowledges the purgative, tonic effects of travel, even as she concedes that the gesture was dictated by rage and premised on a suicidal urge. However, this self-sacrifice, instantiated in the gesture of travel, is ultimately unsatisfactory to West, and in the course of this brief essay she discovers a different value to travel.

West is driven to this gesture not only because she could no longer bear the sordidness of English life but because of the uncertainty she felt over her role in it: "If I had stayed in England any longer I should have become as satisfied as any proprietor of a slaughter-house that God's in His Heaven, all's right with the world" (570). West's rage is generated by the growing consumer culture that pervaded the modern world. She finds on her trip, however, that she is unable to leave this consumer culture entirely behind. On board the train to the Pyrenees, she encounters a German salesman who proceeds to show West his goods. West reacts politely, but inside her rage grows into fury, and she concludes that the problems of the modern world are not limited to London, rendering escape futile: "Our enemy is commerce: The frenetic distribution and exchange of ugly things made by unhappy people confuses the earth. I thanked God that I had no hand in peace and prosperity" (571). The peace enjoyed by Britain in West's mind promoted the production of "ugly things" and precipitated the complacency she felt around her in London.

Against the proliferation of consumer goods, West sets the "trees of gold" of the Castilian heights of Spain. As the train "passed out of the Pyrenean mists," West sees the beauty of the landscape, a beauty that affects her not as death but as a renewal: "I realized that I had come to something that was as important to me as my birth" (571). The beauty of the landscape assaults West's senses, though her description of it foregoes the possibility that it might be a place where she could contemplate "the innocent activities of the natives." Although this landscape is beautiful, it is not peaceful:

> The land throbbed like a bared heart, and here and there a graveyard was the symbol of the valley's desperation. There were four high walls that were not white but pallid like terrified flesh: and above them spread black cypresses, calm as nothing else in that land was calm. . . . The ravaged earth had set itself to prison death, who yet sucked to its prison all the life its passion could create. The mind could grasp that struggle, but not the war between the valley and the naked limestone mountains that marched up from the east and west as proudly as befitted the raw material, the untainted substance of the earth. (571)

West anthropomorphizes the terrain, transforming it into a riven body wracked by pain and the effects of long imprisonment, an image that she recognizes is distorted by her own perceptions and initial anger: "Rage shivered the mountain into peaks and deep distortions so beautiful that it strained this consciousness to perceive them" (572). The rage with which West flung herself out of London is here mirrored in the landscape of the Spanish countryside.

Although the landscape is imbued with her feelings of rage, West's vision of it simultaneously generates in her a "physical misery" as she becomes aware of herself not as a virgin martyr, as she had satirically fantasized at the outset of her trip, but as an intruder on this scene of violent beauty: "I was a grey and disgusting object: I felt as though I was going to die, and I knew that my corpse would be most offensive to the eye" (572). West's own physical presence is here an "ugly thing," like the product of a complacent consumer culture. This contrast, however, does not contribute to her feelings of self-sacrifice but ignites her mind and imagination as she thinks about her own role as recorder of this violent beauty: "I was shattered by excitement. . . . [B]efore I had always worshipped this violent and courageous beauty, which I had never found in people and rarely in art, without any certainty that it existed" (572). This beauty is both foreign and external to her, even as she recognizes in it some urge she has long carried within her, as her own motivation for travel becomes clearer throughout her account.

The gesture of self-sacrifice with which West began her journey is discarded as a kind of betrayal of the violent beauty she sees in Spain. The "fierce splendour" of the landscape offers a more meaningful image than the passive gesture of self-sacrifice or the paradisiacal bliss that she hoped to find in her initial fit of escapist rage. She ends this travel essay describing the rituals of an order of Cistercian nuns she sees who celebrated mass as if it were "a slow court dance." She praises their devotion to Christ because it gives them the means to "cultivate their pride" (573). To West, this community is preferable to the tragic gesture of self-immolation with which she herself began. But whereas she praises the nuns' ritual and devotion, she rejects the image of Christ, whose sacrifice she takes to be a pernicious lesson for the West. Christ chose to save the world "not by a gentle life-time spent sunnily among children and fishermen"—a scene that recalls her initial motivation for leaving England—"but by the nine hours of His passion on the cross; so he damned [the world] by accustoming it to the sight of pain" (573). West here tries to find some middle ground to her escapist fantasy, between a peaceful environment in which she watches cherubim gambol and her realization of the dangers of fruitless pain and pointless self-sacrifice. Further distancing herself from identifying with self-sacrifice, but eagerly wanting to retain the mysteries cultivated by the Cistercian nuns, West takes the "trees of gold" as an image that offers a better example of how to balance "fervent purpose" and the "ritual of rashness and cruelty." The trees of gold are not symbols of self-sacrifice but images of the cruel beauty that West finds both within herself and on her travels. Their beauty lies in a distinctive relationship between the interior and the exterior, "a lichenous growth that gnawed inwards as it glowed outwards" (573).

"Trees of Gold" highlights West's way of seeing as much as it describes what she sees. She is present on the scene variously as martyr, as a "grey and disgusting object," but above all as a traveler who records both the strangeness and the familiarity of foreign landscapes as she attempts to describe what she sees to an England that was mired in its own complacency. Unlike Pound, who further condensed his pre-war travel writing as he found the genre insufficient for recording salient features of the modern world, in *Black Lamb and Grey Falcon* West was to expand this genre and continue to focus on her role as traveler as we see her continually and exhaustively weighing the evidence of her own sight.

BLACK LAMB AND GREY FALCON:
SCREENS AND APORIA

West's narrative style in "Trees of Gold" is dense and the travel account itself compact—centered as it is around the image of the trees of gold—but *Black Lamb and Grey Falcon* is expansive, as West records not only her own motivations for traveling but a range of subjects. As the book opens, West and her husband are on board a train bound for the Balkans, although their immediate location is unclear. The lack of an identifiable point of departure for her journey contributes to the feeling of rootlessness, even as the domestic scene of husband and wife reinforces a sense of stability. West presents her trip as a homecoming to a country where, she assures her husband, "everything was comprehensible" (1). West's desire for comprehension runs parallel to her desire to express the beauty of Yugoslavia to those who haven't seen it and to clarify the complicated foreign political scene for those unfamiliar with Balkan history or current events. Torn between duty to a real homeland and the longing for an imaginary one, West's prologue juxtaposes the foreign and the domestic, the familiar and the unfamiliar, and home and abroad, in order to bring these disparate elements into focus as she considers the possibility of comprehension and the quality of the visible.

As Carl Rollyson points out, the prologue functions much like the "Overture" to Marcel Proust's *Remembrance of Things Past*, as West recedes more and more deeply into her memory before gaining her footing in the present moment (Rollyson, 177). West's personal memories are punctuated by images of public violence, as she charts in these opening pages the growth of her political consciousness. Confronted with her failure to find words to explain to her husband why she felt that in Yugoslavia "everything was comprehensible," West recalls the first time she ever said the word "Yugoslavia." This occurred, we learn, in 1934 when she was in the hospital having a tumor removed. While lying in her hospital room, West hears the news of the assassination of King Alexander Karageorgevitch of Yugoslavia and immediately feels a deep but inarticulate anxiety, even a palpable fear: "We had passed into another phase of the mystery we are enacting here on earth, and I knew that it might be agonizing" (2). This mystery demands probing and inexorably leads West to recall other historical events of similar magnitude but of varying significance as a means of comparison.

As she recalls these earlier political events—and these memories are all political—West recognizes the prevalence of violence in the world and its effects on her and those around her: "For when I came to look back on it my life had been punctuated by the slaughter of royalties, by the shouting of newsboys who have run down the street to tell me that someone has used a lethal weapon to turn over a new leaf in the book of history" (3). In comparing history to a book, West suggests that these events unfold linearly, but more importantly perhaps, she is suggesting that these events can be read again and again and interpreted as one would interpret a text. As she focuses her memory on these events, as she turns the pages of history back, she recalls not only when she first heard of these events but also by what means. She remembers, for instance, hearing indirectly of the death of Empress Elisabeth of Austria through the reactions of others: "I remember when I was five years old looking upward at my mother and her cousin, who were standing side by side and looking down at a newspaper laid on the table" (3). West's memory of this event, though vague as to certain details, was nonetheless powerful as its significance was clearly etched on the features of those around her. West recalls as well in the prologue the murder of Alexander Obrenovitch, the King of Serbia and his wife Draga, which occurred in 1903. Here again the quality of this memory is both vague and bound up with the media that transmitted it: "That murder was just a half-tone square, dimly figured with horror, at the back of my mind: a Police News poster or the front page of a tabloid, seen years ago" (11).

But when West next recalls perhaps the most important historical event of the early twentieth century, the assassination on June 28, 1914, of Archduke Franz Ferdinand of Austria in Sarajevo, an event that sparked the First World War, her memory of it is dim. Although while lying in the hospital, West is aware of the importance of the event, it signified nothing for her when it occurred. She doesn't even recall hearing about it in the media: "Of that assassination I remember nothing at all. Every detail of Elisabeth's death is clear in my mind, of the Belgrade massacre I keep a blurred image, but I cannot recall reading anything about the Sarajevo *attentat* or hearing anyone speak of it" (13–14). These recollections do not show a developing political consciousness so much as they show the deterioration of one, as both West herself and the world at large have grown immune to the violence that increasingly punctuated and ultimately came to define the modern world. West's reasons for recording this deterioration are in part to show how Britain had lost the ability by the time of Ferdinand's death not only to recognize the significance of these events, but also the ability to "see" them at all. Their visibility has been screened by their frequency and by the manner in which they were reported.

When West hears of the death of King Alexander, as she is lying in the hospital in 1934, it is again the manner in which the information reaches her that is as important as the event itself. As she is listening to the radio, she absentmindedly turns to a channel over which she hears the news of the assassination, and it fills her with a vague though palpable anxiety. She calls out to the nurse to "switch on the telephone!" so that she can speak to her husband, both for comfort and for more information. Her husband is unable to answer her questions or allay her fears because he is equally unsure as to what this event might presage. As a result, West resorts not to contemplating the event itself but the technological devices that bring the event to her—the radio and the telephone: "I lay in bed and looked at my radio fearfully, though it had nothing to say that was relevant, and later on the telephone talked to my husband" (14). These devices mock her earnest desire to learn more and ease her fear.

Rather than remaining paralyzed by her fear and uncertainty, however, West manages to get hold of the newsreel, "which had shown with extraordinary detail the actual death of the King of Yugoslavia" (14). In a private viewing room, West views the film again and again hoping to glean something from the spectacle that would tell her not who perpetrated the crime—a fact which she feels comfortable in ascertaining by means of the "rags and tags of knowledge that we all have about us" (2)—but what it might mean. She watches the film "like an old woman reading the tea-leaves in her cup" (15). The newsreel frames the scene for West and makes it uniquely visible and readable. In her description of the beginning of the clip, the familiar and the unfamiliar exist in uncanny proximity:

> First there was the Yugoslavian warship sliding into the harbor at Marseilles, which I know very well. Behind it was that vast suspension bridge which always troubles me because it reminds me that in this mechanized age I am as little able to understand my environment as any primitive woman who thinks that a waterfall is inhabited by a spirit, and indeed less so, for her opinion might from a poetical point of view be correct. I know enough to be aware that this bridge cannot have been spun by a vast steel spider out of its entrails, but no other explanation seems to me as plausible, and I have not the faintest notion of its use.

For West, the features of this mechanized age are as inscrutable as the subsequent event of violence itself, as she becomes aware not only of her ignorance of foreign events but of her ignorance regarding her immediate surroundings and familiar world.

As King Alexander disembarks and enters the view of the camera, West sees in his features, as she saw in the harbor, both familiar and unfamiliar elements. In her description of the king, however, West goes beyond the strictly visible:

> His face is sucked too close to the bone by sickness to be tranquil or even handsome. . . . But he looks like a great man, which is not to say that he is a good man or a wise man, but is to say that he has that historic quality which comes from intense concentration on an important subject. What he is thinking of is noble, to judge from the homage he pays it with his eyes, and it governs him entirely. (15)

This description is not empirical as West describes the "historical qualities" that surround Alexander like an aura. It is the King's eye, his glance, and his countenance that dominate this description, moreover, not West's eye and not even the eye of the camera. His concentration is directed on something exterior to him, and West takes this as evidence of his nobility. It becomes clear in her description of Alexander's features and in her description of the event that follows that West's vision is guided as much by her internal state as by her sensory perceptions. As we saw in "Trees of Gold" where the landscape reflected West's rage over the complacency of English life, in the scene with Alexander what West sees mirrors an inner state. When describing the progression of the royal entourage through the streets of Marseilles, she sees in Alexander's regal distractedness something of her own state of mind while she was in the hospital under anesthesia. She speculates that like her, Alexander's thoughts were of travel, and she repeats the line from Du Bellay with which she began the book, "*Heureux qui, comme Ulyssee, a fait un beau voyage,*" as a means of identifying with the King on his doomed journey.

West does not see the actual moment of Alexander's death on the film because in the heat of the scuffle, just as the event occurs, the camera operator pulls away. At the crucial moment, "the camera leaves him. It recedes. The sound-track records a change, a swelling astonishment, in the voice of the crowd" (16). West's description becomes imprecise and fragmented because the instrument recording it is imprecise and the scene chaotic. We get a series of disconnected images as the carefully framed spectacle at the beginning is reduced to its constituent parts:

> We see a man jumping on the footboard of the car, a soldier swinging a sword, a revolver in the hand of another, a straw hat lying on the ground,

> a crowd that jumps up and down, up and down, smashing something flat
> with its arms, kicking something flat with its feet, till there is seen on the
> pavement a pulp covered with garments. (16)

The camera, unable to focus or direct its gaze, pans back from the act of
violence to reveal a scene of chaos: "A view of the whole street shows people
dashed about as by a tangible wind of death" (16). This scene of violence
and chaos then deteriorates into a ludicrous pantomime, as people scatter in
panic. West describes the scene after Alexander is shot, the final moment of
the newsreel: "He is lying almost flat on his back on the seat, and he is as I
was after the anaesthetic. He does not know that anything has happened, he
is still half rooted in the pleasure of his own nostalgia" (16). What strikes her
above all in the film, and what causes her to view it repeatedly, is Alexander's
reaction to the assassination: "At each showing of the film it could be seen
more plainly that he had not been surprised by his own murder. He had not
merely known of it as a factual possibility, he had realized it imaginatively
in its full force as an event. But in this matter he seemed more intelligent
than his own intelligence" (19). West sees something uncannily familiar
in Alexander's visage, his reactions, and his gestures, but something wholly
unfamiliar in the way in which he not only stoically confronts his death, but
also imagines it as a reality. What she seems unable to determine is how such
realization is generated, whether it springs from self-sacrifice or from a sense of
the "process of life" that West finds visible throughout Yugoslavia.

West emerges from the viewing frustrated over her inability to make any
sense of this event. Like the newspaper accounts of Elisabeth's death or the
history books that recorded Franz Ferdinand's, the camera is unable to render
comprehensible the significance of the death of King Alexander. She says in
frustration, "I could not understand this event, no matter how often I saw
the picture" (17). The film of Alexander's assassination ultimately provides
West with neither the assurance of firsthand accounts ("autopsy") nor the
interpretative authority of a secondhand witness ("hearsay"). The devices of
the modern world bring West no closer to comprehension.

In the Prologue, West's impressions and recollections thus pass through
an arc of her growing awareness of the importance of distant political events,
through her repeated viewing of the nightmarish act of assassination itself
and the ludicrous pantomime ending of those on the film, to an uncanny
identification with the King of Yugoslavia. Although she identifies with
Alexander, however, his body and the manner in which he greets his death
figure as a challenge to West's own impulses, both as she is lying in the hospital
bed and then in the prologue as she is lying in her sleeping compartment in

the wagon-lit bound for Yugoslavia as the book opens. The screen on which she sees this event is an important symbol in West's narrative in that it at once renders the event visible and inscrutable. West evinces both a particular closeness to this event, demonstrated in her identification with Alexander, and an untraversable distance, as she can get no closer to the event than through repeated viewings.

This opening scene, like the scene with the madeleine in Proust's work (to recall Rollyson's apt analogy) establishes the basis for West's journey, but rather than this scene being a portal into the deep recesses of memory and experience, it is instead a kind of aporia, a realization of the inability to understand without further inquiry. And it is this lack of understanding, coupled with this intense desire to know, that sets West in motion. West travels, on one level, to bridge this distance, to bypass the screen that simultaneously renders events visible and acts as a barrier. As she continues on her journey, the symbol of the iconostasis will continue to be important to West, functioning now as a screen, now as a physical barrier, and now as a kind of frame or focal point for the "dramatic rendering" of life as well as for communal worship. For Pound, we saw the ways that the "flimsy brown" partition became the focal point for his rage against the obstructionism of the modern world and how this became the keynote in his lament for a pre-war world. For West, the screen or the iconostasis, in its many manifestations, has a much more complex role, offering West a view not of what had passed forever, but a way of understanding both the complexity of history and what was going on before her eyes as well as the way these two interacted. Although multifaceted in their function, the screen and the iconostasis become powerful symbols through which West contemplates most deeply her political thesis and prepares us for those climactic moments on the Sheep's Field and on the plain of Kossovo, which represent West's most sustained and potent tableaus.

BLESS THE PARTITION:
THE ICONOSTASIS IN BLACK LAMB AND GREY FALCON

On her journey through Yugoslavia, West visits numerous churches, mosques, monasteries, and convents that are spread all over the region. She sees a Serbian Orthodox church in Topola, and a church in Frushka Gora where "the Eastern [Byzantine] idea was still in government" (509). She sees the temple of Aesculapius in Dalmatia, with its fusion of Byzantine and Roman elements; and she sees Mosques in Herzegovina where the remnants of Turkish rule still linger. She visits with priests, nuns, patriarchs, and laity;

she participates in services, and she witnesses various rituals that are a part of the religious life of the people. Often, West takes comfort in the rites of the Orthodox mass, seeing in the highly artificial and dramatic expression an answer to her need for comprehension. One of the main features of the Orthodox Church, and one which West takes particular interest in, is the iconostasis, the screen before the altar that separates the congregation from the sanctuary.

According to the Catholic Encyclopedia, the iconostasis "is built of solid materials such as stone, metal, or wood, and it reaches often (as in Russia) to the very ceiling of the church, thus completely shutting off the altar and the sanctuary from the worshipper." [46] The iconostasis developed in the Greek Orthodox and Catholic Churches in the sixteenth and seventeenth centuries. It was not a part of the Roman altarpiece, nor was it in use in any of the Latin churches in the West. The iconostasis itself consists of a "great screen or partition" that bisects the apse. Its purpose is to separate the sanctuary, in which is kept the Eucharist, from the laity. Whereas in Western European Gothic churches the wall behind the altar, the reredos, was richly decorated, in the East, Greek Orthodox builders, taking their cue from Byzantine Churches, lavished decorations on the partition or iconostasis itself, thus making it a focal point, not a backdrop, as well as a division. According to scholars, however, "the Byzantines never envisioned the separation of the sanctuary from the nave by such a 'material' veil" (626). For West, the iconostasis is an important symbol of the conditions of visibility in Yugoslavia in that it has this dual function as a screen and as a surface on which images are painted.

This physical barrier between the devote worship of the people and the mysteries of the service is sometimes highly decorated and richly ornamented, sometimes plainly designed. Like the screen on which was projected the film that recorded the death of King Alexander in Marseilles, the iconostasis makes manifest a mystery even as it screens it from the viewer, and is thus an apt metaphor, as we will see, for West's portrayal of both empirical reality and historical truth. The iconostasis itself is static and portrays static images, but it acts as a portal through which priests pass during the service. Similarly, West's book contains the empirical descriptions of her travels, her diagnosis of Yugoslavia (as Pound might say), and it allows her to dilate on the history of the region. West sees a number of iconostases on her travels, and these serve as points on her journey as she considers the quality of visibility in Yugoslavia. The iconostasis provides us with an illuminating way of tracing West's movement through the region and her interest in the conditions of the visible.

While in Serbia, West and her company travel to Topola, a small town outside of Belgrade. There they visit an Orthodox Church, "which was full of the dark magic of the Orthodox rite" (491). They are greeted in the church by an old man who gives them a tour of the church and its grounds and then shows them the iconostasis, which "was carved with artless sculptures of holy stories seen through peasant eyes, after the fashion of the fourteenth century, although the wood was new" (491). For West, this artlessness is a sign of the peasants' piety. The old man leads them behind the partition and describes the effort that went into its creation. It was carved, he tells them, by a family of artisans who worked on it for eight years, a task undertaken, he says, to honor the Karageorgeovitch family line. The old man's pride in the craftsmanship, the national sentiment that it stirs, and his religious devotion all merge as he shows them behind the iconostasis:

> He opened the royal door in the iconostasis, that opens on the altar, and his face folded with grief. "Here once God gave us a great mercy. When our King Alexander went to Bulgaria we said mass here day and night during all the three days he was in Sofia, and although there are many Bulgarians who hate us and have evil hearts, nothing happened to him, he came back to us in safety. But, God forgive us, when he went to France we did not say mass for him at all, for we thought he was among friends." (491–92)

The simple movement beyond the iconostasis prompts the old man's grief. His praise of Alexander and the concomitant guilt he feels over failing to pray for the king as he traveled abroad is a sign to West in general of the Serbs' primitivism, in that it evinces a kind of superstitious belief in rituals and magic; but at the same time, that they would reserve space behind the iconostasis for this magic is a sign of their strength. They do not see the King's death as the result of the inevitable laws of history but as part of a larger mystery in which they take part.

West relates to the old man's transformation—his folding into grief—as she herself feels briefly the pull of the inexorable laws of history: "Again history emitted its stench, which was here particularly noisome. Nothing a wolf can do is quite so unpleasant as what can be done to a wolf in zoos and circuses, by those who are assumed not to be wolfish, to be the civilized curators of wolfdom" (492). Although the Serbs are wolfish, their curators— here, the Austrians—are more barbaric in their administration of Serbia as an uncivilized land. The iconostasis preserves for the old man not only the altar on which the ritual of the mass is enacted but also a space where the grief of a people is preserved. There is for West a certain dignity in this preservation, not unlike the dignity she saw on Alexander's face at the moment of his death.

If the altar behind the iconostasis preserves the grief of the people over the death of Alexander, the king's body, the object of this grief, is preserved elsewhere. After visiting the church, they travel a short distance to Oplenats where the physical remains of King Alexander of Yugoslavia and the whole line of Karageorgeovitches are located. Here West confronts the body whose death she had seen on the newsreel. After having pierced the iconostasis in the church, West now in a sense manages to pierce the film screen on which she watched Alexander's death. However, if part of the reason that West traveled was to find out what this event signified, she is still left in doubt after seeing Alexander's body. The mausoleum itself is adorned with mosaics that are copies of frescoes, a mimicry that West finds deceptive, "for the eye is perpetually distracted by its failure to find the conditions which the original design was framed to satisfy" (493). They proceed to the crypt where they see the interred body of Alexander. As when the old man let them behind the iconostasis to see the altar where the mysteries of the mass are enacted and where his grief unfolds, here we get the sense that by seeing the body of Alexander, West will similarly have some better understanding of the mystery that she witnessed on the screen.

Upon seeing the body, more questions are raised. They move closer toward the crypt, which is richly adorned on the inside with real frescoes that depict Serbian history and are, according to the old man, an "encyclopedia of medieval Serbian art" (493). West and her husband are both surprised by the subject matter of the frescoes. Her husband struggles to bring two conflicting views that he has of Alexander into focus:

> Here is a man whom I know only as a Balkan king with an unfortunate tendency to dictatorship. He appears to have conceived a glorious poetic idea, such as only the greatest men of the world have ever had. He recovered the ancient land of his people in the Balkan wars and tried— what was it Constantine once said?—"to graft his dynasty" on the stock of their ancient emperors so that what was dead lived again. It is quite a different idea from mere conquest. Those frescoes say to his people, "This is what you were, so this is what you are." (494)

The frescoes appeal to the history of the people whom Alexander was attempting to unite. West's husband takes such a "poetic idea" to be at odds with the view of Alexander as a dictator, although both he and West seem to accept the coexistence of this dictatorship with this artistic impulse. Her husband wonders, though, if the congregation, to whom the message of the frescoes is addressed, who worship beyond the iconostasis, are able to appreciate Alexander's "poetic idea," especially the young men they have seen, whose thoughts seem to be not of a lived history but of a present misery: "Can those toughs we have seen outside really respond to such an idea?" (494).

Whether or not the young men are able to grasp the message that Alexander, in West's husband's view, had attempted to convey, the rest of the congregation seems quite susceptible to this "poetic idea," which is at heart a nationalist idea. West and her husband see worshipers at Alexander's tomb whose devotion, though inarticulate, is not in doubt, whose gestures speak a language of devotion and duty to which West has mixed reactions:

> Half a dozen men and women were lighting fresh candles and putting them in the stand, were crossing themselves and murmuring and kneeling and bringing their roughness down to kiss the shining onyx; such passion, I have heard, is shown by Lenin's tomb. . . . In this crypt, the foundation of this immense mass of marble erected to a parricide by his descendants, the core of this countryside on which defensive resentments grew like thick forests, all was plaintive and wistful, tender and nostalgic. (495)

Although at the beginning, West described Alexander through the painful nostalgia of Du Bellay's Ulysses, here it is not Alexander's nostalgia but the nostalgia of the congregation that dominates the scene. Like the altar behind the iconostasis that evoked the grief of the old man, Alexander's crypt evokes the nostalgia of a people for a lost past. The comparison with Lenin's tomb and the "marble erected to a parricide," however, make this an ambiguous spectacle, one that is at odds with the view of the benevolent dictator who "grafted his dynasty" on the stock of "ancient emperors." Lenin was a revolutionary who eliminated the tsarist system and replaced it with something new, whereas Alexander attempted to recover for his people an ancient idea of pan-slavicism. Thus, West's comparison here reveals her own uneasiness over how to interpret the figure of Alexander. Closing the distance between the Alexander whom she saw on the screen and the interred body of the king brings West no closer to comprehension than she was before.

The next church they visit and the next iconostasis they see are in the Patriarchate at Karlovsti, a building equally rich in history and tradition, "which had been the headquarters of the Serbian Church since the great migration of Arsenius" (500). Here they not only witness an Orthodox service but they participate in it. They are not led behind the iconostasis on a tour but, more importantly, they witness its crucial role during a mass:

> The priests passed in an out of the royal door in the great iconostasis,
> which framed in gilt the richness of the holy pictures. As they came and
> went there could be seen for an instant the shining glory of the altar,
> so sacred that it must be hidden lest the people look at it so long that
> they forget its nature, as those who stare at the sun see in time not the
> source of light but a black circle. The students' voices affirmed the glory
> of the hidden altar, and declared what it is that makes the adorable, what
> loveliness is and harmony. The unfolding of the rite brought us all down
> on our knees in true prostration, with the forehead bent to the floor.
> (505)

In performing the gestures of the service along with the congregation, West
acknowledges the importance of the ceremony, even if this importance lies
simply in the voluntary adoration of a beautiful idea that is not necessarily
premised on the belief behind it. Such devotion and the spectacle of which it
is a part is for West an indication that despite the violent history of the region,
there was a space in which adoration could maneuver. "We should grudge them
nothing of our love and service," West writes, since the ritual of the mass,
the glimpsed mystery behind the screen, "inoculated man against his constant
and disgusting madness, his preference for the disagreeable over the agreeable"
(505). The iconostasis is both a vehicle and a gateway for such adoration.

At times, for West, the iconostasis is not a separate thing, but is bound up
with that which it intends to either hide or display. It is not only a medium or
a portal, but, as she sees in the next iconostasis that she visits, an important
part of the visibility that is on display throughout the Balkans. In Topola,
West saw the iconostasis and Alexander's body at separate locations: the
iconostasis in the church and the body of the king in a nearby mausoleum.
While still in Serbia, West visits Frushka Gora, a monastery and church
where an iconostasis and the body of another ruler, Tsar Lazar, are in the
same location. Tsar Lazar is the medieval Slav leader whose defeat at the
hands of the Turks at Kossovo in 1389 is the most pervasive national myth in
the region and in *Black Lamb and Grey Falcon*. He is, as well, the subject of
the poem about the grey falcon that West hears when she visits Kossovo and
that is part of the title of her book. According to the legend, as West hears it,
Lazar's troops were massed on the Field of Blackbirds in order to hold off the
advance of the Turkish army. Hopelessly outnumbered, Lazar is visited by the
prophet Elijah in the form of a grey falcon. Elijah offers the Slavs a choice:
to be victorious in battle and gain an earthly kingdom or to suffer defeat and
gain a heavenly kingdom. Lazar chooses the latter, thus memorializing the
spot on which their defeat was brought about and, in West's view, ushering
in centuries of war.

As they enter the church at Frushka Gora, West and her company see both the iconostasis and the body of Tsar Lazar before it. This juxtaposition is important to West. They see his body lying before the great screen, shrunken and withered and yet arrayed in the beautiful garb of the Orthodox Church:

> He lies in a robe of faded red and gold brocade. A dark cloth hides his head and the gap between it and his shoulders. His mummified brown hands, nearly black, are crossed above his loins, still wearing the bright rings of his rank. His dwindled feet have been thrust into modern stockings, and over them have been pulled soft medieval boots of blue silk interwoven with a gold thread. He is shrunken beyond belief; his hipbones and his shoulders raise the brocade in sharp points. (516)

Gazing on Lazar's withered body, West considers the lesson that it offers of self-sacrifice and self-destruction, that "ideal point at which the fulfillment of life must pass into the acceptance of death" (516). At this moment, West is uncertain as to which lesson she takes from Lazar's inert body. In an effort to comprehend, West reaches out and touches his emaciated body:

> I put out a finger and stroked those hard dry hands, that had been nerveless for five hundred years. It is written here that the lot of man is pitiful, since the odds are against him, and he can command the success he deserves only if an infinite number of circumstances work in his favour; and existence shows no trace of such a bias. (516)

He is an image of defeat, though for West this defeat evokes both pity and a deeper feeling of grief. The dead body of this historical figure is laid out for her in front of the screen of the iconostasis, a more powerful symbol than Alexander ever was and yet even more inscrutable. She reads his body like a book or like one of the icons that decorate the partition behind him. But even stronger than her desire to "read" the lesson his body offers is her desire to touch his body, as if only in this way could she gain the comprehension she desired. But this only reinforces the sense of defeat she feels.

If, however, she cannot gain comprehension from either reading or touching his body, she can gain some understanding of the lesson it offers from seeing Tsar Lazar in a larger context, a context in which the iconostasis plays an important role. The church at Frushka Gora is different from the Byzantine church that she visited because of the light that illuminates both the iconostasis and the body of the Tsar, uniting them in a single luminous image: "Direct light shines on the gilded iconostasis and on the multicoloured thrones, and shines back amber from the polished marble pavement. It can be so, for there is no need to manufacture magic here. That already exists inside the coffin lying before the iconostasis" (516). Although at this point West remains ambivalent about the lesson that the Tsar offers, the brightly lit iconostasis and the illuminated coffin are linked together both as an image and in their function in the service. They are at once material, as West demonstrates by touching the Tsar's body, and spiritual, as they provide ritualized approaches to the mystery of the mass. Her comprehension lies in her ability to see the preservation of the Tsar's body and the preservation of the myth that his defeat brought into being as important to the religious life of the people and to their political identity.

The location of the Tsar's body in such a prominent place in the church, before the iconostasis, is unique in the churches that West visits, but the juxtaposition of political and religious elements of the mass is not. Later in her trip, while in Macedonia, West and her company attend an Easter service in a church in Skoplje. West's description of the congregation and the service is again centered on the structure of the iconostasis:

> In this strange building, now full of a deep twilight, stood many people, waiting, holding unlit tapers in their hands. The iconostasis . . . is here a wall surmounted by a cross, a fortification defending the ever-threatened holy things; its height, made gorgeous by icons and gilt carvings, was in this dusk a shadowy richness. (635)

Here, the partition on the altar serves a more explicitly, though equally metaphorical, defensive role, as it harbors the "ever-threatened holy things." The mass itself is a spectacle that explicitly links religion, nationalism, and politics. It begins dramatically as the priest enters through the royal door of the iconostasis. The service itself lacks any tone of peace, aura of asceticism, or even solemn grief that had been a part of the other services that West attended. Instead there is a resolute, if not martial, mood to the service, a mood that runs through the congregation as the flame spreads through the candles that they hold:

> Then, suddenly, the full crash of the Easter ritual was upon us. In an instant the procession of priests came through the door in the iconostasis, there was the gentle lion roar of hymns sung by men of a faith which has never exacted celibacy from its priests nor pacifism from its congregations, and flames had run from wick to wick of the tapers in our hands. (636)

The iconostasis is the medium for the spectacle of the mass and the crowd's attention and worship are directed toward the mystery it hides and defends.

Among the congregation, West sees a peasant woman who was like one of the images on the iconostasis, "like many Byzantine Madonnas to be seen in frescoes and mosaics." The woman was protecting the flame of the candle with her hand, her head bent in devotion. For West this woman represents "the miracle of Macedonia, made visible before our eyes" (637). The totality of the mass—the iconostasis, the dramatic entrance of the priests, the devout congregation—is for West evidence of "a real spiritual process" (638), like that process that she had seen in the port of Korchula. This process is both religious and civic. It urges the population to consider their sufferings throughout history not as a sign of death but as the promise of life; it "prevented doom from becoming degradation" in the face of centuries of rule by foreign powers (639).

This civic message emerges as well in the sermon delivered by the metropolitan—a bishop ranking just below a patriarch—a sermon laced with political messages of a revivified Christian Macedonia. The combination of austere holiness and political speeches was not, according to West, unusual in this setting, although it seems to take her by surprise: "It was in fact straight Yugoslavian propaganda, and most of it could have easily been delivered from a political platform" (640). West finds the combination of secular and sacred to be shocking only to part of her: "It was only our modernity that was shocked. This was not an innovation, but a continuance of the ancient tradition of the Church" (640). Whereas the frescoes that adorned Alexander's crypt and expressed a "poetic idea" of a greater Serbia were strange to West and her husband, here the mass itself expressly links the spiritual and the political. As West ponders this mixture, her hand, still holding the taper, shakes, and she experiences a moment of panic and claustrophobia: "The Metropolitan was still speaking, it was becoming enormously hot" (643). Her panic emanates from a variety of sources, not least of which is the horror of history that she has experienced at numerous times on her trip, but which here is particularly powerful: "There came back to me the fear of fire which I had felt earlier in the service, and this was accompanied by a revulsion from the horror of history, and a dread that it might really be witless enough to repeat itself" (643).

The panic that West feels only subsides when she turns her attention again to the Macedonian woman cradling her flame. The message that this woman offers to West is one that is transmitted silently and one that she is unable to achieve from the newspapers, the police blotters, the radio, or even the Metropolitan's sermon. The woman's gestures and her body make a statement that for West is as profound as that made by Tsar Lazar's inert body, though hers is more comforting, if no easier to articulate: "There was nothing over-positive in her statement. One can shout at the top of one's voice the information that the 11.15 for Brighton leaves from platform 6, but subtler news has to be whispered, for the reason that to drag knowledge of reality over the threshold of consciousness is an exhausting task, whether it is performed by art or by experience" (644). Unlike the withered image of Tsar Lazar's body, this woman offers West hope beyond the inexorable choice between self-sacrifice and self-destruction. In the midst of the mass, before the iconostasis, this woman is the most visible symbol of all that Yugoslavia promises.

Throughout *Black Lamb and Grey Falcon*, as West visits these churches and sees the iconostases that mediate between the human and the divine, she alternately shuns and is repelled by the grim historical view that the worship of the bodies of these dead rulers, lying in the shadow of these partitions, offers. The horror of history greets her on several occasions and affects her physically. But also in the shadow of the iconostasis is the Macedonian woman who is equally capable of participating in the grief, the solemnity, the ritual, and the "magic" that take place somewhere between the hidden mystery of the altar and the daily chore of living. The mediating function of the iconostasis aids her in her worship not by protecting her from the hidden mysteries or protecting the hidden mysteries from her but by providing a forum in which they are that much more potent. For West, the iconostasis serves not just as a metaphor for history where the real is always both masked and enlivened by a screen of words and perspectives but as a site where the very process of history continues as people are drawn to it in prayer and out of ritual. This process itself is multifaceted as is the image of the iconostasis in West's accounts. In Topola, the iconostasis preserved the grief of a people; in Karlovsti, West saw the function of the iconostasis during a mass; in Frushka Gora West sees the iconostasis as part of a single luminous image that involved both the dead Tsar and the congregants; and at Skoplje West sees this holy screen as part of a "real spiritual process" that links the civic and the religious. For West, the iconostasis, like the screen on which she saw the death of Alexander, prompts the very inquiry that is itself a part of the historical process, not separate from it. As West continues on her journey, she sees other rituals in which the element of this "real spiritual process" is also foreground, although this is not always mediated by an iconostasis.

THE CRUEL VISION:
THE SHEEP'S FIELD AND THE PLAIN OF BLACKBIRDS

West begins one of her earlier chapters on Zagreb by complaining that "there is no end to political disputation in Croatia. None" (83). She begins another by lamenting, "Politics, always politics" (104); but such ongoing disputes occur, she finds, not only in the heated conversations that surround her in cafes, restaurants, and on the road, but in the very acts and gestures of worship of the people in the churches and mosques that she visits. Politics comes to manifest itself in ways that are, for West, at times difficult to recognize, at other times all too recognizable. The climax of *Black Lamb and Grey Falcon* comes as West realizes the connections between the religious rituals and the ceaseless political talk. We have seen this connection briefly in the figure of the Metropolitan in Macedonia as he burst forth from behind the iconostasis to deliver a sermon that pitched salvation as a reconstituted Slav state. Although the partition in front of the altar tempered this political argument by framing it as a religious spectacle, it was unabashedly nationalist. We see this connection between the political and the religious most clearly, however, in two scenes toward the end of *Black Lamb and Grey Falcon*, as West leaves Macedonia for Old Serbia—on the Sheep's Field outside of Skoplje and on the Plain of Blackbirds in Kossovo. In both cases, West's view of these locales is unmediated by any sort of manmade technology and thus, on some level, they are the culmination of her journey; these two scenes set the stage for West's most explicit statement on the relationship between the political aspects of her book and her artistic goals.

Schweizer sees in the lessons that West takes from the historical lesson of Serbia's defeat, as chronicled especially in the poem of the grey falcon, evidence of a "strain" of the "logical coherence" of *Black Lamb and Grey Falcon*, as West elicits contradictory messages from these aesthetic portrayals. He shows how West sees in the legend embroidered on a tapestry above the body of Tsar Lazar traces of a "liberationist tradition" in Serbian history, and yet she sees soon after that in the imagery of the poem of the grey falcon, evidence of a strain of defeatism that was symptomatic of the Serbian people and the cause of their long bitterness. Although Schweizer goes on to show the historical inaccuracies and misreadings that shroud West's interpretations, it is important to recognize these fissures in West's text as moments where West's historiographic method is, despite the vehemence of her polemic, open to such contradictions. If these contradictions don't get resolved, we do see, as Schweizer goes on to say, the gradual way in which West "eventually reverted to her earlier interpretation of Serb martyrdom as a form of resistance rather than defeat" (138–39). West's experiences on the Sheep's Field and on the plain of Kossovo offer two divergent emblems or tableaus, which allow West to further dilate on what she has seen and on the political thesis that she has brought with her. Again, how these events are manifest to West as she travels and desires to see for herself the conditions in Yugoslavia is centered around the question of visibility, here construed largely both as the condition of physical sight and as a means of understanding. We see West reacting variously to what she sees, and in this multifaceted reaction to the empirical we can see her arguments about the west emerging. Like she did in "Trees of Gold," West takes the landscape both as a visual reality and as a symbol. As her language becomes more polemical, West's vocabulary becomes more and more centered on whether the scene before her is visible or on how this lack of visibility is indicative of a larger poverty of meaning and a dearth of comprehension. At moments West uses language that makes it seem like all around her is lacking in visibility even as she winds her way through some of the most lush and vivid landscapes that she has encountered. This rhetorical turn is the most important way in which West uses the visual as metaphor, as we see in her pondering of the "conditions of visibility," which at the same time becomes an explicit and simultaneous pondering of the conditions of history.

On the Sheep's Field, West witnesses a religious rite, vivid in its brutality, which is very different from the service that she had seen in Skoplje. Soon after West and her party leave Skoplje, her Serbian guide Constantine takes them to a field outside of town that is for West strikingly visible, both in the landscape and what she sees when they arrive. As they approach, West sees "a new kind of landscape," one with rolling pastures that are overlooked by a hill that "stood alone, magnificent in sharp austerity of cliff and pyramid." This hill and the rolling valley it overlooks give the Sheep's Field an almost dramatic setting, picturesque and vivid. As if in recognition of this, the hill has been named by the people "the witness of God" (821–22). The landscape, in addition to being starkly visible, seems to direct travelers to a location that remains out of sight until they are almost upon it, and in her progress, West is now a part of the tableaus vivant that she has up to now only been witness to. West's journey and her vision coalesce: "It became apparent that we were approaching some focal point, which was not a village. . . . [A] spot which was still not to be discovered by the eye" (822). Their destination, as it turns out, is a large rock in the middle of an open field. The rock is covered with blood since it is the site of animal sacrifice. West and her company finally reach the site, and there they confront this rock directly. West finds this unmediated proximity disturbing, as we see in her description of the rock:

> We were so near the rock that we could see its colour. It was a flat-topped rock, uneven in shape, rising to something like six feet above the ground, and it was red-brown and gleaming, for it was entirely covered with the blood of the beasts that had been sacrificed on it during the night. . . . The spectacle was extremely disgusting. (823)

The rock is compelling: it draws people to it by the sheer force of its presence, just as the landscape seemed to lead them to it and focus their vision. According to West, "the place had enormous authority," (823) an authority that is derived in no small part from the rites that are performed on the rock but also, according to the logic of her prose, because of its commanding visibility.

Once in the presence of the rock, West feels further compelled to witness one of these rituals: "When it had at last been made visible before the eyes as it is—for we are all brought up among disguised presentations of it—it would have been foolish not to stay for a little while and contemplate it" (823). She sees a man carrying a black lamb—the black lamb of the title—perform a brief rite around the rock, and slit the lamb's throat: "A jet of blood spurted out and fell red and shining on the browner blood that had been shed before" (824). The peasant performs this ritual, West learns, because previously, "his wife got [a] child by coming here," and he feels that this ghastly ritual is obscurely linked with his good fortune. For West, this act, which she witnesses in all of its repellent visibility, is "purely shameful" and a "conscious cheat" (826). The meaning of this act of cruelty, in West's view, is the idea that salvation lies in bloody sacrifice. Whereas throughout *Black Lamb and Grey Falcon* West has been receptive to various rites of, for example, the Orthodox Church, especially insofar as they are "dramatically rendered" by the mass, she finds these acts, performed by gipsy Moslems a "beastly retrogression."

In the midst of her revulsion, however, West is overwhelmed by a feeling of recognition similar to what she had felt when she viewed King Alexander's features on the newsreel as he lay dying of his wounds: "I knew this rock well. I had lived under the shadow of it all my life. All our Western thought is founded on this repulsive pretence that pain is the proper price of any good thing" (827). Then, as she had done in "Trees of Gold," West considers the example of another victim of sacrifice, Christ, whom she sees as a prime example of this pointless ritual elevated into religion. She describes how the sacrifice of this "extremely good man" was a symptom of our predisposition for the "disagreeable over the agreeable" (827). The sacrificial urge, she argues, is not merely one of propitiation, but of a deeply ingrained penchant for blood and violence that is not peculiar to the Balkans, although it is particularly visible there on the Sheep's Field. This visible sign of sacrifice and the role that it plays in the daily lives of the people of the region lead West to her most sustained condemnation of the myth of sacrifice in all of its guises, as her recognition leads her to detect the presence of this myth in more familiar places. Speculating on the combination of repulsion and fascination that the rock exercises, West casts her critique in terms of travel: "Since we have traveled thus far from the speechless and thoughtless roots of our stock we should have traveled further. There must be something vile in us to make us linger, age after age, in this unsanitary spot" (830). The compulsion to acknowledge the authority of the rock is all but inescapable.

On the Sheep's Field, West sees the dual urges for self-sacrifice and self-destruction operating both throughout history and within herself as the rite makes visible to her the horror of history. History, in West's view, underwrites the horrible acts that are committed on the rock by bolstering them into myth:

> Here on the Sheep's Field it could be seen where the cleavage lies that can be apprehended to run through art and life: on the one side are the people who are accomplices of the rock and on the other those who are its enemy. It appeared also where the cleavage lay in our human nature which makes us broken and futile. A part of us is enamoured of the rock and tells us that we should not reject it, that it is solemn and mystical and only the shallow deny the value of sacrifice. (831)

Recognizing that the rock makes manifest a division that lies both within and without, West addresses intellectuals and artists, skilled in observation, who nevertheless cannot see the rock for what it is, and at this moment the visible scene of the lamb's slaughter becomes also the occasion for West's attempt to get others to "see." The authority of vision and experience becomes the force behind West's attempt to comprehend. She begins by accusing religious figures such as St. Paul, St. Augustine, and Martin Luther of perpetrating the myth of the rock in their writing by glorifying sacrifice as a means of approaching God; however, she concludes by criticizing artists and writers such as Shakespeare and William Blake who at times, in her view, succumbed to the infatuation for cruelty and bloodshed that the rock made manifest and sanctified. West does not explicitly draw an analogy to the current situation in England at this point, if for no other reason than that the sheer authority of the rock momentarily prevents such lessons from being drawn. Its authority is so pervasive and West is so repelled that it obscures more recent analogous moments of self-sacrifice that West will address later in the epilogue.

In contradistinction to the way in which the Sheep's Field is presents itself so brashly to the eye and therefore to the mind, on the plain in Kossovo we get a similar reliance on descriptive prose but without the sense that what West sees is the same kind of "dramatic rendering" as on the Sheep's Field. Throughout this scene on the plain of Kossovo, West refers frequently to the lack of visibility, the featurelessness of the landscape, even the invisibility of it, as a way not of denying its empirical reality (in fact we get long passages of descriptive prose throughout) but of rhetorically suggesting that the visual alone is insufficient for articulating her political thesis. It is important to recognize this shift from the focus on the visible and the manifest to the abstract at a moment when West simultaneously presents her most clear-cut thesis about the political lesson of Yugoslavia and her most urgent warning to the West. It is as if the landscape before her metaphorically recedes or is occluded or rendered invisible by some symbolic partition, allowing her thoughts of home to assert themselves most clearly and most explicitly for the first time. If the direct visibility here becomes rhetorically impeded, this impediment also leads West to her clearest moment of comprehension, as physical sight is continuous with and leads to deeper understanding.

On the plain of Kossovo, West visits the spot where in 1389 Tsar Lazar was defeated by the Turkish army. It is a place that she finds hard to describe at times because it is lacking in distinctive visual characteristics. Whereas the rock on the Sheep's Field possesses a compulsory visibility for West, one that leads her to consider the pervasiveness of myth and the impact of history, when she visits the Field of Black Birds in Kossovo, it is the landscape's lack of visibility that is most striking. After leaving Macedonia, West and her traveling companions journey to a Serbian Church in Grachanitsa, where they look out over the plain where Tsar Lazar was defeated. She sees a landscape that is eerily still and supine: "The land lies loosely, like a sleeper, in a cradle of featureless hills." The plain is blank and desolate: "It is obviously prostrate and passive, it has none of the active spirit which makes mountains and forest and the picturesque valley" (837). The sky hangs over this landscape and it mirrors this blankness, a "vault visible yet of no colour except space" (838). Such inscrutable blankness for West is a depressing sight: "Kossovo speaks only of its defeats." Unlike the Sheep's Field, where the stark landscape and the vivid and imposing rock offered themselves up, as did the rites that were performed by the locals in that vivid "dramatic rendering," "here is the image of failure, so vast that it fills the eye as failure sometimes fills an individual life, an epoch" (841). What fills the eye is not what is before it, but rather what has been abstracted from the historical record and perpetuated through story and chronicle, the lesson of defeat learned through this "image of failure." The Plain of Kossovo provides a lesson of defeat through the inscrutability of the landscape, and from this lesson, according to West, all Serbian history has emanated.

One of the reasons, perhaps, why West describes both the landscape and the events that have been memorialized on it as "invisible" is that they are so remote in time from lived experience. She sees a memorial on which is etched the "appalling words": "To the heroes who fell for the honest cross, freedom, and the right of the people, 1389–1912." Of these words and the memorial, West writes: "It made the head ache with its attempt to commemorate people who were utterly outside the scope of memory" (904). We see West equate as well a lack of material visibility with a kind of historical blindness: "If the battle of Kossovo was invisible to me it was because it had happened too completely" (905). Whereas West was unable to comprehend the meaning of Alexander's death through what she could see on the screen, here there was too much meaning, or rather one overwhelming and unavoidable meaning; the defeat at Kossovo had trumped all other accounts of Serbian history and become a myth by which all subsequent political action was defined. The two opposite poles of visibility and comprehension that West had hoped to encounter in the Balkans had collapsed into the sameness of myth. However, at the same time, the lesson she learns from the sequence of these two locales provides West with her most sustained moment of comprehension, as thoughts of home begin to dominate.

Desperate to elicit some further meaning from the lesson of defeat that the landscape at Kossovo memorializes, West draws a brief and preliminary parallel between Tsar Lazar's fate and the current political situation in England. West's guides show her the battlefield and expect her to be moved by the solemn historical lesson that it offers. At this point West first hears the poem of the grey falcon, who was Elijah in disguise and who came from Jerusalem offering the Tsar a choice between holy defeat and earthly victory. When West viewed Lazar's body earlier on her trip she was uncertain as to what significance his defeat had on the people, but here amidst the desolate and inscrutable landscape of Kossovo, the scene of this defeat, the meaning of this poem and of Lazar's importance to Serbian history gradually becomes manifest to her.[47] She accuses Lazar of being mistaken in his choice of death over life, because this choice involved the sacrifice of his entire people, a futile gesture akin to the slaughter of the lamb on the rock at Sheep's Field. But her feelings vacillate as she weighs the implications of this choice:

> He should have chosen damnation for their sake. No, what am I saying? I am putting the state above the individual, and I believe that there are certain ultimate human rights that must have precedence over all others. What I mean is rather that I do not believe in the thesis of the poem. I do not believe that any man can procure his own salvation by refusing to save millions of people from miserable slavery. (911)

For the first time, West links Lazar's predicament, his impossible choice, with the predicament of England in the years leading up to the Second World War, as she claims somewhat sarcastically, "Lazar was a member of the Peace Pledge Union." West is referring here to the organization formed in 1934 by

Dick Sheppard in response to the continued ineffectiveness of the Treaty of Versailles in 1919. The Peace Pledge Union was one of the major organizations within the British peace movement and in West's view was ineffective in its response to the rise of Hitler to power, a point she argues more forcefully in the epilogue. The sense of recognition that West has vaguely felt throughout her trip, for example in the gestures and physical features of Alexander, here takes on a more concrete expression as the parallels between home and abroad make themselves felt.

Upon hearing the poem and seeing the desolate landscape that was the occasion of its utterance, West realizes the source of her recognition. She realizes why "this poem had stirred me," and what was familiar to her when she had "touched Prince Lazar's mummified hand." It was those figures in England who had made a similar choice, opting for their own salvation over a communal good, "that company loving honour and freedom and harmony," but that refused to realize these in the world. Like Lazar, they allow the phrases of virtue and the belief of innocence to dictate the way they see the world. West mentions in this instance Herbert Fisher, former Education Minister and author of a three-volume *History of England*; Lord Cecil, one of the architects of the League of Nations; and Gilbert Murray, classics scholar at Oxford and Chairman of the League of Nations Union, as examples of those who speak in "accents of sincerity and virtue" but who never act "as if power would be theirs tomorrow and they would use it for virtuous action." For West, these figures "want to be right, not to do right" (912–13).

Whereas the field of Kossovo doesn't offer the "dramatic renderings" that West had come across elsewhere, her visit ends with a very visible and potent symbol. She sees an Albanian man carrying a black lamb, like the lamb she had seen sacrificed on Sheep's Field. Suddenly this visible image causes everything else she has seen to make sense. In a flash, "the meaning of Kossovo was plain": "The black lamb and the grey falcon had worked together here. . . . This I had learned in Yugoslavia, which writes obscure things plain, which furnishes symbols for what the intellect has not yet formulated" (914). The sacrifice of innocents and the self-sacrifice that Lazar had practiced were similar in their "primitive" doctrine of belief that such bloodletting is a precondition for atonement. As they leave, these abstract concepts become suddenly more real. Briefly distracted by the lessons these visual symbols present to her, West is surprised when abruptly the black lamb "stretched out its neck and laid its cold twitching muzzle against my bare forearm" (917). Oddly reminiscent of the scene where West reaches out and touches the arm of Tsar Lazar, it is as if by nuzzling West's arm the lamb has completed a circuit and allowed life to assert itself over death.

In the epilogue to *Black Lamb and Grey Falcon,* the most expressly political and polemical part of the book, West ties together all that she has seen and learned in the Balkans. As she and her husband leave Yugoslavia through Zagreb in Croatia, where they first arrived, visibility and scrutability depart: "The people around us were colourless and inexpressive. Their clothes did not tell us where they came from or what they were. . . . Here, we thought as we lay ungratefully in our comfortable beds, the life of the soul would not, as in the other Slav lands, take forms visible to the corporeal eye" (1075). But to retain the corporeal visibility that she found so engrossing in the Balkans, West recalls all of her experiences in order that they may achieve some memorable shape in her mind:

> I resolved to put on paper what a typical Englishwoman felt and thought in the late nineteen-thirties when, already convinced of the inevitability of the Second Anglo-German war, she had been able to follow the dark waters of that event back to its source. . . . I was obliged to write a long and complicated history, and to swell that with an account of myself and the people who went with me on my travels, since it was my aim to show the past side by side with the present it created. And while I grappled with the mass of my material during several years, it imposed certain ideas on me. (1089)

The imposition of these ideas came not from the Yugoslav Press Bureau or from the British Council, though these no doubt were influential, but from the desperate need to remember her journey, from the struggle with historical events that would not remain stable, and from the sights that offered to her mind more than simply what was visible. West draws all of her material together in the epilogue in her most explicit argument for opposing Hitler's imperial goals. She sees England as a vast Kossovo: "In England there was such a stillness, such a white winter of the spirit, and such a prolongation of it that death was threatened. . . . It was as though a pall of nullity covered all the land, as if the springs of the national will were locked fast in frost" (1115). This nullity arose from the refusal of her British contemporaries to recognize Hitler's ambition or their own incapacity to act in the face of his ambition.

She recalls again the poem that told of Lazar's fateful choice and concludes, "so it had been at Kossovo, and so it was in England" (1124). However, whereas the choice at Kossovo had been made in the distant past, for England this choice was being offered now. It is for this reason that West's tone takes on such urgency, though West is aware of the danger of her advice and of her readings of history, as she has been aware all along of the danger of accepting the advice of her various guides. She ends by speculating on the nature of her own book: "In writing this book I have been struck again and again by the refusal of destiny to let man see what is happening to him, its mean delight in strewing his path with red herrings" (1128). These red herrings are not only the numerous contested meanings that can be drawn from particular historical events, but the deliberate misrepresentations of these events by dishonest guides. For West, it is foolish to confront the unfamiliar terrain of a foreign country or of history alone without mediation, but equally foolish to put ultimate faith in either guides or the firsthand accounts of others: "The few guides that man has been allowed to help him on his way out of the darkness come to him surrounded by traitors, dressed in their guise, indistinguishable. It is not possible to exaggerate the difficulty of man's lot. Therefore no page in history, not even the bloodiest recorded in this volume, should be contemned" (1128–29). West's value as a guide lies in the way she reveals the very process whereby she attempts to make sense of the tapestry of the Balkans that she sees unfurled before her. West's re-deployment of the modernist techniques that made "Trees of Gold" more than just an escapist text mired in its own subjectivity make *Black Lamb and Grey Falcon* an exemplary text in the way that it links this private dream with the public discourse of modernity.

CONCLUSION:
"A FAITHFUL MIRROR"

In a 1945 letter to Leonard Woolf, in response to his praise of *Black Lamb and Grey Falcon*, West thanks him and takes the opportunity to revisit some of the themes of the book in the light of subsequent events. In this letter, West nostalgically hopes for the renewal of Central Europe, wrecked by war since she had seen it last. In this letter she presents her book both as a mirror and as a screen:

> I am so glad you liked my book. It is at any rate a faithful mirror, because what has happened since isn't incongruous with what I wrote. I don't know if you remember what I wrote about the body of King Lazar in one of the Monasteries of Frushka Gora—The Germans stripped the tomb of its jewel-work and threw the body into the river, from which it was rescued and taken to Belgrade, where it was reburied before the Cathedral, and is now the object of a cult, but, of course, more fervent than in the first days after Kossovo. What is the use of thinking about human beings as if such things were not done, and are not of value?
>
> I don't see any possible re-education of Central Europe and Italy save by renewal of poetry, that is to say, of religion, a transformation of Judaism

and Christianity. I mean the symbolic representation of what is real,
behind which a reasonable pattern is always to be assumed and sought.
(*Letters*, 195)

West sees her book as a rich and detailed screen that draws attention to the
pattern in life, a pattern she never detected but always sought, and failing to
find it, constructed one of her own. According to West at the end of *Black
Lamb and Grey Falcon*, the artist's only directive is to revisit events either
physically or imaginatively. "I will make that event happen again," she has an
imaginary artist say, "altering its shape, which was disfigured by its contacts
with other events, so that its true significance is revealed" (1127); yet West,
"never sure of the reality of what [she] sees," is at the same time anxious that
such distortion not be a betrayal of the visible.

It is perhaps no accident that in the forties and fifties, after the details of
the horrors of the Second World War were becoming more evident, and as
the country she had traveled to and come to love continued to suffer from the
effects of war, the subject of treason would dominate West's writing. For West,
the visible, what can be witnessed and testified to, was of utmost importance
as the numerous meanings it offers up constantly change under the burden
of memory, the weight of interpretation, and anxiety over and hope for the
future.

West composed the prologue to *Black Lamb and Grey Falcon* last, as bombs
were falling on London. In it, as West views the death of Alexander, she
thinks again about her journey, asking the question that Hartog says is central
for the travel writer: "What is it that I have seen?" As the train crawls through
the countryside at the very beginning of the book, West sees Yugoslavia again:

> I saw the blue lake of Ochrid, the mosques of Sarajevo, the walled town
> of Korchula, and it appeared possible that I was unable to find words
> for what I wanted to say because it was not true. I am never sure of the
> reality of what I see, if I have seen it only once; I know that until it
> has firmly established its objective existence by impressing my senses and
> my memory, I am capable of conscripting it into the service of a private
> dream. (23)

Ultimately, West is unable and perhaps unwilling to claim the authority
necessary to make sense of the events that she has witnessed and read about;
however, she has fixed with greater precision their most salient features,
sometimes distorting them in order to make them stand out more clearly, and,
like the woman in the church in Skoplje in Macedonia, she cradles this image
of Yugoslavia—part private dream, part political reality—more closely.

Conclusion

AFTERMATHS AND LATE MODERNISM

& all rds have an ending

—Ezra Pound, *A Walking Tour*

The end is nothing; the road is all.

—Willa Cather, *Interviews, Speeches, and Letters*

B Y ALL ACCOUNTS, TRAVEL WRITING DURING THE INTERWAR years was unique in its preponderance and variety. That there was such preponderance and such variety was due in part to the fact that travel itself had become a much more common activity with the developments in transportation technology and the growth of infrastructure that made the world a smaller place. Travel captured the public mind as well as the imaginations of writers and intellectuals from across the artistic and political spectrum because of the way it offered a connection with the world "out there." It was both a reinvigoration of the public sphere and a prerequisite for globalism. During these same years, the movement we know as modernism, a movement that began in the not-so-distant and yet in many ways altogether unrecognizable period just before the First World War, underwent its own dramatic changes as well, as the focus shifted from the interiority of subjective experience to the exteriority and new forensics of politics and public life, which was often just as experimentally rendered.

And yet despite the scientific, technological, and social advances that promised an era of progress and optimism, the general trend was toward a skepticism that emerged from doubts over whether such interaction could lead to a new age. That was one lesson from the First World War. Critical approaches to the literature of the early twentieth century have long recognized the special nature of the interwar years, but only recently has there been a recognition of the ways in which the dual impulses of mobility and modernism impacted on one another and how this impact can help us better read these years. This study has taken this crucial intersection of mobility and modernism as its main focus and in so doing has tried to read the travel writing and travel experience of Pound, Cummings, Lewis, and West as works that shed some light on these individual authors, on modernism, and on the period between the wars.

One way I have done this is by employing the phrase "late modernism," which has been used in recent years to describe the literature written up to and during the Second World War. At first, the introduction of a new term such as "late modernism," may seem to be a faddish impulse, an unnecessary subdivision of an already complex and subdivided field, or yet another grand narrative where grand narratives already abound; but it is helpful for the way it frees us from being bound by language provided by the very originators and participants of the movement it is being used to describe. As both Tyrus Miller and Marina MacKay have shown, it is not enough to treat the complicated public events and multifaceted history of the years of the Second World War in the critical light of incipient pronouncements about what "modernism" was intended to be (a renaissance, a revolutionary literary movement, a radically new way of seeing). MacKay suggests that we cannot have an "adequate definition of modernism" without taking into account the "self-referential and historiographic late phase" (14). This study has tried to contribute to the still-emerging definition of modernism by drawing on this vocabulary of late modernism when investigating the travel writing of certain modernist writers. In so doing, I have sought to engage modernism both as a self-defined movement, by those who were either its architects or there at its founding, and as an academic and critical period, where various genealogies and histories have been and continue to be usefully refined.

Just as the category and phrase "late modernism" has allowed us to revisit the travel literature of these four writers, so has the field of travel studies, especially those studies that have focused on the politically engaged writing of the interwar period, allowed us to read these modernist texts in their particular historical context. The travel writing of the interwar years, no matter what its political orientation or artistic affiliation, is notable for the way that it engages with a larger interwar community, shapes its argument for its audience, and is often as polemical as it is descriptive. As Helen Carr points out, the intersection between modernism and travel writing during these years is of a special texture: "Modernist texts register a new consciousness of cultural heterogeneity, the condition and mark of the modern world; in both imaginative and travel writing, modernity, the meeting of other cultures, and change are inseparable" (74).

One way of registering this change and further demonstrating this point about the interrelationship between modernist studies and travel studies is to consider the impact that travel had on these writers' later careers, and more generally in what ways the results of travel—what they saw—was processed and transformed into literature. In what follows, and as a way of concluding, I want to dwell briefly on certain moments after their journeys were long over, where we see them revisiting particular themes that emerged from their travels. I do this as a way of showing how travel itself was not the ultimate answer to their shifting understanding of the world they were living in and traveling through, but rather a means to a much more important end, that of gaining a deeper comprehension of this world and this experience, a comprehension that at times translated back into their imaginative work. Whereas the earlier optimism of modernism's goals were intertwined with the boastful sentiment of "make it new," in the years up to the Second World War what was new to these traveling modernists was already saturated with history.

We have already seen in the chapter on Pound how those early travels had such a lasting impact, how the details of his journey provided both immediate illumination of some tough scholarly puzzle and some lingering difficulties, both of which shaped his larger political views during the interwar years. The partition that Pound had damned in his 1927 *Nation* article remained very real in retrospect. In May of 1958, after twelve years, Pound was officially discharged from St. Elizabeths, and by July he was sailing to Italy.[1] The treason charges had been dismissed with the help of Dr. Winfrid Overholser, the Director of St. Elizabeths, who had also written the state department on Pound's behalf to help him get his passport back. During this period of incarceration, Pound's poetry gained a deeper obscurity. In 1955, Pound published the latest installment of his epic poem including history in a limited edition in Milan called "Section: Rock-Drill 85–95 de los cantares." We see a return to the language of obscurity and partitions in the very title of this volume, as Pound conjures again his immediate frustrations over the modern world. Rather than a simple outburst designed to penetrate the partition at the London consulate, Pound here envisions all the modern world as an impenetrable barrier that requires the industrial force of his poetry to pierce.

In *Eimi* Cummings defends and validates his poetic calling in a world in which the individual, he felt, was being subsumed by a collective identity. He maintained his distrust and even hatred of the Soviet system well after his journey to Moscow in 1931, suggesting that he was not just a disgruntled tourist, but that he had always had a larger ideological point. In 1947, in response to a Moscow radio commentator who suggested that the war writing of American and British poets was "superficial," that it was the result either of "a feeling of loneliness and confusion or a profound indifference to the outside world" and that Cummings in particular in his account of Russia "did not refrain from the biggest lies about the Soviet Union," Cummings stated brusquely that "to be called a liar by anyone even remotely associated with the present Russian tyranny is, in my proud and humble opinion, a strictly unmitigated honor."[2] His hatred of the Soviet system had not abated over time, nor had his characteristically fluid use of language and paradox to reposition his own identity ("my proud and humble opinion"). Style remains the fortification in Cummings' defense of poetry, even if the book is clearly neither prose nor poetry.

For Pound and Cummings, as these two very brief examples show, the negative effects of their journeys lingered, but I want to conclude this inquiry into the subject of modernist travel writing by briefly examining two later works by Lewis and West: Lewis's 1954 novel *Self-Condemned* and West's 1943 short story, "The Second Commandment: Thou Shalt Not Make Any Graven Images," published in a collection of short stories by writers who were responding to the events of the Second World War. [3] In these works, we can see traces of the impact of their interwar journeys on their artistic efforts.

SELF CONDEMNED:
LEWIS AND THE ARTIST-HISTORIAN

Some of the material that Lewis gathered on his trip to Morocco eventually appeared in his 1932 novel *Snooty Baronet* as a backdrop to the title character's trip through Persia.[4] Snooty is a famous London-based writer whose literary agent organizes a journey to exotic northern Africa as a promotional gimmick for his latest book. Lewis's use of his travel experiences in this manner indicates that he continued to question his own original motivation for traveling, as his agent appeals to the "exoticist's infatuation" that Lewis had described in *Hitler*. Having originally claimed in a letter to his publisher that he was traveling to Morocco to gain inspiration for a long-promised sequel to *The Childermass*, Lewis wound up presenting an ironized treatment of his subject matter in *Snooty Baronet*. However, at the same time, Lewis gained a new understanding in Morocco and in writing about his travels there both of history and of the contemporary European political landscape. If in his postwar polemical works of the twenties, Lewis saw history, especially in the hands of Oswald Spengler, as heavily politicized and frequently employed to reinforce the belief that the modern world was in decline, after traveling to Morocco and as political events in the thirties became more urgent, he began to rethink his notion of how past events impinged on the present moment. In particular, Lewis advanced a theory of history that avoided Splenglerean doomsaying, while, perhaps contradictorily, retaining Spengler's selective and subjective view of history.

Lewis's Morocco trip represents a significant transition in his thinking about history that has some bearing on his work after the Second World War. In his 1954 novel *Self Condemned*, Lewis attempts to wrest history from the historians and give it to the artists. In this novel, Renee Harding, a Professor of History and author of *The Secret History of World War II*, introduces a radical view of history that he feels makes him an outcast in the academic community. In a review of his book, written and read aloud by his friend Rotter, Harding's philosophy of history is contrasted to that of the real-life historian R. G. Collingwood. According to Rotter, Collingwood sees the actions of humanity as "in general irrational," and favors a historical viewpoint that is radically positivist: "For [Collingwood] the true historian must go to these happenings, of whatever kind, without any prejudice relating to ethics, taste, intellectual fastidiousness etc." (92). In contrast, according to Rotter, Harding's history is rife with judgment and bias. Harding's view "is that we should reject anything (notwithstanding the fact that it undoubtedly happened) which is unworthy of any man's attention, or some action which is so revolting that it *should not* have happened, and must not be encouraged to happen again" (93). Insofar as Harding's views can be attributed to Lewis, something in this philosophy of history speaks as much of personal trauma as it does of the "revolution in history" that Harding proposes it to be. Two world wars interrupted Lewis's hopes—as they did Pound's and a generation of writers—for an age in which art and artists would flourish as would their connectedness to history. Harding's philosophy records this disenchantment with its brutal rejection of "unworthy" fact.

Harding feels that the prevailing view of history as the record of political figures is nothing more than "police court news." Discussing his new version of history with a colleague in Momaco, the imaginary city in Canada where he resides, Harding states his reasons why historical accounts should not focus on politicians and those in power: "It is an essential feature of my programme that the egotistical, the anti-social type should cease to fascinate the multitude . . . and the more or less enlightened will greatly increase in number and influence. Then ultra-barbarous wars should have the opposite effect from leading to a more barbarous state of mind, which is what happens at present. A crescendo of violence should, rather, lead away from it" (319). This brief sketch of Harding's program recalls Lewis's own career, a career that was launched with the manifesto *Blast,* that crescendo of violence and energy that fizzled as the First World War began, and continued through 1931 when he visited what he thought would be the "barbarous state of mind" of North Africa. But what he had found in Morocco was not nearly as barbarous as the interwar European society that he had left behind; in fact, he saw in Moroccan society a worthy model for the West. Lewis was not a war writer so much as he was a postwar writer.

West:
The Manifestation of History and the Second World War

In *Black Lamb and Grey Falcon,* West described current events and Balkan history, both of which were for her complex and malleable substances. And whereas she also saw her book as grounded in a particular historical moment and as an urgent call to arms, the malleable nature of history and current events is what stands out and what lingers. For example, in the epilogue to *Black Lamb and Grey Falcon* West harshly criticizes the policies of the Yugoslav regent Prince Paul as pro-German: in 1941, Paul signed a pact with the Axis powers that managed to keep his country out of the war. West saw this pact as akin to Chamberlain's appeasement of Hitler and suggested that Paul was betraying the Yugoslavian people, but according to Victoria Glendinning, rather than being a sign of weakness or capitulation as West characterized it, the pact was the shrewd maneuvering of a statesman, since it "was relatively favourable to Yugoslavia in that it deprived German troops of the right to use Yugoslavia as a corridor, a fact not publicized at the time."[5] When this information was revealed to West years later, she protested that there was no way that she could have known of this when she was writing her book; in subsequent editions, however, she declined to correct her characterization of Paul in the light of this information. The book, it seems, had ironically achieved a certain form in her mind that she was reluctant to change, suggesting that her argument was more important and more permanent than the historical facts out of which it was made. West's refusal to alter her book seems unpardonable in a writer who was so concerned about the impact of history; but at the same time it reveals both the situatedness and the urgency with which she wrote *Black Lamb and Grey Falcon.* This refusal also suggests that the potential errors and misreading of history were both revealed and replicated in her book. Thus West's own mistakes as a fallible recording subject become a part of the story.

Throughout her trips to Yugoslavia, West was guided in part by a desire to apprehend that "quality of visibility" that made "the Balkans so specially enchanting" (202). But the quality of visibility did not pertain only to a particular locale, although it was with great affection that West recorded the Balkan scene; rather it also had to do simply with knowing which way to direct her glance, what to look at, and how to articulate ideas that would promote the agreeableness of life in the face of much that was disagreeable. In a short story written after the Second World War, "The Second Commandment: Thou Shalt Not Make Any Graven Image," West again focuses on this quality of visibility.

This story was a contribution to a volume published in 1943 and edited by Armin L. Robinson called *The Ten Commandments: Ten Short Novels of Hitler's War Against the Moral Code*, a collection that gathered together ten stories on the commandments by ten celebrated writers of the time, including Thomas Mann, Jules Romain, and Franz Werfel. Robinson expresses his hope in the introduction that the collection will "help to open the eyes of those who still do not recognize what Nazism really is" (v). In her essay "Rebecca West's Shadowy Other," Phyllis Lassner reads this story as a kind of culminating testimony on West's part of the dangers of disengagement, a testimony that emerged from the lengthier historical disquisition and empirical evidence that she assembled in *Black Lamb and Grey Falcon*.[6] Lassner sees this story as a bridge between West's Balkan book and her reporting from Nuremberg in *A Train of Powder*. And we do see in the plot and substance of this 1943 story an important way in which immediate experience demands both action and contemplation.

In "The Second Commandment," West tells the fate of Elisaveta, a successful actress living in Copenhagen during the Nazi invasion of Denmark, and her two dramatist friends, Egon and Nils. As the Nazis gradually assert control over the town under the guise of keeping order, the three friends find themselves learning to endure this hostile invading force. Their strategy at first is a passive resistance, in which they go about their business and act as if nothing had changed, as if life could simply go on. They hope that by this silent resistance they will be able to neutralize the effects of the Nazi presence. However, as the Nazi violence intensifies, their strategy becomes ineffective. The three friends are drawn closer together and comfort one another as they try to make sense of both Nazi brutality and the presence of violence in general. In response to her question, "Why is God doing this to us?" Egon invokes the abstract virtues of Love, Justice, and Truth, and assures her of the perpetuity of these despite aggression and suffering, separating as he does an abstract world of ideas from the physical world: "You cannot reverse the meaning of an abstract noun by an event on the material plane" (198). When she asks Nils what he believes in and how he accounts for suffering and horror, Nils dismisses Egon's faith in abstract concepts and his radical break between the ideal and the real. He stammers in response: "'My belief,' he said, 'my belief . . . why, Elisaveta, it is written behind all my plays. . . . I do not know how to put it into words directly." But although at a loss for words, Nils does what West had done when trying to describe to her husband the beauty of Yugoslavia: "There's no use merely talking about these things. They must be made visible" (200). Nils takes Elisaveta to a church service in which she sees a congregation worshiping together with a new sense of devotion. She is surprised at how powerfully she is moved by the simple service even as she finds its elements to be mundane. Egon's reliance on abstract principles and Nils's on the visible and the manifest represent dual ways of knowing and of understanding the world.

Later on during a party that is briefly interrupted by a Nazi officer who claims that "we have discovered the way of living that is right for mankind," Egon, Nils, and the other townspeople discuss the Nazis, who believed "they could draw a picture of God's mind, and another picture of man's mind" (209). The discussion turns to the second commandment of the title, which prohibits graven images of God from being worshiped instead of God. Nils clarifies his position on this matter:

> For me that commandment means that man must never pretend to have accomplished that task which will be unfinished so long as he himself exists. He was set upon earth in order that he may acquaint himself with reality, which is an impossible task, since reality creates itself anew as fast as the learner learns. . . . It seems to me that a man's work is dead and a man's soul is ideas, if he does not make this admission that all sacred truth is still veiled, for this relationship between us and a mystery is what constitutes life. Why need we go on living if all is known? (209)

Nils's description of what "constitutes life" is reminiscent of West's description throughout *Black Lamb and Grey Falcon*, especially on those occasions where she visited the Orthodox churches and participated in the masses. West has Nils describe truth as veiled and our relationship to it as a mystery that once again evokes the image of the screen. For both Nils and West there is always something more to be known.

Nils's desire nonetheless to make certain things visible extends both to the mystery of the church and to the crimes of the Nazis. Their strategy of passive resistance to the Nazis failing in the face of increased and indiscriminate violence, Egon and Nils publish a manifesto that they post around the city overnight. The purpose of this manifesto is twofold: it charges the Nazi invaders with crimes against the residents of the city, and it reminds residents of what their lives had been like before the Nazis came: "It set down in black and white what the city had been, and what the Germans were" (213). This manifesto, true to its definition, urges residents to see what is before their eyes. Written both by the idealist Egon and the realist Nils, it appeals both to an abstract reason and to a visible reality, here the printed text.

Egon and Nils are subsequently arrested on charges of sedition when it is discovered that they are the authors of the manifesto, and Elisaveta is arrested along with them as a known associate and the widow of a Jew. Elisaveta, Egon, and Nils are deported from Copenhagen and eventually taken to a prison camp outside of Denmark. As they leave Copenhagen, they are overcome with a sense not only of fear but of foreignness as they leave their home: "But now that they were over the frontier and the railwaymen spoke a foreign language, so that they felt as if they were a stage nearer the end of their journey, which would be the extremity of foreignness" (219). Their journey ends when the railway car in which they are transported is derailed in a bleak and barren area. In the wreck, Egon is fatally wounded. Elisaveta comforts him until he dies and then turns her attention to Nils, who is also near death. Elisaveta cradles Nils in her arms as he gradually deteriorates. He fixes his gaze beyond Elisaveta: "I want to look at the sky. I am watching a great battle" (220). Elisaveta follows his gaze, but realizing he is near death, turns back to him. Nils, as if unable to decide where to look when so close to death, shuts his eyes, turning his gaze inwards instead: "'No,' said Nils, and shut his eyes. 'It is no use. One cannot see the battle. The sky is too small a frame'" (220). As Nils's life departs, his eyes alternately open and shut in what seems to be a paroxysm of death, but which also, in its apparent indecisiveness, replicates the various ways of knowing that the visible offers. Nils's wandering glance suggests that he is unable at this crucial moment to decide what it is that he sees.

ENDING IN EARNEST

West confronts the problems of history and of the empiricism of travel by foregrounding and interrogating the related issues of visibility, what can be seen, and history, what can be determined by other kinds of evidence; in other words, both what we see and what we *make of* what we see. In the prologue to *Black Lamb and Grey Falcon*, as West and her husband travel by train to

Yugoslavia—he for the first time—she reassures him of the beauty of what they will find. Her husband, not out of disbelief or doubt but in recognition of West's sincere yet inarticulate devotion, asks, "Is it so wonderful there?" West's response calls into question one of the primary functions of the travel genre, the ability to describe a foreign country: "It is more wonderful than I can tell you" (22–23). She attempts to describe for her husband and for her readers what she has seen on her previous trips, but when trying to find the words, she despairs over the possibility of her success: "The thing I wanted to tell him could not be told, however, because it was manifold and nothing like what one is accustomed to communicate by words" (23). This leads West to consider the elusive nature of the visible and the uncertainty of her own memory and knowledge: "It appeared possible that I was unable to find words for what I wanted to say because it was not true. I am never sure of the reality of what I see, if I have seen it only once; I know that until it has firmly established its objective existence by impressing my senses and my memory, I am capable of conscripting it into the service of a private dream" (23). Throughout *Black Lamb and Grey Falcon*, this double urge—to show others and to see again in order to confirm and ratify the contents of her own memory—is always present as West attempts to give shape to her various journeys and meaning to what she sees. As often as not, West extrapolates these memories and experiences in the form of symbols, often in the form of a concrete image or object or a tableau. The way that West's experience establishes its "objective existence" in her mind is through the abstraction of material reality and empirical description into these powerful symbols. Although the primary motivation for West's journey may be to seek out this experience and use that as the ground for her authority, this experience is also abstracted for the benefit of her audience back home. This abstraction is a key function of her art.

For these writers who had come into their own in the years during the First World War, the events of the period were difficult to process, difficult to render, and sometimes difficult to even recognize or see. For all the missteps, misperceptions, and faulty judgments, these writers portrayed these countries with an effort and devotion similar to the effort and devotion with which they had rendered their own complex interior lives. We see in Pound's jottings and in the more substantial travel writing of Cummings, Lewis, and West, not simply forgotten or overlooked works that need to be restored to an ever growing canon of writers and texts, or curiosities from an interim period, but important efforts at understanding both their own modernist inheritance and the wider world. These writers couldn't possibly have gained total comprehension of the countries they traveled to after such relatively brief trips.

Their demands for comprehension of both the modern world and their own roles in it was often met with further uncertainty and even aporia. However, their desire to know, to seek out through inquiry and firsthand experience, and their efforts to render what they saw can help us better understand the period, the movement, these writers' own later works, and even the countries they visited. To Pound, Cummings, Lewis, and West, comprehension would come—or not—later, in the recesses of "home" and in the stasis of art.

Introduction

1. See Helen Carr, "Modernism and Travel (1880–1940)," in *The Cambridge Companion to Travel Writing*, ed. Peter Hulme and Tim Youngs, 73. Further references will be cited parenthetically in the text. Carr traces a transition from the Romantic notion of travel and travel writing from the nineteenth century and through the period leading up to the Second World War, focusing especially on how travel writing emerged from the frank didacticism of nineteenth-century realism into a particularly literary genre; and yet the "Modernism" of her title is not so much the narrow literary movement, which I discuss here, as it is a wider term used for many of the writers who produced travel accounts during this period of the West's modernity.

2. Throughout, I spell Cummings's name in capital letters, following the advice of Norman Friedman in his essay "NOT 'e. e. cummings.'" Friedman finds no evidence that Cummings consistently signed his name in lowercase. He cites a letter from Cummings's widow, Marianne Moorehouse, where she insists that Cummings had never had the name legally changed and that it would be erroneous to designate him in this manner. Following Moorehouse's advice, Friedman wrote in a letter to his publisher his reasons for agreeing with this view: "I think that Cummings could do what he wanted to do about capitals, but that we should follow the standard forms, since we are not poets in this" (116).

3. Pound's statement, "an epic is a poem including history," comes from the essay "Dateline," published in 1934. See *Literary Essays of Ezra Pound*, ed. T. S. Eliot, 86. Further references to *Literary Essays* will be cited parenthetically in the text.

4. Tyrus Miller, *Late Modernism: Politics, Fiction, and the Arts between the World Wars*. Further references will be cited parenthetically in the text.

5. Marina MacKay, *Modernism and World War II*, 14. Further references will be cited parenthetically in the text.

6. Paul Fussell, *Abroad: British Literary Traveling between the Wars*. Further references will be cited parenthetically in the text.

7. Bernard Schweizer. *Radicals on the Road: The Politics of English Travel Writing in the 1930s*. Further references will be cited parenthetically in the text. See also *At Home and Abroad in the Empire: British Women Write the 1930s*, especially the introduction by Robin Hackett and Gay Wachman, for a discussion of how the political nature of travel writing influenced modernism's development throughout the 1930s.

8. See Schweizer, "Introduction," in *Rebecca West Today: Contemporary Critical Approaches*, ed. Schweizer, 21–42.

9. According to Lynne Whitey in *Grand Tours and Cook's Tours: A History of Leisure Travel, 1750–1915*, "Roads improved substantially in the second half of the [eighteenth] century, regular coaches and cross-Channel ferry routes were established, and a few entrepreneurs began providing services designed specifically to aid the tourist" (8–9). For more on the rise of tourism see Dean McCannell, *The Tourist: A New Theory of The Leisure Class*, and Dennis Porter, *Haunted Journeys: Desire and Transgression in European Travel Writing*.

10. See Joel H. Wiener, ed., *Great Britain, the Lion at Home: A Documentary History of Domestic Policy, 1689–1973*, 2947–48, and Gilman Udell, ed. *Passport Control Acts*, 3–4. Daniel C. Turack, in *The Passport in International Law*, points out that "the Constitution of the United States does not expressly guarantee the right to travel. Prior to 27 May 1941, the date on which the president proclaimed the existence of a national emergency, it was not illegal for United States citizens to leave their country without a passport except for a brief duration during World War I when the passport requirement was obligatory"(9).

11. John Maynard Keynes, *The Economic Consequences of the Peace* (1920), 5.

12. Oswald Spengler, *The Decline of the West*, trans. Charles Francis Atkinson.

13. For more on Spengler's influence on the intellectual climate of the post-war years as well as the fierce debate that surrounded the publication of *The Decline of the West*, see Tomislav Sunic, "History and Decadence: Spengler's Cultural Pessimism Today," *Clio: A Journal of Literature, History, and the Philosophy of History*, 51–62; John Farrenkopf, "Hegel, Spengler, and the Enigma of World History: Progress or Decline?" *Clio: A Journal of Literature, History, and the Philosophy of History*, 331–44.

14. T. S. Eliot, *The Waste Land*, 67. For a discussion of the way that Eliot's style elsewhere draws on the realities of war, see Vincent Sherry, *The Great War and the Language of Modernism*. For example, Sherry says of Eliot's "Gerontion," "If the cunning passages and contrived corridors in this disquisition on history were meant to be part of the speaker's experience of war, some critics and literary historians might counter, these verbal images must invoke instead the maze of trenches networked across the midsection of the European continent" (6).

15. For a discussion of the connection between Keynes's views and the rhetoric he employs in *The Economic Consequences of the Peace* and the language of *The Waste Land*, see Michael Levenson, "Does *The Waste Land* Have a Politics?"

16. Lesley Higgins and Marie-Christine Leps describe the problematic nature of these laws in their analysis of the role of travel documents in the modern world:

[T]he hegemonic recognition of individual freedom of movement, its prominent place in the structure of feelings of Western countries . . . is contradicted by the extensive range of government prerogatives where passports are concerned. Each state retains the authority to dispense travel documents (passports, visas, work permits) at will, simply through bureaucratic regulations, and thereby reserves the right to locate and control individuals and peoples according to the changing demands of economic, social, and political contingencies. ("'Passport, Please': Legal, Literary, and Critical Fictions of Identity," 95)

17. For a critique of Fussell's views, see Jonathan Culler, "The Semiotics of Tourism," in Culler, *Framing the Sign: Criticism and Its Institutions*, 153–67. Part of Fussell's argument about interwar travel is to distinguish real travel from the tourism that arose throughout the nineteenth century. In his view, the British literary travelers writing between the wars were motivated by a desire to reclaim real travel in the face of encroaching mass culture and commercialism, especially as represented by the tourist industry. Culler critiques Fussell's distinctions between "real travel" and "tourism," suggesting that such binaries have always been implicit in travel: the "repetition and displacement of the opposition between tourist and traveler suggest that these are not so much two historical categories as terms of an opposition integral to tourism" (157).

18. In *A Sinking Island: The Modern British Writers*, Hugh Kenner similarly describes this changing way of life. Although he doesn't attribute this change to the increase in travel at the beginning of the century specifically, Kenner does see it in terms of a new internationalism in letters: "English by about 1930 had ceased to be simply the language they speak in England. It had been split four ways. It was (1) the language of International Modernism, having displaced French in that role. And it was (2) the literary language of Ireland, and (3) of America, and yes, (4) of England, countries which International Modernism bids us think of as the Three Provinces" (3–4). Kenner also examines the importance of travel to modernist writers in another work, *The Elsewhere Community*.

19. Samuel Hynes, *The Auden Generation: Literature and Politics in England in the 1930s*. Further references will be cited parenthetically in the text. Hynes focuses primarily on the generation of writers "born in England between 1900 and the First World War" (9), but his description of the literature written in the thirties is important for the way it expresses the overall anxiety of the postwar years. For other discussions of the literature of the period see Valentine Cunningham, *British Writers of the Thirties*.

20. See for instance "The 'Chronological' Philosophy of Spengler," in *Time and Western Man*, 252–86.

21. Ezra Pound, "Augment of the Novel," in *Ezra Pound's Poetry and Prose: Contributions to Periodicals*, vol. 8, *1940–1954*, ed. Lea Baechler, A. Walton Litz, and James Longenbach, 96. Further references will be cited parenthetically in the text. For more on Pound's use of the term "diagnosis" when describing the function of prose and the relationship of his critical methods to the methods and terminology of science, see Ian Bell, *Critic as Scientist: The Modernist Poetics of Ezra Pound*, especially 5–16. See also Herbert Schneidau, *The Image and the Real*. Schneidau describes how

Pound's promotion of imagism, which stressed precision and accuracy of perception, and his focus on the presentation of detail as a way of constructing a long poem, were influenced by the prose tradition of Henry James and, more particularly, Ford Madox Ford. See especially chapter 1, "Imagism as Discipline: Hueffer and the Prose Tradition."

22. Michael André Bernstein, in *The Tale of the Tribe: Ezra Pound and the Modern Verse Epic*, describes Pound's anxiety over the role of epic poetry in the modern world, especially as he saw it competing with the novel, as an anxiety over the most effective way to portray the complex tapestry of modern life. According to Bernstein, Pound claimed for poetry both the diagnostic aspect of prose and the creative aspect of the traditional verse epic. Because Pound did not believe in the autonomy of literary discourse, and because he was convinced that the words of a fictional text *both* reflect and help shape the society within which it is created, he was unwilling to abdicate the full range of either literature's "diagnostic" or potentially "curative" powers (23).

23. Although these sequels were not to appear until the fifties, some of the materials from his Morocco trip emerged as background for parts of another novel, the 1932 *Snooty Baronet*. Other sections of what was to become *Filibusters in Barbary* were first published as articles in various periodicals in 1931 and 1932.

24. Wyndham Lewis, *Men Without Art*, 95.

25. Ezra Pound, "How to Read," in *Literary Essays of Ezra Pound*, 25. Pound's comments on imagism are from an essay entitled "A Retrospect," in a section called "A Few Don't's," which first appeared in *Poetry* 1, no. 6 (March 1913). For "A Retrospect," see *Literary Essays*, 3–4.

26. The other categories of poetry Pound describes are "melopoeia" and "logopoeia." Melopoeia he defines as when "words are charged, over and above their plain meaning, with some musical property, which directs the bearing or trend of that meaning"; and logopoeia he defines as "the dance of intellect among words," "ironic play." While Pound does not necessarily give priority to phanopoeia, he does suggest that phanopoeia "can be translated almost, or wholly, intact. When it is good enough, it is practically impossible for the translator to destroy it save by very crass bungling" (*Literary Essays*, 25).

27. For Eliot on the "objective correlative," see "Hamlet and His Problems," in *T. S. Eliot: Selected Essays*, 124–25.

28. Virginia Woolf, "Mr. Bennet and Mrs. Brown," in *The Gender of Modernism: A Critical Anthology*, ed. Bonnie Kime Scott, 634–41.

29. Michael Levenson, *A Genealogy of Modernism: A Study of English Literary Doctrine, 1908–1922*. Further references will be cited parenthetically in the text.

30. Vincent Sherry, *Ezra Pound, Wyndham Lewis, and Radical Modernism*; Reed Way Dasenbrock, *The Literary Vorticism of Ezra Pound and Wyndham Lewis: Toward the Condition of Painting*. Further references to Sherry and Dasenbrock will be cited parenthetically in the text. Both Dasenbrock and Sherry provide important correctives to the prevalent view of modernism as either reflecting or reconstituting an oral culture, as a movement that recounts, in Pound's words, "the tale of the tribe." Sherry addresses this issue explicitly as he confronts the legacy of Pound-centered versions of modernism, especially that of Hugh Kenner. According to Kenner in *The Pound Era*, the chief achievement of the modernists was their recovery of oral

traditions, traditions that manifest themselves in the widespread invocations of the Homeric bard, from Joyce's Ulysses, through Pound's Cantos, to Eliot's *The Waste Land*. According to Kenner, one sign of the modern renaissance is the recovery of the oral affiliations of poetry and prose: "The norm is now Speech, which binds men, which flows through minds and cultures" (qtd. in Sherry, *Ezra Pound*, 6). Although Sherry acknowledges, as must we, that the musical aspect of language and speech is important to the literature of the period, he finds it to be ultimately incommensurate with the "social elitism that Pound and Lewis came to espouse" and that manifested itself in the sharp, jagged aspect of Pound's poetry and in the forbidding surfaces of Lewis's prose (7).

31. For more on the "primary pigment" as well as on the importance of imagism and Vorticism in the history of modernism, see Levenson, *Geneaology*, 103–36.

32. François Hartog, *The Mirror of Herodotus: The Representation of the Other in the Writing of History*. Further references will be cited parenthetically in the text.

33. Carl E. Schorske, *Thinking with History: Explorations in the Passage to Modernism*. Schorske describes Hartog's method as valuable for the way it shows

> how Herodotus constructed a picture of the Scyths that would serve as a kind of magic mirror for defining Hellenic identity, one that would reinforce the Greek cultural values that Herodotus shared. The 'other' itself, Scythian culture, is swallowed in the Greek view of it; and the Greek view in turn is swallowed in Herodotus's mental and literary construct, the text. (224)

34. Cecil Frank Melville, *The Truth about the New Party*. Melville says of Lewis: "Politically he has in [the matter of examining National Socialism] shown himself to be an Intellectual Innocent Abroad" (2).

35. Lawrence Rainey, *Ezra Pound and the Monument of Culture: Text, History, and the Malatesta Cantos*, 223.

36. Jürgen Habermass, *Habermas: Critical Debates*, ed. David Held and John Thompson, 192.

Chapter 1

1. For Pound's use of the phrase "luminous detail," see "I Gather the Limbs of Osiris," *Selected Prose, 1909–1965*, 19–44. Pound's definition of "luminous detail" is intended to counter the traditional language and methods of historiography, privileging as he does salient facts over their use in a larger narrative structure. He writes, "Any fact is, in a sense, 'significant.' Any fact may be 'symptomatic,' but certain facts give one a sudden insight into circumjacent conditions, into their causes, their effects, into sequence, and law" (22).

2. In *Provence and Pound*, Peter Makin describes Pound's interest in this verse form and provides a useful definition: "*Trobar clus*, which means 'enclosed,' perhaps hermetic composition, is the name given to the art of those troubadours who put hidden meanings in their songs; at times Pound took it that these meanings were not strictly esoteric, but simply deep" (160).

3. Richard Sieburth, *A Walking Tour in Southern France: Ezra Pound among the Troubadours*, viii. Further references will be cited parenthetically in the text.

4. Ezra Pound, *Pound/Ford, The Story of A Literary Friendship: The Correspondence between Ford Madox Ford and Ezra Pound*, 172. Further references will be cited parenthetically in the text. In his recent biography of Pound, David Moody refers to this scene as well, though he sees much it as evidence more of Pound's own self-fashioning than anything. See Moody, *Ezra Pound: Poet. A Portrait of the Man and His Work*, vol. 1, *The Young Genius, 1885–1920*.

5. Ezra Pound, "Ford Madox (Hueffer) Ford; Obit," in *Selected Prose, 1909–1965*, 462.

6. Ezra Pound, *Ezra Pound and Dorothy Shakespear: Their Letters, 1909–1914*, ed. Omar Pound and A. Walton Litz, 155.

7. For Pound's description of the epic as a "poem including history," see Introduction, Note 7 above.

8. See Introduction for a discussion of the various passport control acts that were in existence at this time.

9. Robert Spoo, "Copyright Protectionism and Its Discontents: The Case of James Joyce's *Ulysses* in America," 634; see also Timothy Redman, *Ezra Pound and Italian Fascism*. Redman points out that though the gestation of Pound's interest in these and related matters—copyright law, passports, and the 18th Amendment (prohibition)—

> did not represent as yet a commitment to politics on Pound's part. Instead Pound was responding to certain actions by governments or bureaucracies that impinged upon his sensibility or freedom as an artist. Pound himself insisted that his campaign about these matters was "civil not political." . . . Pound's civic sense foreshadowed a broader political interest to come. (89)

10. E. P. Walkiewicz and Hugh Witemeyer, eds., *Ezra Pound and Senator Bronson Cutting: A Political Correspondence*, 23. Further references will be cited parethetically in the text.

11. In *The Life of Ezra Pound*, Noel Stock suggests, however, that Pound was to a degree deceived into believing that he knew more about what was going on in the states than he in fact did, due to the nature of the information that he was getting: "Because he received letters from aspiring writers who kept him in touch with their quarrels with the established publishing system, Pound believed that he was well informed about America as he would be if he lived there" (282).

12. Guy Davenport, *Cities on a Hill: A Study of I–XXX of Ezra Pound's "Cantos,"* 7.

13. Humphrey Carpenter, *A Serious Character: The Life of Ezra Pound*, 32. Further references will be cited parenthetically in the text.

14. Ezra Pound, *The Spirit of Romance*, n.p.

15. "Patria Mia" appeared in installments in *The New Age* from September 1912 through June 1913. Pound revised the essays for publication in 1913. The revised essay, which I cite here, appears in Pound, *Selected Prose*, 99–142. Further references to this version will be cited parenthetically in the text.

16. See "The Passport Nuisance," *The Nation*, November 30, 1927, p. 341. This essay has been reprinted in *Ezra Pound's Poetry and Prose: Contributions to Periodicals*, vol. 4, *1920–1927*, ed. Lea Baechler, A. Walton Litz, and James Longenbach, 389–90. Further references to this essay will be to the reprinted version and will be cited parenthetically in the text.

17. Ezra Pound, "Troubadours, Their Sorts and Conditions," in *Literary Essays of Ezra Pound*, ed. T. S. Eliot, 94.

18. See "Henry James," in *Literary Essays*, 295–338. Further references to this essay will be cited parenthetically in the text.

19. John Espey, in *Ezra Pound's Mauberley: A Study in Composition*, quotes this line (49). In his study, Espey rejects the traditional interpretation of the character of "Mauberley" being simply a Yeatsian mask for Pound. He argues instead that Pound "uses a foundation of his own experience for the poem, interpreting it through the attitudes revealed in his recent 'Baedekers' of Henry James [. . .] and Remy de Gourmont" (14).

20. According to Carpenter, many of the initial reviews found the poem to be difficult, even, in one reviewer's words "needlessly obscure" (*A Serious Character*, 364).

21. This essay, originally published separately as "Aeschylus" in *The Egoist* 6, no. 1 (January–February 1919), and no. 2 (March–April 1919), was later included as part of a larger essay entitled "Translators of Greek: Early Translators of Homer." I cite the combined essays, which have been reprinted in *Literary Essays*, 249–75.

22. Ezra Pound, *Selected Letters of Ezra Pound to John Quinn, 1915–1924*, 195. Further references will be cited parenthetically in the text.

23. See, for example, Daniel Pearlman, *The Barb of Time: On the Unity of Ezra Pound's "Cantos."* Regarding Canto 7, Pearlman argues that Pound "has been speaking of a nostalgia for a dead poetic style from whose 'empty rooms' Beauty no longer answers to the modern poet's needs." He explains the partition as follows: "An outmoded poetic style is the paper partition which must be torn aside if 'buried beauty' is to be revived" (79). Ronald Bush, in *The Genesis of Ezra Pound's "Cantos,"* writes that "Canto VII completes Pound's triptych of the failed will" (220); and while he does not address these lines specifically, Bush nevertheless reiterates Pearlman's claim that Canto 7 is a lament for the past. See also Robert Spoo and Omar Pound, eds., *Ezra Pound and Margaret Cravens: A Tragic Friendship 1910–1912*: "A lament for lost love and friendship, for 'buried beauty' (and indirectly for companions like T. E. Hulme and Gaudier-Brzeska, killed in the war), Canto 7 is also an elegy for the Europe Ezra knew before August 1914, when the 'flimsy and damned partition' went up" (146).

24. Ezra Pound, *The Cantos*, 25.

25. Joel H. Wiener, ed., *Great Britain, the Lion at Home: A Documentary History of Domestic Policy, 1689–1973*, 2947.

26. Gilman Udell, ed., *Passport Control Acts* , 3–4.

27. See E. P. Walkiewicz and Hugh Witemeyer, eds., *Ezra Pound and Senator Bronson Cutting: A Political Correspondence 1930–1935*, 8–10.

28. Ezra Pound, "The Passport Nuisance," *The Chicago Tribune* (Paris), November

9, 1929, 4. Reprinted in *Contributions to Periodicals*, vol. 5, *1928–1932*, 189.

29. Julien Cornell, *The Trial of Ezra Pound: A Documented Account of the Treason Case by the Defendant's Lawyer Julien Cornell*, 157–59. Further references will be cited parenthetically in the text.

30. This letter contradicts Carpenter's claim that this scene never occurred. In a footnote explaining this scene, Carpenter writes:

> Telling the story to D. G. Bridson at St. Elizabeths, Ezra claimed that the passport official had tried to refuse him re-entry to Britain on the grounds that the U. S. Government wanted all citizens to return home. This scarcely seems likely; he may have been confusing whatever happened in 1919 with a row he had at the American Consulate in Rome during the Second World War, when this was indeed official policy. (*A Serious Character*, 346)

31. "Ezra Pound Still Sees Mad World Out of Step," *The Washington Star* (April 30, 1958), n.p., reprinted in *A Casebook on Ezra Pound*, 144–48; Ezra Pound, "Post-postscript," *The Spirit of Romance*, 9.

32. According to Pound in "The Passport Nuisance," while he was living in London and attempting to travel to France one time, the passport official told him that he could not proceed unless he had business in France. Furthermore, insisted the official, once there, he would be unable to move about freely. Upon arriving in France Pound discovered this information was wrong: "I went to France. When I got to Toulouse I found, as I had suspected, that the under-sub-vice-assistant's information was false. The young chap at the *marie* told me I could do as I liked, and that I was free to walk into the Pyrenees" (*Contributions to Periodicals*, Volume 4 1920–1927. 390).

33. Whitman Bassow, *The Moscow Correspondents: Reporting on Russia from the Revolution to Glasnost*, 9.

34. William C. Bullitt, *The Bullitt Mission to Russia: Testimony before the Committee on Foreign Relations, United States Senate*, 111.

35. E. Fuller Torrey, in *The Roots of Treason: Ezra Pound and the Secrets of St. Elizabeths*, cites Colum's account of this meeting (120).

36. Ezra Pound, *A Draft of XVI Cantos For the Beginning of a Poem of Some Length* (Paris: Hours Press, Three Mountains Press, 1925). In what follows, I cite from the 1986 version of *The Cantos*. According to Ronald Bush in *The Genesis of Ezra Pound's Cantos*, "These Cantos [I–XVI] were generally the same as the first sixteen Cantos in later editions."

37. Walter Benn Michaels, ""Lincoln Steffens and Pound," 209–10.

38. In his *ABC of Reading*, Pound says that "Literature is News that STAYS news" (29).

39. Letter from Steffens to Mrs. J. James Hollister, dated December 6, 1919. See Steffens, *The Letters of Lincoln Steffens*, vol. 1, ed. Ella Winter and Granville Hicks, 494.

40. Ezra Pound, "Augment of the Novel," in *Contributions to Periodicals*, vol. 8, *1940–1954*, 91–98. Further references will be cited parenthetically in the text.

41. Ezra Pound, *Guide to Kulchur*, 96. Further references will be cited parenthetically in the text.

42. Barry Ahearn, ed., *Pound/Cummings: The Correspondence of Ezra Pound and E. E. Cummings*, 24.

43. "E.E. Cummings Alive," in *Contributions to Periodicals*, vol. 6, *1933–1935*, 225–26. This essay originally appeared in *The New English Weekly* 6:10 (December 20, 1934), 210–11.

44. Ezra Pound, *If This Be Treason*, 6, 10.

45. Neal Ascherson, *Black Sea*, 100, 101. Further references will be cited parenthetically in the text.

CHAPTER 2

1. Ezra Pound, "Augment of the Novel," in *Ezra Pound's Poetry and Prose: Contributions to Periodicals*, vol. 8, *1940–1954*, Lea Baechler, A. Walton Litz, and James Longenbach, eds., 95. Further references will be cited parenthetically in the text.

2. François Hartog, *The Mirror of Herodotus: The Representation of the Other in the Writing of History*, Janet Lloyd, trans., 268. For a more detailed discussion of Hartog's terms see above, Introduction, pp. 20–22.

3. See above, Chapter 1, Note 31. According to Richard Kennedy, in *Dreams in the Mirror: A Biography of E. E. Cummings*, "very few people had visited Russia and seen what was happening there, for the situation of being beleaguered by the Great Powers had created an isolationist paranoia on the part of the Soviet leaders. Access to or observation of Russia under the Reds was tightly restricted, and almost all the information that was given to the world came carefully filtered from headquarters in Moscow" (306). Further references to Kennedy's book will be cited parenthetically in the text.

4. For more on the relationship between western writers and intellectuals and the Soviet Union, in addition to Fussell, Hynes, and Schweizer mentioned above, see Valentine Cunningham, *British Writers of the Thirties*; Philip Dodd, "The View of Travelers: Travel Writing in the 1930s." in *The Art of Travel: Essays on Travel Writing*, 127–38; Paul Hollander, *Political Pilgrims: Western Intellectuals in Search of the Good Society*; Daniel Aaron, *Writers on the Left: Episodes in American Literary Communism*.

5. In his recent biography of Cummings, *E.E. Cummings: A Biography*, Christopher Sawyer-Lauçanno describes how the Communist Aragon urged Cummings to visit the Soviet Union. Writing of their time together in Paris in 1930s, Sawyer-Lauçanno says: "Their talk that winter often focused on the Soviet Union. Aragon and Triolet [Russian-born novelist and friend of Aragon's], firm believers in Stalin's vision for radical transformation of his country, urged Cummings to see for himself the wonders of the new Communist state" (341).

6. Richard Kennedy, *Dreams in the Mirror: A Biography of E. E. Cummings*, 307. Further references will be cited parenthetically in the text.

7. Richard Kennedy, *E. E. Cummings Revisited*, 84.

8. According to Kennedy, Cummings obtained this "without party" visa with the assistance of John Dos Passos.

9. Norman Friedman, *e.e. cummings: The Growth of a Writer*, 20. Further references will be cited parenthetically in the text.

10. Sawyer-Lauçanno also mentions the expansion from diary to book, from "about fifty typed pages" to "over four hundred printed pages," and notes the difference between the two as being more one of tone than of structure. Sawyer-Lauçanno says elsewhere of the tension between political posturing and descriptive prose in *Eimi*, "At the same time, *Eimi* is not propaganda, except perhaps when it came to championing the importance of the individual over the masses. He was too wise (and too much of an artist) to write a tract denouncing the excesses of Communism. Instead, he preferred to allow his portrayal of incident and individuals to make the point much more adequately" (355). While rightly focusing on Cummings's preference for art over ideology in his revisions to *Eimi*, where these two things brushed against one another closely, Sawyer-Lauçanno's seems to ascribe neutrality to Cummings's move toward individualism, even as he labels it a kind of "propaganda" itself.

11. E.E. Cummings, "Introduction," *Eimi*, ii. Further references will be cited parenthetically in the text.

12. E.E. Cummings, *The Enormous Room*. Further references will be cited parenthetically in the text.

13. For more on Timothy Redman's distinctions between Pound's civic-mindedness and his political interests, see above Chapter 1, Note 9.

14. See above, pp. 50–53.

15. For Pound's definition of literature as "news that STAYS news," see *ABC of Reading*, 29.

16. Marianne Moore, "A Penguin in Moscow," 278.

17. Eugene Lyons, *Assignment in Utopia*, 418.

18. Francis Fergusson, "When We Were Very Young," 702.

19. See, for example, Lisa Nunn, "Cummings in Context: *Eimi*," 132–40.

20. T. S. Eliot, "Ulysses, Order, and Myth," *Selected Prose of T. S. Eliot*, 177–87.

21. Austin Patty, "Cummings' Impressions of Communist Russia," 21. Further references will be cited parenthetically in the text.

22. William Troy, "Cummings's Non-land of Un-," 72.

23. Paul Headrick, "'Brilliant Obscurity': The Reception of *The Enormous Room*," 46–76.

24. Robert Wegner, *The Poetry and Prose of E. E. Cummings*, 24–25.

25. Ezra Pound, "Shop Girl," *Personae: The Shorter Poems of Ezra Pound*, 116.

26. Commenting on the theme of the voyage to the underworld, Kennedy suggests that Cummings's allusions to Dante's *Divine Comedy* are more of a casual frame of reference than a rigid structural device: "Although Cummings does not strive to duplicate the complexity of the allegorical points in Dante's poem, he picks up correspondences wherever he can in order to give shape and extra dimension to his book" (*Dreams in the Mirror*, 329).

27. "E. E. Cummings Reads," performed by E. E. Cummings.

28. E. E. Cummings, *Complete Poems 1904–1962*, 897.

CHAPTER 3

1. Rebecca West, "Fierce People, These Two Wyndham Lewises!" Further references will be cited parenthetically in the text.

2. As Lewis's biographer Paul O'Keefe points out, Lewis was keenly aware of the confusion caused by the similar names. He notes in particular that Lewis had gone so far as to publish an article in his short-lived journal *The Enemy* entitled "What's in a Namesake?" that addressed precisely this issue. As O'Keefe further points out: "Mistaken identity was to be a recurring joke and was to result in a great deal misdirected mail for the rest of Lewis's life." See O'Keefe, *Some Sort of Genius: A Life of Wyndham Lewis*, 269. Further references will be cited parenthetically in the text.

3. Lewis published magazines with both of these titles in the twenties. See *The Tyro: A Review of the Arts of Painting, Sculpture, and Design*, and *The Enemy*.

4. See *Time and Western Man*, especially chapter 6, "The Revolutionary Simpleton." Further references will be cited parenthetically in the text.

5. See "The Prose Song of Gertrude Stein," in *Time and Western Man*, 59–63.

6. See Introduction above.

7. Wyndham Lewis, "Introduction," in *Journey into Barbary*, ed. Cy Fox, xvi.

8. Wyndham Lewis, *Men without Art*, 99.

9. Wyndham Lewis, *Paleface*, 256–57.

10. Hugh Kenner, *Wyndham Lewis*, 2.

11. Bonnie Kime Scott, *Refiguring Modernism*, vol. 1, *The Women of 1928* 103. Further references will be cited parenthetically in the text.

12. Vincent Sherry, *Ezra Pound, Wyndham Lewis, and Radical Modernism*, 6.

13. Fredric Jameson, *Fables of Aggression: Wyndham Lewis, the Modernist as Fascist*, 176.

14. See SueEllen Campbell, *The Enemy Opposite: The Outlaw Criticism of Wyndham Lewis*, xiii. Further references will be cited parenthetically in the text.

15. Wyndham Lewis, *The Complete Wild Body*, xiii.

16. For a discussion of Borrow's influence on Lewis, see Peter Carter, "Lewis, Borrow, John, and The Gitanos," *Wyndham Lewis Annual 2*, 23–30.

17. Lewis, *Complete Wild Body*, 90.

18. W. K. Rose, ed., *The Letters of Wyndham Lewis*, 99.

19. See Ezra Pound, "Augment of the Novel," in *Ezra Pound's Poetry and Prose: Contributions to Periodicals*, vol. 8, *1940–1954*, Lea Baechler, A. Walton Litz, and James Longenbach, eds., 91–98; and above, pp. 50–53.

20. Wyndham Lewis, *Hitler*, 32. Further references will be cited parenthetically in the text.

21. Paul O'Keefe cites a review of *Hitler* from *Everyman* written by Clennell Wilkinson, who calls the book a "mere write up of the Nazi case, entirely uncritical, vague and unsubstantial. It was positively a feat to fill so many pages and give so little information" (qtd. in O'Keefe, *Some Sort of Genius*, 302). Such reactions, according to O'Keefe, were typical: "[*Hitler*] was criticized for being biased, sloppily written,

badly researched and inaccurate. But nowhere was it condemned as morally tainted" (*Some Sort of Genius*, 302).

22. See Cecil Frank Melville, *The Truth about the New Party*. Melville says of Lewis: "Politically he has in [the matter of examining National Socialism] shown himself in many respects to be an Intellectual Innocent Abroad" (2).

23. Douglas Porch, *The Conquest of Morocco*, 5.

24. Paul Rabinow, *French Modern: Norms and Forms of the Social Environment*, 277.

25. See Cy Fox, "Lewis as Travel Writer: The Forgotten *Filibusters in Barbary*," in *Wyndham Lewis: A Revaluation*, ed. Jeffrey Meyers, 166–80. According to Fox, Lewis did "extensive preparatory reading" on Northern Africa. Further references will be cited parenthetically in the text.

26. Henry Adams *The Education of Henry Adams*, 382.

27. Quoted in Rowland Smith, "Snooty Baronet: Satire and Censorship," in Meyers, *A Revaluation*, 183.

28. See *Wyndham Lewis, Satire & Fiction*, and Robert T. Chapman, *Wyndham Lewis: Fictions and Satires*.

29. Bradford Morrow and Bernard Lacourcad, *A Bibliography of the Writings of Wyndham Lewis*, 67.

CHAPTER 4

1. Wyndham Lewis, *Thirty Personalities and a Self-Portrait*.

2. See Wyndham Lewis, *Journey into Barbary: Morocco Writings and Drawing*, ed. C. J. Fox, 24. Fox's edition of Lewis's book includes two essays that were not included in the original edition. Further references to Fox's edition will be cited parenthetically in the text.

3. Hugh Kenner, *Wyndham Lewis*, 85.

4. Yeats made this comment in a letter to T. Sturge Moore. See Ursula Bridge, ed. *W. B. Yeats and T. Sturge Moore: Their Correspondence, 1901–1937*, 115.

5. See Walter Michel, *Wyndham Lewis: Paintings and Drawings*, 439.

6. See T. S. Eliot, "Tradition and the Individual Talent," in *The Sacred Wood: Essays on Poetry and Criticism*, 47–59.

7. Letter to Bernard Lafourcade, January 27, 1972. In Rebecca West Collection, University of Tulsa McFarlin Library Special Collections. Series I: Box 29: Folder 7.

8. Rebecca West, review of *Tarr*, by Wyndham Lewis, *The Nation*, 67–69; *The Dithyrambic Spectator*, by Wyndham Lewis, *Daily Telegraph*, n.p.

9. Rebecca West, "On Making Due Allowances for Distortions," review of *Paleface*, by Wyndham Lewis, *Time and Tide*, 623–24.

10. For more on West and her use of myth in *Black Lamb and Grey Falcon*, see Marina MacKay's *Modernism and World War II*, 62–70. MacKay says of West's use of myth: "West posits a different kind of national story: defensive rather than aggressive, self-scrutinising [sic] rather than expansionist. Suggesting the modernist championing of myth against materialism, but unpacking for the first time myth's nation-making origins and implications, she argues that groups unite defensively

around the stories they invented to define themselves in the face of foreign occupation" (64).

11. See Introduction above, pp. 20–22.

12. For more on the Peace Pledge Union, see Samuel Hynes, *The Auden Generation: Literature and Politics in England in the 1930s*, 194. Hynes points out that there were at least two separate peace movements at the time: the English Pacifist movement, organized by Viscount Cecil, and the Peace Pledge Union initiated by canon Dick Sheppard. Both movements reflected the mood of the country and indicated that "very large numbers of ordinary Englishmen in 1936 were afraid that a war was coming; but neither was much more than a widespread expression of feeling, and neither developed a programme that was politically intelligent" (194).

13. See Carl Rollyson, *Rebecca West: A Saga of the Century*, 148. Further references will be cited parenthetically in the text.

14. I borrow this phrase from Pound's description of his long poem *The Cantos*. See Introduction, Note 7 above.

15. George Meredith, "Modern Love," *The Works of George Meredith, Volume 24*, 181–230.

16. Evidence of this move from recovery to assessment and re-assessment can be found most clearly in the volume *Rebecca West Today: Contemporary Critical Approaches*, ed. Bernard Schweizer, a collection of essays valuable for the wide range of critical approaches as well as the wide variety of West's works addressed. In addition to examining issues such as West's relationship to modernism or postmodernism or the nature of her feminism, the collection is notable for how authors seek to incorporate West into the classroom. See for example Bonnie Kime Scott's afterword, "Unresolvable Pedagogy: Teaching Rebecca West," where she aligns West with a number of critical and intellectual trends of the twentieth century, as well as pointing out the way that West's life paralleled the development of English Studies itself as a discipline (247).

17. Jane Marcus, *The Young Rebecca: Writings of Rebecca West, 1911–1917*. Further references will be cited parenthetically in the text.

18. See especially Ann Norton's study of West, *Paradoxical Feminism*, where she sees West's feminism often colliding with her sympathetic views of the rigid gender roles that she associates with a vitality that was lost to the West, a view that we see especially in *Black Lamb and Grey Falcon*. In his introduction to *Rebecca West Today*, Bernard Schweizer addresses Norton's skepticism over West's feminist credentials, suggesting that this very paradox "signifies the ardent struggle of a new consciousness trying to overcome older, socially ingrained ideas about gender and sexuality" (28).

19. Quoted in Scott, *Refiguring Modernism, Volume 1: The Women of 1928* 126.

20. Loretta Stec, "Female Sacrifice: Gender and Nostalgic Nationalism in Rebecca West's *Black Lamb and Grey Falcon*," in *Narratives of Nostalgia, Gender, and Nationalism*, 138–58.

21. Quoted in Margaret Diane Stetz, "Rebecca West and the Visual Arts. 44.

22. Rebecca West, "What is Mr. Eliot's Authority as a Critic?" in *The Gender of Modernism: A Critical Anthology*, ed. Bonnie Kime Scott, 587–92. This essay originally appeared in *The Daily Telegraph* (September 30, 1932), 6.

23. See Wyndham Lewis, *Blasting and Bombardiering*, 254.

24. See Schweizer, "Introduction," in *Rebecca West Today*, ed. Schweizer, 28.

25. Erin Carlston, *Thinking Fascism: Sapphic Modernism and Fascist Modernity*, 7. Further references will be cited parenthetically in the text. Carlston refers here to Reed Way Dasenbrock's essay, "Wyndham Lewis's Fascist Imagination and the Fiction of Paranoia," in *Fascism, Aesthetics, and Culture*, 81–97.

26. For a discussion of the epic status of West's work see Bernard Schweizer's *Rebecca West: Heroism, Rebellion, and the Female Epic*, as well as his essay "Epic Form and (Re)Vision in Rebecca West's *Black Lamb and Grey Falcon*," in *Approaches to the Anglo and American Female Epic, 1621–1982*, 69–81. Schweizer argues in the latter essay that West's book fulfills certain definitions of the epic, especially "elements of the 'epic apparatus,' a focus on nation-founding, and authoritative pronouncements about collective moral spiritual values" (*Approaches*, 70).

27. See Joachim Du Bellay, *The Regrets*, translated by C. H. Sisson, 99. Written while Du Bellay was in Rome, this sonnet gives expression to his longing to see his home province of Anjou once again, to see again the places with which he was most familiar. The irony in Du Bellay's lines is that Ulysses was anything but happy upon his return to Ithaca, as his home was overrun with suitors competing for his wife and property. Ulysses' journeys thus takes place, Du Bellay slyly reminds us, between two conflagrations: the war in Troy and the scene of violence at home in Ithaca.

28. See, for example, W. B. Stanford, *The Ulysses Theme: A Study in the Adaptability of a Traditional Hero*, and Stephen Sicari, *Pound's Epic Ambition: Dante and the Modern World*.

29. T. S. Eliot, *The Waste Land*, in *The Complete Poems and Plays, 1909–1950*.

30. Karen Lawrence, *Penelope Voyages: Women and Travel in the British Literary Tradition*, 1. Further references will be cited parenthetically in the text.

31. See Katherine Woods, "Rebecca West's Brilliant Mosaic of Yugoslavia Travel," 4, 39.

32. Schweizer sees the portrayal of Gerda and Constantine as evidence of the mythological method that West employed, and as further evidence of the epic quality of *Black Lamb and Grey Falcon*. Schweizer writes that "the 'fabula' or myth, together with the creation of quasi literary characters such as Constantine and Gerda, intrude to shape the tale." See Schweizer, "Epic Form and (Re)Vision in Rebecca West's *Black Lamb and Grey Falcon*," in *Approaches to the Anglo and American Female Epic, 1621–1982*, 69–81.

33. Ultimately, for Schweizer West fuses such oppositions in *Black Lamb and Grey Falcon* as she demonstrates the ability to "overcome antitheses" (*Approaches* 140).

34. For more on the initial reception of *Black Lamb and Grey Falcon*, see Carl Rollyson, *Rebecca West: A Saga of the Century*, 180–84.

35. *Selected Letters of Rebecca West*, 189. Further references will be cited parenthetically in the text.

36. Vesna Goldsworthy, "*Black Lamb and Grey Falcon*: Rebecca West's Journey through the Balkans."

37. Robert Kaplan, *Balkan Ghosts: A Journey through History*. Further references will be cited parenthetically in the text.

38. See, for example, David Fromkin. *Kossovo Crossing: American Ideals Meet Reality on the Balkan Battlefields*; David Owen, *Balkan Odyssey*.

39. In a "Note on Pronunciation" at the beginning of *Black Lamb and Grey Falcon*, West writes: "Kossovo I have written Kossovo, though the Serbo-Croat language uses no double consonants, because we take them as a sign that the preceding vowel is short." Unless I am quoting directly from West, I spell the word Kossovo, as this is the more common spelling today.

40. Richard Holbrooke, *To End a War*.

41. David Remnick, *The New Yorker*, June 14, 1999, 94. Remnick calls Kaplan's book "an essentialist account, a description of unchanging types and patterns. It also turned out to be a marvelous alibi for inaction." Taking into account Kaplan's own statement of influence regarding *Black Lamb and Grey Falcon*, Remnick goes on to call West's book a "classic of fatalism."

42. Letter to Lt. Colonel Charles Bridge, June 9, 1936, Rebecca West Collection. McFarlin Library. Series I: Box 8: Folder 3.

43. Letter to Lt. Colonel Charles Bridge, June 4, 1936. Rebecca West Collection. McFarlin Library. Series I: Box 8: Folder 3.

44. In *Radicals on the Road*, Schweizer sees in Kaplan's determinism evidence of an underlying humanitarianism, and he credits him remaining open to the experience around him and seeing his work as "harboring the seed for a new kind of cross-cultural rhetoric, one that is rooted in a self-reflexive kind of inquiry that constantly questions the premises of its own ideological and epistemological apparatus" (184).

45. "Trees of Gold," in *Gender of Modernism*. Further references will be cited parenthetically in the text.

46. *The Catholic Encyclopedia* 1967, s.v. "iconostasis."

47. Schweizer sees in this moment a return to the optimism that West had begun her travels with, and this scene as trumping the defeatism that had overcome West earlier when she sees Tsar Lazar's body. See *Radicals on the Road*, 139.

Conclusion

1. See Humphrey Carpenter, *A Serious Character: The Life of Ezra Pound*, 846.

2. *New York Times* January 6, 1947, sec. 35, p. 2; E. E. Cummings, Letter to the Editor, *New York Times* January 7, 1947, sec. 25, p. 2.

3. Rebecca West, "Thou Shalt Not Make Any Graven Images," in *The Only Poet and Short Stories*, ed. Antonia Hill. Further references will be cited parenthetically in the text. Wyndham Lewis, *Self-Condemned*. Further references will be cited parenthetically in the text.

4. Reed Way Dasenbrock documents the inclusion of the material of Lewis's Moroccan trip in *Snooty Baronet*. See Dasenbrock, "Lewis's Sources for the Persian Settings of *Snooty Baronet*."

5. Victoria Glendinning, *Rebecca West: A Life*, 171.

6. Phyllis Lassner, "Rebecca West's Shadowy Other," in *Rebecca West Today: Contemporary Critical Approaches*, ed. Bernard Schweizer, 43–63.

Aaron, Daniel. *Writers on the Left: Episodes in American Literary Communism.* New York: Columbia University Press, 1992.

Adams, Henry. *The Education of Henry Adams.* Edited by Ernest Samuels. New York: Houghton Mifflin Harcourt, 1972.

Ahearn, Barry, ed. *Pound/Cummings: The Correspondence of Ezra Pound and E. E. Cummings.* Ann Arbor: University of Michigan Press, 1996.

Ascherson, Neal. *Black Sea.* New York: Hill and Wang, 1995.

Bassow, Whitman. *The Moscow Correspondents: Reporting on Russia from the Revolution to Glasnost.* New York: W. Morrow, 1988.

Bell, Ian. *Critic as Scientist: The Modernist Poetics of Ezra Pound.* New York: Methuen and Co., 1981.

Bernstein, Michael André. *The Tale of the Tribe: Ezra Pound and the Modern Verse Epic.* Princeton, N.J.: Princeton University Press, 1980.

Bridge, Ursula. *W. B. Yeats and T. Sturge Moore: Their Correspondence, 1901–1937.* London: Routledge and Kegan Paul, 1953.

Bridson, D. G. *The Filibuster: A Study of the Political Ideas of Wyndham Lewis.* London: Cassell, 1972.

Brown, Dennis. *Intertextual Dynamics within the Literary Group—Joyce, Lewis, Pound, and Eliot.* London: Macmillan Press Ltd., 1990.

Bullitt, William C. *The Bullitt Mission to Russia: Testimony before the Committee on Foreign Relations, United States Senate.* New York: Huebsch, 1919. Reprint, Westport, Conn.: Hyperion Press, 1977.

Bush, Ronald. *The Genesis of Ezra Pound's "Cantos."* Princeton, N.J.: Princeton University Press, 1976.

Buzard, James. *The Beaten Track: European Tourism, Literature, and the Ways to Culture, 1800–1918.* Oxford: Clarendon Press, 1993.

Campbell, SueEllen. *The Enemy Opposite: The Outlaw Criticism of Wyndham Lewis.* Athens: Ohio University Press, 1988.

Carlston, Erin. *Thinking Fascism: Sapphic Modernism and Fascist Modernity.* Stanford, Calif.: Stanford University Press, 1998.

Carpenter, Humphrey. *A Serious Character: The Life of Ezra Pound.* London: Faber and Faber, 1988.

Carr, Helen. "Modernism and Travel (1880–1940)." In *The Cambridge Companion to Travel Writing,* edited by Peter Hulme and Tim Youngs. Cambridge: Cambridge University Press, 2002, 70–86.

Chapman, Robert T. *Wyndham Lewis: Fictions and Satires.* New York: Barnes and Noble, 1973.

Cornell, Julien. *The Trial of Ezra Pound: A Documentary Account of the Treason Case by the Defendant's Lawyer Julien Cornell.* London: Faber, 1967.

Culler, Jonathan. *Framing the Sign: Literature and Its Institutions.* Norman: University of Oklahoma Press, 1988.

Cummings, E. E. *Eimi.* New York: Grove Press Inc., 1933.

———. *The Enormous Room.* New York: Liveright, 1922.

Cunningham, Valentine. *British Writers of the Thirties.* New York: Oxford University Press, 1988.

Dasenbrock, Reed Way. "Lewis's Sources for the Persian Settings of *Snooty Baronet.*" *Enemy News: The Journal of the Wyndham Lewis Society.* (Spring 1986): 42–49.

———. *The Literary Vorticism of Ezra Pound and Wyndham Lewis: Toward the Condition of Painting.* Baltimore: Johns Hopkins University Press, 1985.

———. "Wyndham Lewis's Fascist Imagination and the Fiction of Paranoia." In *Fascism, Aesthetics, and Culture,* edited by Richard J. Golsan. Hanover: University Press of New England, 1992. 81–97.

Davenport, Guy. *Cities on a Hill: A Study of I–XXX of Ezra Pound's "Cantos."* Ann Arbor, Mich.: UMI Research Press, 1983.

Dodd, Philip, ed. *The Art of Travel: Essays on Travel Writing.* London: Franck Cass and Co. Ltd., 1982.

Du Bellay, Joachim. *The Regrets.* Translated by C. H. Sisson. Manchester: Carcanet Press, 1984.

Duranty, Walter. *Duranty Reports Russia.* New York: Viking Press, 1934.

Durham, Mary Elizabeth. *The Struggle for Scutari.* London: Edward Arnold, 1914.

Edwards, Paul. Afterword to *Time and Western Man*, by Wyndham Lewis. Santa Rosa: Black Sparrow Press, 1993.

———. *Wyndham Lewis Painter and Writer*. New Haven, Conn.: Yale University Press, 2000.

Eliot, T. S. *The Complete Poems and Plays 1909–1950*. New York: Harcourt Brace & Company, 1980.

———. *The Sacred Wood: Essays on Poetry and Criticism*. New York: Methuen, 1960.

———. *Selected Essays*. New York: Harcourt Brace and World,. 1964.

———. "Wyndham Lewis." *Hudson Review* 10 (1957): 167–70.

Elliot, Robert C. *The Power of Satire: Magic, Ritual, Art*. Princeton, N.J.: Princeton University Press, 1960.

Espey, John. *Ezra Pound's Mauberley: A Study in Composition*. Berkeley: University of California Press, 1955.

Farrenkopf, John. "Hegel, Spengler, and the Enigma of World History: Progress or Decline?" *Clio: A Journal of Literature, History, and the Philosophy of History* 19, no. 4 (Summer 1990): 331–44.

Farrington, Jane. *Wyndham Lewis*. London: Lund Humphries in association with the City of Manchester Art Galleries, 1980.

Fergusson, Francis. "When We Were Very Young." *Kenyon Review* 12, no. 4 (Autumn 1950): 701–5.

Fox, C. J. "Lewis as Travel Writer: The Forgotten *Filibusters in Barbary*." In *Wyndham Lewis: A Revaluation*, edited by Jeffrey Meyers, 166–80. London: Athlone Press, 1980.

Friedman, Norman. *e. e. cummings: The Growth of a Writer*. Carbondale: Southern Illinois University Press, 1964.

———. "NOT 'e.e. cummings.'" *Spring: The Journal of the E. E. Cummings Society* 1 (Spring 1992): 114–21.

Fromkin, David. *Kosovo Crossing: American Ideals Meet Reality on the Balkan Battlefields*. New York: Free Press, 1999.

Fussell, Paul. *Abroad: British Literary Traveling between the Wars*. New York: Oxford University Press, 1980.

———. "Travel, Tourism, and 'International Understanding.'" In *Thank God for the Atom Bomb and Other Essays* (New York: Ballantine Books, 1988), 124–46.

Glendinning, Victoria. *Rebecca West: A Life*. London: Weidenfeld and Nicolson, 1987.

Goldsworthy, Vesna. "*Black Lamb and Grey Falcon*: Rebecca West's Journey through the Balkans." *Women: A Cultural Review* 8, no. 1 (Spring 1997): 1–11.

Habermas, Jürgen. *The Philosophical Discourse of Modernity. Twelve Lectures.* Translated by Frederick Lawrence. Cambridge, Mass.: MIT Press, 1990.

Hackett, Robin, et al., eds. *At Home and Abroad in the Empire: British Women Write the 1930s.* Newark: University of Delaware Press, 2009.

Hartog, François. *The Mirror of Herodotus: The Representation of the Other in the Writing of History.* Translated by Janet Lloyd. Berkeley: University of California Press, 1988.

Headrick, Paul. "'Brilliant Obscurity': The Reception of *The Enormous Room.*" *Spring: The Journal of the E. E. Cummings Society* 1, no. 1 (October 1992): 46–76.

Habermas, Jürgen. *Habermas: Critical Debates.* Edited by David Held and John Thompson. Cambridge: MIT Press, 1982.

Herodotus. *The History.* Translated by David Grene. Chicago: Chicago University Press, 1987.

Higgins, Lesley, and Marie-Christine Leps. "'Passport, Please': Legal, Literary, and Critical Functions of Identity." *College Literature* 25, no. 1 (Winter 1998): 94–138.

Hoisington, William A. *Lyautey and the French Conquest of Morocco.* New York: St. Martin's Press, 1995.

Holbrooke, Richard. *To End a War.* New York: Modern Library, 1998.

Hollander, Paul. *Political Pilgrims: Western Intellectuals in Search of the Good Society.* New York: Oxford University Press, 1981.

Homberger, Eric. *John Reed.* Manchester: Manchester University Press, 1990.

Hynes, Samuel. *The Auden Generation: Literature and Politics in England in the 1930s.* London: The Bodley Head, 1976.

Jameson, Fredric. *Fables of Aggression: Wyndham Lewis, the Modernist as Fascist.* Berkeley: University of California Press, 1979.

Kaplan, Justin. *Lincoln Steffens.* New York: Simon and Schuster, 1974.

Kaplan, Robert. *Balkan Ghosts: A Journey through History.* New York: St. Martin's Press, 1993.

Kennedy, Richard. *Dreams in the Mirror: A Biography of E. E. Cummings.* New York: Liveright Publishing Corp., 1980.

———. *E. E. Cummings Revisited.* New York: Twayne Publishers, 1994.

Kenner, Hugh. *The Elsewhere Community.* Concord, Ont.: House of Anansi Press Ltd., 1998.

———. *The Pound Era.* Berkeley: University of California Press, 1971.

———. *A Sinking Island: The Modern English Writers.* Baltimore: John Hopkins University Press, 1987.

———. *Wyndham Lewis.* Norfolk, Conn.: New Directions, 1954.

Keynes, John Maynard. *The Economic Consequences of The Peace.* London:

Macmillan, 1920.

Lassner, Phyllis. *British Women Writers of World War II: A Battleground of Their Own*. New York: St. Martin's Press, 1998.

———. "Rebecca West's Shadowy Other." In *Rebecca West Today: Contemporary Critical Approaches*, edited by Bernard Schweizer. Newark: University of Delaware Press, 2006.

Lawrence, Karen R. *Penelope Voyages: Women and Travel in the British Literary Tradition*. Ithaca, N.Y.: Cornell University Press, 1994.

Levenson, Michael. *A Geneology of Modernism: A Study of English Literary Doctrine, 1908–1922*. New York: Cambridge University Press, 1984.

———. "Does *The Waste Land* Have a Politics?" *Modernism/Modernity* 6, no. 3 (September 1999): 1–13.

Lewis, Wyndham. *The Apes of God*. Santa Barbara, Calif.: Black Sparrow Press, 1981.

———. *Blast*. London: John Lane, 1914.

———. *Blasting and Bombardiering*. 1937. Reprint, London: John Calder, 1982.

———. *The Complete Wild Body*. Edited by Bernard Lafourcade. Santa Barbara: Black Sparrow Press, 1982.

———. *Journey into Barbary: Morocco Writings and Drawing*. Edited by C. J. Fox. Santa Barbara, Calif.: Black Sparrow Press, 1983.

———. *Men Without Art*. Edited by Seamus Cooney. Santa Rosa: Black Sparrow Press, 1987.

———. *Paleface: The Philosophy of the Melting Pot*. London: Chatto and Windus, 1929.

———. *Rude Assignment: An Intellectual Autobiography*. Edited by Toby Foshay. Santa Barbara, Calif.: Black Sparrow Press, 1984.

———. *Satire & Fiction*. Folcroft, Pa.: Folcroft Library Editions, 1973.

———. *Self-Condemned*. Santa Barbara, Calif.: Black Sparrow Press, 1983.

———. *Snooty Baronet*. Edited by Bernard Lafourcade. Santa Barbara, Calif.: Black Sparrow Press, 1984.

———. *Tarr*. London: Penguin, 1982.

———. *Thirty Personalities and a Self-Portrait*. London: Desmond Harmsworth, 1932.

———. *Time and Western Man*. Edited by Paul Edwards. Santa Rosa, Calif.: Black Sparrow Press, 1993.

———. *The Wild Body*. New York: Haskell House, 1970.

———, ed. *Blast 2*. Santa Barbara, Calif.: Black Sparrow Press, 1981.

Lyons, Eugene. *Assignment in Utopia*. New York: Harcourt Brace and Company, 1937.

MacKay, Marina. *Modernism and World War II*. New York: Cambridge University Press, 2007.

Makin, Peter. *Provence and Pound*. Berkeley: University of California Press, 1978.

Marcus, Jane. *The Young Rebecca: Writings of Rebecca West, 1911–17*. Bloomington: Indiana University Press, 1989.

Materer, Timothy. *Vortex: Pound, Eliot, and Lewis*. Ithaca, N.Y.: Cornell University Press, 1979.

———. *Wyndham Lewis the Novelist*. Detroit: Wayne State University Press, 1976.

Maurois, Andre. *Lyautey*. Translated by Hamish Miles. London: John Lane, 1931.

McCannell, Dean. *The Tourist: A New Theory of the Leisure Class*. New York: Schocken Books, 1976.

Melville, Cecil Frank. *The Truth about the New Party*. London: Wishart, 1931.

Meredith, George. *The Works of George Meredith*. New York: Scribner's Sons, 1909–12.

Meyers, Jeffrey. *The Enemy: A Biography of Wyndham Lewis*. London: Routledge and Kegan Paul, 1980.

———, ed. *Wyndham Lewis: A Revaluation, New Essays*. London: Athlone Press, 1980.

Michaels, Walter Benn. "Lincoln Steffens and Pound." *Paideuma: A Journal Devoted to Ezra Pound Scholarship* 2 (1973): 209–10.

Michel, Walter. *Wyndham Lewis: Paintings and Drawings*. Berkeley: University of California Press, 1971.

Miller, Tyrus. *Late Modernism: Politics, Fiction, and the Arts between the World Wars*. Berkeley: University of California Press, 1999.

Moody, David. *Ezra Pound, Poet: A Portrait of the Man and His Work*. Vol. 1, *The Young Genius, 1885–1920*. New York: Oxford University Press, 2007.

Moore, Marianne. "A Penguin in Moscow." *Poetry* 42 (April–September 1933): 277–80.

Morrow, Bradford, and Bernard Lafourcade. *A Bibliography of the Writings of Wyndham Lewis*. Santa Barbara, Calif.: Black Sparrow Press, 1978.

Norton, Ann. *Paradoxical Feminism: The Novels of Rebecca West*. International Scholars Publications, 1999.

Nunn, Lisa. "Cummings in Context: *Eimi*." *Spring: The Journal of the E. E. Cummings Society* 7 (Fall 1998): 132–40.

O'Connor, William Van and Edward Stone eds. *A Casebook on Ezra Pound*. New York: Thomas Y. Crowell, 1959.

O'Keefe, Paul. *Some Sort of Genius: A Life of Wyndham Lewis.* London: Jonathan Cape, 2000.

Ouditt, Sharon. *Fighting Forces, Writing Women: Identity and Ideology in the First World War.* London: Routledge, 1994.

Owen, David. *Balkan Odyssey.* New York: Mariner Books, 1996.

Patty, Austin. "Cummings' Impressions of Communist Russia." *Rendezvous: A Journal of Arts and Letters* 2, no. 1 (1967): 15–22.

Pearlman, Daniel. *The Barb of Time: On the Unity of Ezra Pound's "Cantos."* New York: Oxford University Press, 1969.

Perrino, Mark. *The Poetics of Mockery: Wyndham Lewis's "The Apes of God" and the Popularization of Modernism.* London: W. S. Manley and Son Ltd., 1995.

Porch, Douglas. *The Conquest of Morocco.* New York: Knopf, 1983.

Porter, Dennis. *Haunted Journeys: Desire and Transgression in European Travel Writing.* Princeton: Princeton University Press, 1991.

Pound, Ezra. *Ezra Pound's Poetry and Prose: Contributions to Periodicals.* 10 vols. Edited by Lea Baechler, A. Walton Litz, and James Longenbach. New York: Garland Publishing Inc., 1991.

———. *The Cantos.* New York: New Directions, 1986.

———. *Ezra Pound and Dorothy Shakespear: Their Letters, 1909–1914.* Edited by Omar Pound and A. Walton Litz. New York: New Directions, 1984.

———. *Guide to Kulchur.* London: Faber and Faber, 1938.

———. *If This Be Treason.* Nuova Siena, Italy: Tip, 1948.

———. *Literary Essays of Ezra Pound.* Edited by T. S. Eliot. London: Faber and Faber, 1954.

———. *Personae: The Shorter Poems of Ezra Pound.* New York: New Directions, 1990.

———. *Pound/Ford, The Story of a Literary Friendship: The Correspondence between Ford Madox Ford and Ezra Pound.* London: Faber and Faber, 1982.

———. *Selected Letters of Ezra Pound to John Quinn, 1915–1924.* Edited by Timothy Materer. Durham, N.C.: Duke University Press, 1991.

———. *Selected Prose, 1909–1965.* Edited by William Cookson. New York: New Directions, 1973.

———. *The Spirit of Romance.* New York: New Directions, 1968.

———. "Wyndham Lewis." *The Egoist* 1, no. 12 (June 15, 1914): 133–34.

Pound, Omar, and Robert Spoo, eds. *Ezra Pound and Margaret Cravens: A Tragic Friendship, 1910–1912.* Durham: Duke University Press, 1988.

Rabinow, Paul. *French Modern: Norms and Forms of the Social Environment.* Chicago: University of Chicago Press, 1989.

Rainey, Lawrence. *Ezra Pound and the Monument of Culture: Text, History, and the Malatesta Cantos*. Chicago: University of Chicago Press, 1991.

———, ed. *A Poem Containing History: Textual Studies in "The Cantos."* Ann Arbor: University of Michigan Press, 1997.

Ray, Gordon N. *H. G. Wells and Rebecca West*. New Haven, Conn.: Yale University Press, 1974.

Redman, Timothy. *Ezra Pound and Italian Fascism*. New York: Cambridge University Press, 1991.

Reed, John. *Ten Days that Shook the World*. 1919. Reprint, New York: Bantam Classics, 1987.

Rollyson, Carl. *Rebecca West: A Saga of the Century*. London: Sceptre, 1995.

Rose, W. K., ed. *The Letters of Wyndham Lewis*. London: Methuen and Co. Ltd., 1963.

Rosenstone, Robert. *Romantic Revolutionary: A Biography of John Reed*. New York: Alfred A. Knopf, 1975.

Sawyer-Lauçanno, Christopher. *E. E. Cummings: A Biography*. Naperville: Sourcebooks Inc., 2004.

Schneidau, Herbert. *The Image and the Real*. Baton Rouge: Louisiana State University Press, 1969.

Schorske, Carl E. *Thinking with History: Explorations in the Passage to Modernism*. Princeton, N.J.: Princeton University Press, 1998.

Schweizer, Bernard. *Approaches to the Anglo-American Female Epic, 1621–1982*. Burlington: Ashgate Publishing Company, 2006.

———. *Radicals on the Road: The Politics of English Travel Writing in the 1930s*. Charlottesville: University Press of Virginia, 2001.

———. *Rebecca West: Heroism, Rebellion, and the Female Epic*. Westport, Conn.: Greenwood Press, 2002.

———, ed. *Rebecca West Today: Contemporary Critical Approaches*. Newark: University of Delaware Press, 2006.

Scott, Bonnie Kime. *Refiguring Modernism*. Vol. 1, *The Women of 1928*. Vol. 2, *Postmodern Feminist Readings of Woolf, West, and Barnes*. Bloomington: Indiana University Press, 1995.

Sherry, Vincent. *Ezra Pound, Wyndham Lewis, and Radical Modernism*. New York: Oxford University Press, 1993.

———. *The Great War and The Language of Modernism*. New York: Oxford University Press, 2003.

Sicari, Stephen. *Pound's Epic Ambition: Dante and the Modern World*. Albany: State University of New York Press, 1991.

Sieburth, Richard. *A Walking Tour in Southern France: Ezra Pound among the Troubadours*. New York: New Directions, 1992.

Spengler, Oswald. *The Decline of the West*. Translated by Charles Francis Atkinson. New York: Alfred A. Knopf, 1926–1928.

Spoo, Robert. "Copyright Protectionsim and Its Discontents: The Case of James Joyce's *Ulysses* in America." *Yale Law Journal* 108, no. 3 (December 1998): 633–67.

Stanford, W. B. *The Ulysses Theme: A Study in the Adaptability of a Traditional Hero*. New York: Barnes and Noble, 1964.

Steffens, Lincoln. *The Autobiography of Lincoln Steffens*. New York: Harcourt and Brace, 1931.

———. *The Letters of Lincoln Steffens. 2 Volumes*. Edited by Ella Winter and Granville Hicks. New York: Harcourt Brace and Company, 1938.

Stec, Loretta. "Female Sacrifice: Gender and Nostalgic Nationalism in Rebecca West's *Black Lamb and Grey Falcon*." In *Narratives of Nostalgia, Gender, and Nationalism* (New York: New York University Press, 1997), 138–58.

Stetz, Margaret Diane. "Rebecca West and the Visual Arts." *Tulsa Studies in Women's Literature* 8, no. 1 (Spring 1989): 43–62.

Stock, Noel. *The Life of Ezra Pound*. San Francisco: North Point Press, 1982.

———. Tomislav, Sunic. "History and Decadence: Spengler's Cultural Pessimism Today." *Clio: A Journal of Literature, History, and the Philosophy of History* 19, no. 1 (Fall 1989): 51–62.

Torrey, E. Fuller. *The Roots of Treason: Ezra Pound and the Secret of St. Elizabeths*. New York: McGraw Hill, 1984.

Tretyakov, Sergei. *Roar China*. Translated by F. Polianovska and Barbara Nixon London: Martin Lawrence, 1931.

Troy, William. "Cummings's Non-land of Un-." In *E. E. Cummings and the Critics*, edited by S. V. Baum, 71–72. East Lansing: Michigan State University Press, 1962.

Turack, Daniel C. *The Passport in International Law*. Lexington, Mass.: Lexington Books, D. C. Heath and Company, 1972.

Veit, Karin. "Journey and Gender—Diversity in Travel Writing." In *Feminist Contributions to the Literary Canon: Setting Standards of Taste*, edited by Susanne Fendler. Lewiston: The Edwin Mellen Press, 1997.

Wagner, Geoffrey. *Wyndham Lewis: A Portrait of the Artist as Enemy*. New Haven, Conn.: Yale University Press, 1957.

Wegner, Robert. *The Poetry and Prose of E. E. Cummings*. Harcourt, Brace, and World, 1965.

West, Rebecca. *Black Lamb and Grey Falcon: A Journey through Yugoslavia*. New York: Penguin Books, 1982.

———. "Fierce People, These Two Wyndham Lewises!" *Daily Telegraph*, July

8, 1932.

———. "Indissoluble Matrimony." *Blast*. London: John Lane, 1914.

———. "On Making Due Allowances for Distortions." *Time and Tide*, May 10, 1929. 623–24.

———. "The Second Commandment: Thou Shalt Not Make Any Graven Image." In *The Only Poet and Short Stories*, edited by Antonia Hill, 179–220. London: Virago Press, 1992.

———. *A Train of Powder*. 1955. Reprint, London: Virago Press, 1984.

———. "Trees of Gold." In *The Gender of Modernism: A Critical Anthology*, edited by Bonnie Kime Scott. Bloomington: Indiana University Press, 1990.

White, Stephen K. *The Recent Work of Jürgen Habermas: Reason, Justice and Modernity*. Cambridge: Cambridge University Press, 1988.

Whitey, Lynn. *Grand Tours and Cook's Tours: A History of Leisure Travel, 1750–1915*. New York: William Morrow and Company Inc., 1997.

Wiener, Joel H., ed. *Great Britain, the Lion at Home: A Documentary History of Domestic Policy, 1689–1973*. New York: Chelsea House Publishers, 1974.

Woods, Katherine. "Rebecca West's Brilliant Mosaic of Yugoslavia Travel." *New York Times*, Oct. 26, 1941, BR4.

Woolf, Virginia. "Mr. Bennett and Mrs. Brown." In *The Gender of Modernism: A Critical Anthology*, edited by Bonnie Kime Scott, 634–41. Bloomington: Indiana University Press, 1990.